Instant Notes on Horticultural Sciences

About the Author

Nilesh Sharma currently, working as Professor at Department of Agriculture, Mandsaur University, Mandsaur, M.P. He received his B.Sc. (Horti.) from Rajmata Vijaya Raje Scindia Krishi Vishwa Vidhyala (RVSKVV), Gwalior, M.P. He received his M.Sc. (Ag in Horti.) degree with specialized in Vegetable from the Jawaharlal Nehru Krishi Vishwa Vidhyala (JNKVV), Jabalpur, M.P. and also qualified NET (ASRB, ICAR). He has published some valuable national and international research papers. He has published technical articles and abstracts in different areas of horticulture. He attempted many National and International seminars.

Instant Notes on Horticultural Sciences

Nilesh Sharma
Assistant Professor
Department of Agriculture
Mandsaur University
Mandsaur-458001, Madhya Pradesh

New Delhi – 110 034

A Paperback Division of
NEW INDIA PUBLISHING AGENCY
101, Vikas Surya Plaza, CU Block, LSC Market
Pitam Pura, New Delhi 110 034, India
Phone: + 91 (11) 27 34 17 17 Fax: + 91 (11) 27 34 16 16
Email: info@nipabooks.com
Web: www.nipabooks.com

Feedback at feedbacks@nipabooks.com

ISBN: 978-93-89130-21-8

Composed and Designed by NIPA

Dedicated to
my Father and my Teachers

Preface

Horticulture is gaining importance as it gives more return per unit area and also gives nutritious food to human being thereby improves quality of life and enhances the aesthetic beauty in nature. Considering the recent trends in exams, all these examination are mostly based on objective type questions and students always look for study material that is ready to use and easy to grasp. Keeping in view, each topic is briefly explained in point wise so that students can easily grasp the concepts and the emphasis is given to the most important topic.

Though many books of horticulture are available in the markets, most of these books are written in highly elaborative manner which is time consuming for the students who are preparing for competitive exams. All the chapters in the book had been properly covered according to their families and relative importance.

I express my sincere thanks to my friend Rahul Singh Rajput for encouraging me to write this book. I hope that this book will be a useful reference material for the teachers, practitioners and students searching their careers in ICAR institutions, State Agricultural/Horticulture Universities and for competitions like ARS/SRF/JRF/NET along with entrance examinations for B.Sc, M.Sc and Ph.D Degree in Horticulture.

I will always welcome any comments and suggestions for improvements of this book.

Nilesh Sharma

Acknowledgements

First of all I would like to express my happiness for my guide Dr. B.P. Bisen (Assistant Professor, Dept. of Horticulture, JNKVV, Jabalpur). He always helped me.

I wish to pay highly indebted thanks from the core of my heart to my respected father Shri Subhash Sharma and mother Smt. Mohini Sharma for their regular encouragement and moral support throughout my career.

I would like to give a special thanks to Dr. R.A Sharma (Director Agriculture, Mandsaur University, M.P.) who has been my inspiration and motivation for continuing to improve my knowledge and move my career forward. He also helped me whenever needed during completion of this book.

I pay a special thanks to my colleagues Rahul Singh Rajput, Chetan Patel, Shambhu Nayma, Deepak Kumar Verma, Kamlesh Patidar, Om Soni, Vinod Mahore, Shrishti Bilaiya, Manisha Mishra, Alka Pawaiya, Trapti Mandliya and Bhagyashree Ojha who helped me especially in different sections.

Contents

Section 'A'
Fundamentals of Horticulture

1

Importance and Scope of Horticulture

- The Total Horticulture production of the country is estimated to be an impressive level of 314.87 Million Tonnes during 2018–19.
- Production of fruits is estimated to be about 97.38 million tonnes during 2018–2019.
- Production of vegetables is estimated to be about 187.36 million tonnes during 2018–2019.
- Production of spices is estimated to be about 8.61 million tonnes during 2018–2019.
- Plantation crops are another potential sector with lot of opportunities for employment generation, foreign exchange earnings and overall supporting livelihood sustenance of mankind at large.
- In short and sweet horticulture supplies quality food for health and mind, more calories per unit area, develops better resources and yields higher returns per unit area.
- It also enhances land value and creates better purchasing power for those who are engaged in this industry. Therefore, horticulture is important for health, wealth, hygiene and happiness.
- Similar to forest trees these horticultural trees will maintain the ecosphere. They help in transforming the micro climate.
- It provides shelter to birds, reptiles and other micro organisms and add to the geo–ecological diversity on the land.

Scope of horticulture

Scope of horticulture depends on incentive it has for the farmers, adaptability of the crops, necessity and facilities for future growth through inputs availability and infrastructure for the distribution of produce/marketing etc.

Incentive for the farmer

- The biggest incentive for the farmer is money.
- Horticultural crops provide more returns in terms of per unit area of production, export value, value addition compared to agricultural crops.

Adaptability

- India is bestowed with a great variety of climatic and edaphic conditions as we have climates varying from tropical, subtropical, temperate and within these humid, semi–arid, arid, frost free temperate etc.
- Likewise we have soils from loam, alluvial, laterite, medium black, rocky shallow, heavy black, sandy etc., and thus a large number of crops can be accommodated with very high level of adaptability. Thus, there is lot of scope for horticultural crops.

Necessity

- After having achieved the self sufficiency in food, nutritional security for the people of the country has become the point of consideration/priority.
- To meet the nutritional requirement in terms of vitamins and minerals horticulture crops are to be grown in sufficient quantities to provide a bare minimum of 85 g of fruits and 300 g of vegetables per head per day.
- Good land is under pressure for stable food, industry, housing, roads and infrastructure due to population explosion and only wasteland had to be efficiently utilized where cultivation of annuals is a gamble due to restricted root zone and their susceptibility of abiotic stress. These lands can be best utilized to cultivate hardy horticultural crops like fruits and medicinal plants.
- At present our share in international trade of horticultural commodities is less than one per cent of total trade. Moreover, these commodities (spices, coffee, tea etc.,) fetch 30 times more foreign exchange per unit weight than cereals and therefore, taking advantage of
- Globalization of trade, nearness of big market and the size of production, our country should greatly involve in international trade which would provide scope for growth.

Export value

- Among fresh fruits–mangoes and grapes; in vegetables– onion and potato; among flowers, roses; among plantation – cashewnut, tea , coffee, coconut, arecanut, and spice crops like black pepper, cardamom, ginger, turmeric, chillies, etc., constitute the bulk of the export basket.

- European and gulf countries are major importer of horticultural produce.
- In the recent past communication and transport system have improved, investment in food industry has increased which will support growth of horticulture through quick deliverance and avoidance of waste.

Human Nutrition

- Fruits and vegetables play an important role in balanced diet.
- These provide not only energy rich food but also provide vital protective nutrients/elements and vitamins.
- Comparatively fruits and vegetables are the cheapest source of natural nutritive foods.
- Realizing the worth of fruits and vegetables in human health, Indian Council of Medical Research (ICMR) recommended the use of 120g fruits and 280g vegetables per capita per day.

Functions of fruits and vegetables in human body

- Fruits and vegetables provide palatability/ taste
- Improves appetite and provides fibre to overcome constipation.
- They neutralize the acids produced during digestion of proteins and fatty acids.
- They improve the general immunity of human body against diseases, deficiencies etc.
- They are the important source of vitamins and minerals for used in several bio–chemical reactions occur in body.
- Fruits and vegetables provide higher energy value per unit area compared to cereals.

Scenario of horticulture

- India is one of the leading producers of horticultural crops in the Globe.
- Horticultural crops cover more than 17% of the total area under agriculture and contribute to about 30.4% of the GDP.
- These crops accounts for 37% of the total exports of agricultural commodities.
- Due to planned emphasis laid on horticulture, India is accredited as the second largest producer of fruits and vegetables,
- India exports fruits, vegetables, processed products, flowers, seeds and planting materials, spices, cashew nut, tea, coffee etc.

2

Horticulture Zones in India

The Indian subcontinent is bestowed with a great variety of climate and soil conditions.

- Broadly the country can be divided into Tropical, subtropical and temperate regions.
- Within each broad category there are differences due to rainfall, humidity, altitude etc.
- Considering these aspects six different horticultural zones have been identified so that appropriate choice of the crops can be made and development is planned. They are;
- **Temperate:** Kashmir, Himachal Pradesh, North Uttarakhand, Sikkim and part of Arunachal Pradesh.
- **N.W. Subtropical:** Punjab, Haryana, Rajasthan, Central Uttar Pradesh and North M.P.
- **N.E. Subtropical:** Bihar, Jharkhand, Assam, Meghalaya, Nagaland, Manipur.
- **Central tropical:** South Madhya Pradesh, Chattisgarh, Gujarat, Maharashtra, Orissa and West Bengal.
- **Southern tropical:** Karnataka, Andhra Pradesh and Tamil Nadu.
- **Coastal tropical humid:** Konkan, Goa, Kerala, Western Ghats, Eastern Ghats in Tamil Nadu, Andhra Pradesh and Orissa.

The fruit growing zones are classified based on the climate factors

Tropical fruit zone

- This class includes fruit crops which are ever green unable to endure cool temperature but can tolerate warm temperature of about 100 °F.
- The fruit plants of this zone need strong sunshine warm and humid climate and a very mild winter.
- They cannot stand against frost.
- Areas under this zone include West Bengal, Parts of Punjab, Haryana, Rajasthan Orissa, Maharastra, AP, Karnataka, TN and Kerala.

- Fruits crops: Banana, Pineapple, Sapota, Papaya, Cashew, Pomegranate.

Sub-tropical fruit zone

- This class includes fruit crops intermediate characters to tropical and temperatures.
- The summer is hot and dry and winter is less mild.
- They may be either deciduous or ever green & are usually able to withstand a low temperature but not the frost
- Some require chilling for flower bud differentiation the fruits grow mostly in plains,
- This fruit zone covers the plains of Punjab, UP, Parts of Bihar, MP, WB, Maharastra, Rajasthan, Karnataka, AP, TN, Kerala, Orissa. etc.
- Fruits crops: Citrus, Grapes, Phalsa, Fig, Guava, Pomegranate, Banana etc.

Temperate fruit zone

- This class of fruits grows successfully in cold regions where temperature falls below freezing point during winter.
- During the cold season, the trees shed their leaves and go into rest period.
- For breaking the rest/dormant period, a definite chilling period is required. This chilling temperature helps the plants to put forth new growth, flowering and fruiting with the onset of spring season.
- The regions under this zone are J&K, Kuluvally, HP, Parts,
- Peaches, Plum, Cherries, Almond, Walnut, Strawberry, Apricot, Persimmon, Pecan nut, Kiwi fruit etc.

Arid zone

- The arid zone has an extreme climatic condition, high temperature low humidity, rainfall is very low and its distribution is erratic, poor textured soil.
- The area of Rajasthan (62%) and Gujarat (20%) parts of the Punjab, Haryana, Karnataka & Maharashtra
- The crops are Phalsa, Date palm, Pomegranate, Ber, Custard apple, Tamarind etc.

Semi– arid zone

- This region exhibits low and erratic rainfall, low humidity and high temperature
- Fruits of arid region can be cultivated in this zone also Mango, Sapota, Guava, Jack, Avocado, Ber, Pomegranate and Tamarind etc.

- 15 North– Eastern sub–Tropical zone:
- All tropical and sub–tropical fruits are grown in this region.
- The parts are Bihar, Assam, Meghalaya, Manipur, Parts of WB and UP etc.

North– Western region

- Parts of J&K, HP, hills of UP, South of Punjab and Haryana
- It is again classified into four regions;

1. Temperate– low winter temperature
2. Dry temperature– highly cold condition
3. Sub– Temperate– winter temperature and lesser cold
4. Low hill valley– low winter temperature and lesser cold

Central tropical fruit zone

- This region covers Southern parts of MP, Maharastra Orissa, parts of AP, WB, Gujarat etc.
- South tropical fruit zone: Karnataka, TN, Kerala and AP
- Coastal tropical fruit zone: Kerala, Goa, Diu–Daman, Tripura, Coastal parts of Maharastra, AP, WB, TN, Orissa, and Karnataka.

Humid zone fruit crops

- This region is characterized by low temperature and high humidity.
- The crops are Litchi, Strawberry, Avocado, Mangosteen, Passion fruit etc.
- Apart from these fruit zones, India has been classified in to 21 agro ecological regions based on the physiography of soils, bioclimatic types and growing periods.

3

Hi-tech Horticulture

- It is the technology of intensive production system.
- In which modern, less environmental dependent and capital–intensive but with a capacity to improve productivity and farmer income.
- Use of plastics, protected cultivation, precision farming, high density planting (HDP), integrated nutrient management (INM), integrated pest management (IPM), mechanization etc., are important facets of hi-tech horticulture. There are many practices which helps to enhance horticulture production:

Micro–irrigation

Definition:–Application of water to the plant by drippers/emitters, sprinklers, micro-jets, micro tuber misters, foggers, fat-jets etc is called micro-irrigation

- This technology increasing productivity by 30–100% while saving water to the extent of 70% and enhanced water use efficiency
- About 275.8 lakh ha area has been brought under micro irrigation.

Plasticulture

Definition:- Use of plastic in horticulture for production and post harvest handling of crops is called plasticulture.

- Plastics are used in green house, Net house, nurseries, roof top gardening, off-season cultivation, mulching, micro-irrigation, propagation etc.

Grades of plastics

- Low density polyethylene (LDPE)
- High density polyethylene (HDPE)
- Pipe for drip irrigation
- Plastic sheet of varying thickness for mulch
- Ultra violet (UV) radiation film for cladding in greenhouse

Uses

- It minimizes maintenance of the system
- Efficient management of water and energy
- Minimize wastage of crop residue
- Controlled soil erosion,
- Minimize temperature and moisture fluctuation
- Better nutrient application etc.

Protected cultivation

Definition:- Protective cultivation practices can be defined as cropping techniques where in the micro climate surrounding the plant body is controlled partially/ fully, as per the requirement the plant species grown, during their period of growth.

- The various types of protective cultivation practices have been adopting based upon the prevailing climate condition. Among them, green house/polyhouse is extremely useful for round the year in temperate condition.
- Protected cultivation is also known as controlled environmental agriculture (CEA) is highly productive, conservation of water and land and also protective of the environmental.
- A variety of vegetable, short duration –short growing fruits and flowers have been found suitable for green house cultivation. Strawberry, capsicum, tomato, cucumber, rose, gerbera, chrysanthemum, cactus, orchids etc are under cultivation in green house.
- The technology being worth increasing yield by as high as 300%.

Precision farming

Definition:- Precision farming or precision agriculture is about doing the right thing, in the right place, in the right way, at the right time. Managing crop production inputs such as water, seed, fertilizers etc to increase yield, quality, profit, reduce waste and becomes eco-friendly.

- It enhances productivity and prevents soil degradation in cultivation land.
- Dissemination of modern farm practices to improve quality, quantity and reduce cost of production in horticulture crops.
- Micro–propagation, micro-irrigation, fertigation, mulching, protected cultivation, organic farming, integrated nutrient, water, pest and diseases management, use of modified crop varieties, high tech post harvest handling etc form the part of precision farming.

High Density Planting (HDP)

Definition:- High density planting is techniques is a modern method of fruit cultivation involving planting of fruit trees densely, allowing small or dwarf trees with modified canopy for better light interception and distribution and ease of mechanized field operation.

- HDP and meadow orcharding offers high productivity per unit area both in short duration as well as perennial horticulture crops. It is achieved by resorting use of dwarf rootstock, adoption of dwarf scion varieties, use of growth regulators, proper training and pruning, suitable cropping system.
- In HDP, plant density is:
  - Semi–intensive 500–1000 trees/ha
  - Intensive 1000–10,000 trees/ha
  - Meadow orcharding/ Super intensive 20,000–1,00,000 trees/ha

4

Classification of Horticultural Crops

I. Classification of fruit crops

1. Based on botanical relationship

S. No.	Family	Crop name	Botanical name	C. N.
1.	**Arecaceae**	Coconut	Cocus nucifera	32
		Arecanut	Areca catechu	32
		Oil palm	Ealias guinensis	32
		Palmyra palm	Borasus flaballifer	32
		Date palm	Phoenix dactylifera	36
2.	**Bromeliaceaea**	Pineapple	Annanas comosus	50
3.	**Musaceae**	Banana	Musa paradisica	22, 33, 44
4.	**Anacardiaceae**	Mango	Mangifera indica	40
		Cashew nut	Anacardium occidentale	42
		Pistachio nut	Pistachia vera	30
5.	**Annonaceae**	Custard apple	Annona squamosa	14
		Bulloc's heart	Annona reticulate	14
6.	**Raosaceae**	Apple	Malus domestica	34
		Plum	Prunus domestica	16,48
		Pear	Pyrus communis	34
		Loquat	Eriobotrya japonica	34
		Almond	Prunus communis	16
		Cherry	Prunus avium	16
		Peach	Prunus Persia	16
		Apricot	Prunus armeniaca	16
		Straw berry	Fragaria ananasa	56
7.	**Rutaceae**	Bael	Aegle marmelos	18
		Wood apple	Feronia limonica	18
		Mandarin	Citrus reticulate	18
		Sweet orange	Citrus sinensis	18
		Kagzi lime	Citrus aurantifolia	18
		Lemon	Citrus limon	18
		Grapefruit	Citrus paradise	18
		Citron	Citrus medica	18

S. No.	Family	Crop name	Botanical name	C. N.
		Tahati lime	Citrus latifolia	18
		Rangpur lime	Citrus limonica	18
8.	Caricaceae	Papaya	Carica papaya	18
9.	Myrtaceaea	Guava	Psidium guajava	22
		Jamun	Syzygium cumunii	40
10.	Moraceae	Jackfruit	Artocarpus heterophyllus	56
		Fig	Ficus carica	56
11.	Apocynaceae	Karona	Carrisa carandas	22
12.	Rhamnaceae	Ber	Zizyphus mauritiana	48
13.	Punicaea	Pomegranate	Punica granatum	18
14.	Euphorbiaceae	Aonla	Emblica officinalis	28
15.	Leguminoceae	Tamarind	Tamarindus indica	24
16.	Juglandaceae	Walnut	Juglans regia	32
		Pecanut	Carya illieonsis	36
17.	Sapindaceae	Litchi	Litchi chinensis	30
18.	Sapotaceae	Sapota	Achrus sapota	26
19.	Tilliaceae	Phalsa	Grewia subnequalis	36
20.	Vitaceae	Grape	Vitis vinifera	38
21.	Sterculaceae	Cocoa	Theobroma cocoa	20
22.	Rubiacea	Coffee	Coffee robusta/ C. Arabica	22
23.	Theaceae/Camaliaceae	Tea	Camelia sinensis	30
24.	Actinidaceae	Kiwifruit	Actinidia deliciosa	58
25.	Ebenaceae	Persimmon	Diospyras kaki	90
26.	Guttiferae	Mangosteen	Garcinia mangosteena	24
27.	Lauraceae	Avocado	Persia Americana	24
28.	Oxilidaceae	Carambola	Averrhoea carambola	24
29.	Passifloraceae	Passion fruit	Passiflora indica	18
30.	Proteaceae	Macadamia nut	Macadamia ternifolia	48

2. Based on ripening behaviour

a. **Climacteric:** Increasing respiration rate after harvesting resulting they continue to ripen. During the ripening process the fruit emit ethylene along with increase rate of respiration.

b. **Non-climacteric:** There is no characteristic increased rate of respiration or production of carbon dioxide. These fruit once harvested do not ripen further. They produce very small amount of ethylene and do not respond to ethylene treatment.

Climacteric fruits			Non–climacteric fruits	
Mango	Guava	Plum	Citrus	Litchi
Banana	Papaya	Fig	Cherry	Strawberry
Sapota	Apple	Annona	Grape	Ber
Pear	Peach		Pineapple	Jamun
			Pomegranate	Cashew

3. Based on photoperiodic response

Long day plant	Short day plant	Day neutral plant
(Light period of 12 hr. Or more.)	(Light period of 12 hr. Or less)	(No effect of light on the plant)
Apple, Banana, Passion fruit	Strawberry, Pineapple, Coffee	Papaya, Guava

4. Based on salinity tolerance

Highly tolerant		Moderate tolerate		Sensitive	
Ber	Date palm	Fig	Orange	Apple	Pear
Aonla	Guava	Lemon	Mango	Peach	Plum
Coconut	Khirni	Grapefruit	Grape	Apricot	Almond
Pomegranate	Phalsa	Cashew	Jamun	Avocado	Strawberry
Custard apple					

5. Based on acid tolerance

Highly tolerant			Moderate tolerant		Sensitive
Strawberry		Raspberry	Pineapple	Avocado	
Fig	Bael	Plum	Litchi		

6. Based on Self incompatability

a. **Heteromorphic:** No fruit crops

b. **Heteromorphic:** There are two types of heteromorphic self incompatability

1. **Sporophytic:** Mango, Cocoa, Aonla
2. **Gametophytic:** Ber, Loquat, Pineapple, Apple, Pear, Apricot Almond, Cherry

7. Based on Dichogamy

a. **Protoandry:** Coconut, Pecanut, Walnut, Aonla, Annona Muricata, Passion fruit

b. **Protogyne:** Banana, Fig, Pomegranate, Plum, Annona spp, Sapota, Strawberry, Avocado

c. **Heterodichogamy:** Pecanut, Pistachionut

d. **Duodichogamy:** Chestnut

e. **PDSD:** Avocado [PDSD: Protogynous, Diurnally Synchronous Dichogamy]

f. **Heterostyle:** It have two type of flower in this dichogamy

1. **Distyle flower**
2. **Tristyle**

1. **Distyle flower: There are also two types of flowers**
   Pin type: Pomegranate, Sapota, Litchi
   Thrum type: Almon, Carambola
2. **Tristyle flower:** Primula

8. Based on pollination

a. **Self pollination:** There are some types of mechanism which favours self pollination.

- **Cleistogamy:** Grape, Papaya, Sapota
- **Homogamy:** Apricot, Citrus, Peach, Phalsa, Dwarf coconut

a. **Cross pollination:** There are some types of mechanism which favours cross pollination.

- **Monoecious:** Muscadine grape *(V. Rotundifolia)*
- **Dioecious:** Papaya, Date palm, kiwi fruit, Palmyrah, Grape
- **Gynodioecious:** Fig

9. Based on ploidy level

a. **Allo–polyploid:** These types of fruits have different type of ploidy level.

- **Allo–tetraploid/ Amphidiploid:** Mango
- **Allo–Hexaploid:** European plum
- **Allo– Octaploid:** Strawberry, Villiacolumban var. of Mango

b. **Auto–polyploid:** These types of fruits have different type of paddy level.

- **Autotriploid:** Tahati lime
- **Auto tetraploid:** Aonla, Bael, Litchi, Jackfruit, Phalsa, Umran var. Ber
- **Auto Hexaploid:** Persimon, Kiwifruit
- **Auto–Octaploid:** Gola and Illaichi var. Ber

10. Based on type Parthenocarpy

Vegetative	**Stimulative**	**Sternospermocarpy**
Banana Fig Pineapple	Litchi Bread fruit Black corianth var. of grape	Grape Sindhu var. of Mango

11. Based on Apomixis

Parthenogenesis	Recurrent apomixes	Nonreccurent/Nucellar/ Polyembryony
Mangosteen	Apple Raspberry	Mango-Adventive Citrus-Nucellar Jamun-Nucellar

12. Based on fruit morphology

1. Simple fruit:
   (a) Berry
   (b) Modified berry-Balausta, Amphisaraca, Pepo, Pome, Drupe/Stone, Hespiridium, Nut, Capsule
2. Aggregate fruit:
   (a) Eteario of berries
   (b) Eteario of achene
3. Multiple fruit:
   (a) Sorosis
   (b) Syconus

S. No.	Fruit type	Fruits name
1.	Berry	Grape, Banana, Papaya, Sapota, Arecanut, Avocado
2.	Balausta	Pomegranate
3.	Amphisaraca	Wood apple, Bael
4.	Pome	Apple, Pear, Quince, Loquat
5.	Pepo	Water melon
6.	Drup/Stone	Mango, Ber, Coconut, Coffee, Cocoa, Cherry, Peach, Plum
7.	Hespiridium	Citrus group
8.	Nut	Litchi, Walnut, Chestnut, Pecanut, Rambutan
9.	Capsule	Aonla, Carambola
10.	Eteario of berry	Custard apple, Raspberry
11.	Eteario of achene	Strawberry
12.	Sorosis	Jackfruit, Mulberry, Breadfruit
13.	Syconus	Fig

13. Based on edible part

S. No.	Edible part	Fruits name
1.	Mesocarb-Endocarp	Banana, Aonla, Apricot
2.	Mesocarp-Epicarp	Olive, Karonda, Jamun, Peach, Plum, Phalsa, Persimon
3.	Pericarp	Avocado, Ber, Custard apple, Date palm
4.	Mesocarp	Mango, Mulberry, Papaya, Passion fruit, Tamarind, Sapota
5.	Fleshy thalamus	Apple, Pear, Quince, Loquat, Strawberry, Guava

S. No.	Edible part	Fruits name
6.	Cotyledon	Almond, Cashewnut, Pecanut, Pistachionut
7.	Endosperm	Coconut
8.	Fleshy receptacle hair	Fig
9.	Juicy hair	Citrus group
10.	Juicy seed coat/ Aril	Pomegranate
11.	Succulent placenta	Bael, Wood apple
12.	Pericarp, Placenta	Grape
13.	Bracts/Perianth	Pineapple, Jackfruit
14.	Fleshy aril	Litchi
15.	Fleshy peduncle	Custard aapple

14. Based on bearing habit

a. **Terminal bearing**

New season growth: Bael, Jackfruit, Pecannut, Loquat

Old season growth: Banana, Pineapple, Litchi, Mango

b. **Axillary bearing:**

New Season growth: Papaya, Guava, Coconut, Passion fruit, Mulberry, Fig, Phalsa, Ber, Aonla, Sapota, Karonda.

Old season growth: Apple, Pear, Peach, Plum, Custard apple, Tamarind

c. **Mixed bearing:**

New season growth: Pomegranate, Citrus, Carambola

15. Based on Placentation

a. **Axil:** Banana, Citrus

b. **Marginal:** Litchi

c. **Parietal:** Papaya

d. **Basal:** Ber

16. Based on Acidic nature

a. **Citric acid:** Citrus, Guava, Pineapple, Pear, Berries

a. **Malic acid:** Apple, Banana, Cherry, Plum, Melon

17. Based on Vivipary

Grape fruit, Cocoa, Jackfruit

18. Based on centre of origin

S. No.	Centre of Origin	Fruit crops
1.	India	Bael, Ber, Jackfruit, Kagzilime, Phalsa
2.	Indo–Burma	Mango
3.	Indo–Malaya	Jamun, Carambola
4.	Indo–China	Aonla, Walnut
5.	China	Sweet orange, Mandarin, Mulberry, Litchi, Peach, Japanese plum, Persimon, Loquat, Apricot, Tea
6.	South east Asia	Banana, Coconut, Lemon, pummel, Quince
7.	Brazil	Passion fruit, Cashewnut, Pineapple
8.	Tropical America	Custard apple, Papaya
9.	Mexico	Avocado, Sapota
10.	Peru	Guava
11.	Iraq	Date palm, Fig
12.	Afganisthan	Almon
13.	Iran	Pomegranate
14.	USA	Pecanut
15.	Asia minor/Himalayan India	Apple
16.	Black Caspian sea	Grape
17.	Europe	Pear
18.	Japan	Plum
19.	Ethopia	Coffee
20.	South America	Cocoa
21.	West Africa	Oil palm
22.	Tropical Africa	Palmyra palm

19. Based on Growth curve

S. No.	Sigmoid curve	Fruit crops
1.	Single sigmoid curve	Seeded Banana
2.	Double sigmoid curve	Seedless Banana, Ber, Papaya, Sapota, Guava, Fig, Grape, Plum
3.	Triploid sigmoid curve	Kiwifruit

20. Based on Alternate bearing

- Apple, Mango, Olive, Date palm, Pecanut, Persimon, European plum

21. Based on respiration rate

a. **Very low:** Nut, Dried fruit and vegetable, Potato, Onion

b. **Low:** Apple, Citrus, Grape, Cucumber, Turnip, Sweet potato

c. **Medium:** Mango, Banana, Peach, Pear, Fig, Carrot

d. **High:** Strawberry, Avocado, Cauliflower, Lettuce, Radish

e. **Very high:** Cut flower, Leek, Brussels sprout, Snap melon

f. **Extremely high:** Spinach, Asparagus, Green peas, Mushroom, Broccol

22. Based on sex ratio

S. No.	Fruit crops	Male:Female
1.	**Date palm**	3:100
2.	**Aonla**	1:307/1:197
3.	**Apple**	33:67
4.	**Papaya**	1:20
5.	**Mango**	65–100:1–35

II. Classification of plantation crops

1. Based on cotyledon:

a. Monocot: Coconut, Arecanut

b. Dicot: Tea, Coffee, Rubber, Cocoa, Black pepper, Cinnamon, Clove, Nutmeg, Cashewnut

2. Based on growth behaviour

a. Vine: Vanilla, Black pepper,

b. Shrub: Tea

c. Tree: Cashew nut

3. Based on utility

a. Food: Coconut, Cashew nut

b. Industrial: Rubber, Arecanut, Oil palm

4. Based on extent of growing

a. Homestead plantation: Coconut, black pepper

b. Estate plantation: Tea, Coffee, Rubber

5. Based on intensity of cultivation

a. Single–storeyed: Clove, Nutmeg

b. Multi–storeyed: Coconut

III. Classification of vegetable crops

1. Based on botanical relationship

S. No.	Family	Crop name	Botanical name	C. No.
1.	**Alliaceae (Amaryllidaceae)**	Onion Garlic Leek Shallot Chive	Allium cepa Allium savtivum Allium porum Allium ascalonicum Allium schoenoprasum	16 16 32 16, 24, 32

S. No.	Family	Crop name	Botanical name	C. No.
		Multiplier potato onion	Allium cepa var. aggregatum	16
		Top tree onion	Allium cepa var. viviparum	16
		Welsh onion	Allium fistulosum	16
2.	**Araceae**	Elephant foot yam	Amorphophyllus campanulatus	26
		Taro/Arvi	Colocasia esculenta	26
		Tannia	Xanthosoma sagitifolium	26
3.	**Dioscoraceae**	Greater yam	Dioscorea alata	40
		Lesser yam	Dioscorea esculenta	40
		White yam	Dioscorea rotundata	40
4.	**Lilliaceae**	Asparagus	Asparagus officinalis	20
5.	**Amaranthuaceae**	Amaranthus	Amaranthus spp	32
6.	**Chenopodiaceae**	Beet root/ Sugarbeet	Beta vulgais	18
		Palak/Beet leaf	Beta vulgaris var. bengalensis	18
		Swiss chard	Beta vulgaris var. cicla	
		Spinach	Spinacea oleracea	12
7.	**Basillaceae**	Indian spinach	Basella rubra	24
8.	**Aizoaceae**	New Zealand palak	Tetragonia expansa	
9.	**Compositae**	Lettuce	Lactuca sativa	18
		Globe artichoke	Cynara scolymus	34
		Jerusalem artichoke	Helianthus tuberosus	102
		Chicory	Cichorium intybus	
		Endive	Cichorium endivia	
10.	**Convolvunaceae**	Sweet potato	Ipomea batatas	90
11.	**Criciferae (Brassicaceae)**	Cauliflower	Brassica oleracea var. botrytis	18
		Cabbage	B. oleracea var. Capitata	18
		Brussel's sprout	B. oleracea var. gemmifera	18
		Sprouting broccoli	B. oleracea var. italic	18
		Knol–khol	B. oleracea var. caolorapa	18
			B. oleracea var. gongylodes	
		Kale	B. oleracea var. acephala	18
		Rutabaga	B. oleracea var. napobrassica	
		Chinese cabbage	Brassica chinensis	20
		Turnip	Brassica rapa	20
		Radish	Raphanus sativua	18
		Horse radish	Armoracia rusticana	
12.	**Cucurbitacea**	Cucumber	Cucumis sativus	14
		Musk melon	Cucumis melo	24
		Snapemelon	Cucumis melo var. momordica	24

S. No.	Family	Crop name	Botanical name	C. No.
		Long melon (kakkri)	C. melo var. utillisimus	24
		Gherkin	Cucumis anguria	24
		Water melon	Citrullus lanatus	22
		Round melon (Tinda)	Citrullus lanatus var. fistulosus	22
		Pumpkin	Cucurbita moschata	40
		Summer squash	Cucurbita pepo	40
		Winter squash	Cucurbita maxima	40
		Bottle gourd	Lagenaria siceraria	22
		Bitter gourd	Momordica charantia	22
		Sponge gourd	Luffa cylindrical	26
		Ridge gourd	Luffa acutangula	26
		Pointed gourd/ Parval	Trichosanthus dioca	22
		Snake gourd	Trichosanthus anguina	22
		Sweet gourd	Momordica cochinchinensis	36
		Spine gourd	Momordica dioca	36
		Ash/Wax gourd	Benincasa hispida	24
		Ivy gourd	Coccinia indica	24
		Chow-chow	Sechium edule	28
13.	**Euphorbiaceae**	Cassava	Manihot esculenta	36
		Chekurmanis	Saropus androgynous	
14.	**Labitae**	Chinese potato	Coleus pervriflorus	
15.	**Leguminoceae**	Pea	Pisum sativum	14
		Cowpea	Vigna unguiculata	22
		French bean	Phaseolus vulgari	22
		Cluster bean/ Guar	Cyamopsis tetragonolobus	
		Lima bean	Phaseolus lunatus	14
		Winged bean	Psophocarpus tetragonolobus	18
		Dolichus bean/ Sem	Dolichus lablab/Lablab purpureus	22
		Broad bean	Vicia faba	12
		Agathi	Sesbania grandiflora	24
		Fenugreek	Trigonela foenu graceum	16
16.	**Malvaceae**	Okra	Abelmoschus esculentus	130
17.	**Solanacea**	Potato	Solanum tuberosum	48
		Tomato	Lycopersicon esculentum	24
		Brinjal	Solanum melongena	24
		Chilli	Capsicum annum	24
18.	**Moringanacea**	Drumstick	Moringa oleifera	28

S. No.	Family	Crop name	Botanical name	C. No.
19.	**Apiaceae (umbeliferae)**	Carrot	Daucus carota	18
		Coriander	Coriandrum sativum	22
		Celery	Apium graveolens	22
		Parsley	Petroselinum crispum	
		Parsnip	Pastinaca sativa	
20.	**Lauraceae**	Bay leaf	Paurus nobilis	
21.	**Polygonaceae**	Rhubarb	Rheum rhapontium	44
		Sorrel	Rumex vesicarius	

2. Based on hardness or temperature tolerance

- **Cool season vegetables:** Consumed vegetative part other than fruit.

Example: Root and tuber crops, Leafy vegetable crops, Cole crops, Pea, Broad bean etc

- **Warm season vegetables:** Consumed immature fruit or pod or seed.

Example: Tomato, Brnjal, Cucurbits, Beans, Okra, Sweet potato, New Zealand palak etc

3. Based on tolerance to soil acidity

Less tolerance (pH–6.8–6)	Moderate tolerance (pH–6.8–5.5)	Highly tolerance (pH–6.8–5)
Cole crops, Okra, Onion, Musk melon	Tomato, Brinjal, Chilli	Potato, Sweet potato, Water melon, Rhubarb, Fennel, Endive

4. Based on tolerance to soil salinity

Less tolerance (pH–7.25–7.5)	Moderate tolerance (pH–7.5–7.8.0)	Highly tolerance (pH–8.0–8.5)
Potato, Sweet potato, Brinjal, Radish, Pea	Tomato, Chilli, Onion, Cole crops	Bitter gourd, Ash gourd, Palak, Turnip, Lettuce, Beet root, French bean

5. Based on edible part

- **Leafy vegetables:** Spinach, Spinach beet, Amaranthus, Bathua, Lettuce, Radish leaves, Pea twigs etc
- **Stem vegetables:** Knol–khol, Asparagus
- **Modified stem vegetables:** Potato
- **Bulb vegetables:** Onion, Garlic
- **Root and tuber vegetables:** Radish, Carrot, Turnip, Beet root, Elephant foot yam, Sweet potato, Tapioca, Taro, yams etc

- **Fruit vegetables:** Tomato, Brinjal, Chilli, Okra, Cucurbits, Beans
- **Flower vegetables:** Cauliflower, Broccoli, Globe artichoke etc

6. Based on raising

- **Direct sown crops:** Okra, Pea, Cucurbits, Garlic, Beans etc
- **Nursery crops:** Tomato, Brinjal, Chilli, Cole crops, Onion, celery etc

7. Based on rooting depth

- **Very shallow (15–30cm):** Onion, Lettuce, Small radish
- **Very deep (120–180cm):** Sweet potato, Water melon, Pumpkin, Tomato, Asparagus, Cluster bean
- **Moderate deep (80–100):** Brinjal, Chilli, Musk melon, Turnip

8. Based on rate of respiration

Very high	High	Moderate	Low	Very low
Asparagus Broccoli Pea Spinach	Bean Lettuce Lima bean	Beet root Carrot Celery Cucumber	Cabbage Sweet potato Turnip	Onion Potato

9. Based on photoperiodic response

Long day plant (required >12 hrs light)	Short day plant (required <12 hrs light)	Day neutral plant (No effect of light)
Potato, Onion, Cabbage Cauliflower, Radish Lettuce, Spinach Palak, Turnip Carrot, Beet	Sweet Potato Indian spinach Dolichus bean Cluster bean Winged bean	Tomato, Brinjal Chilli, Okra Cucurbits, Amaranthus French bean, Cowpea Sweet pepper

10. Based on acid present

- **Citric acid:** Tomato, Potato, Beet root, Leafy vegetables, Legumes
- **Malic acid:** Carrot, Celery, Lettuce, Onion, Broccoli

11. Based on ripening behaviour

Climacteric vegetables	Non–climacteric vegetables
Tomato, Brinjal, Chilli, Gourd crops, Water melon, Musk melon etc	Cucumber

12. Based on pollination

Self pollination	Often cross pollination	Cross pollination
Tomato, Pea, Cowpea, Broad bean, Fenugreek, Lettuce, Globe artichoke	Okra, Brinjal, Chilli, Lima bean	Cole crops, Cucurbits, Radish, Carrot, Turnip etc

13. Based on Aroma

- **Cucumber** : Nonadienal
- **Cabbage** : Raw-Allyll isothiocynate
  Cooked-Dimethyl disulphide
- **Potato** : Dimethyl pyrazine
- **Radish** : Isothio cynate
- **Onion** : Allyl propyl disulphide
- **Garlic** : Diallyl disulphide

14. Based on Sex form

- **Monoecious** : Cucurbits, Amaranthus, Sweet corn, Cassava
- **Dioecious** : Pointed gourd, Spine gourd, Asparagus, Spinach, Yams, Beet root, Scarlet gourd
- **Male sterility** : Tomato, Brinjal, Chilli, Onion, Carrot, Sweet Potato
- **Protogyne** : Cole crops
- **Protoandry** : Onion, Carrot, Beet root, Leek, Celery
- **Sporophytic self incompatability** : Colr crops, Radish, Turnip, Beet
- **Gametophytic self incompatability** : Tomato

15. Based on isolation distance

Crop name	Foundation seed (m)	Certified seed(m)
Cole crops	1600	1000
Turnip, Radish	1600	1000
Beet root	1600	800
Carrot	1000	800
Spinach beet/ Palak	1600	1000
Spinach	1600	1000
Cucurbits	1000	500
Okra	400	200
Chilli	400	200
Brinjal	200	100
Tomato	50	25
Cowpea, Cluster bean, French bean, Indian bean Lima bean, Fenugreek	50	25

Crop name	Foundation seed (m)	Certified seed(m)
Pea	10	5
Potato, Sweet potato	10	5
Ginger, Turmeric	10	5

16. Based on origin

S. No.	Centre of Origin	Vegetable crops
1.	India	Brinjal, Amaranthus, Cucumber, Pointed gourd, snake gourd, Cluster bean, Basella, Dolichus
2.	Central Asia	Onion, Garlic, Leek, Pea
3.	Sri lanka	Taro
4.	Indo–burma	Yams, Bitter gourd, Chekurmanis
5.	Europe	Asparagus, Radish
6.	Tropical Africa	Musk melon, Long melon, Snape melon, Water melon, Round melon, Gherkin
7.	Mediterranean region	Beet root, Cole crops, Globe artichoke, Bay leaf, Lettuce
8.	USA	Jerusalem artichoke
9.	South America	Sweet potato, Potato, Tomato
10.	Indo china	Palak
11.	Iran	Spinach
12.	China	Chinese cabbage, Turnip
13.	Mexico	Pumpkin, Summer squash, Winter squash, Chow-chow, French bean, Chilli, Sweet pepper
14.	India/South Africa	Bottle gourd
15.	Asia	Ridge gourd
16.	Assam	Sponge gourd
17.	Japan	Ash gourd
18.	Brazil	Cassava
19.	Africa	Cow pea, Chinese potato, Winged bean, Okra,
20.	Africa/India	Drum stick
21.	Guate mala	Lima bean
22.	Afganisthan	Carrot
23.	New Zea land	New Zea land spinach

iv. Classification of spices

1. Based on Botanical relationship

S. No.	Family	Crops name	Botanical name	C. No.
1.	Piperaceae	Black peper	Piper nigrum	128
2.	Zingiberacea	Turmeric Ginger Cardamom Large cardamom	Curcuma longa Zingiber officinale Elettaria cardamomum Amomum subulatum	62 22 48
3.	Lauraceae	Cinnamon	Cinnamomum verum	24

S. No.	Family	Crops name	Botanical name	C. No.
4.	Myristicaceae	Nutmeg	Myristica fragrance	
5.		Clove	Syzygium aromaticum	44
6.	Myrtaceae	All spice	Pimenta dioca	
7.	Solanaceae	Capsicum	Capsicum annum	24
8.	Rutaceae	Curry leaf	Murraya koenigi	18
9.	Iridaceae	Saffron	Crocus sativus	
10.	Orchidaceae	Vanilla	Vanilla planifolia	
11.	Fabaceae	Fenugreek	Trigonella foenum graceum	
12.	Guttiferae	Kokum	Garcinia indica	24
13.	Apiaceae	Coriander Cumin Fennel Asafoetida Dill/Suwa Sweet flag Aniseed	Coriander sativum Cuminum cyminum Foeniculum vulgare Ferulla foetida Anethum graveolns Acorus calamus Pimpinella anisum	22 14

2. Based on completion of life cycle

- **Annual:** Cumin, Fennel, Coriander, Fenugreek, Chilli, Aniseed, Ajwain, Dill, Garlic,
- **Biennial:** Onion, Garlic, Ginger, Turmeric, Radish, Carrot, Turnip
- **Perennial:** Saffron, Tejpat, Cinnamon, Tamarind, Curry leaf, Vanilla, All spice

3. Based on growth behaviour

Herbaceous: Cumin, Coriander, Fenugreek, Onion, Garlic, Turmeric, Ginger

Shrubaceous: Black pepper, Cardamom

Tree: Cinnamon, Tejpat, Nutmeg, Clove

4. Based on part used

Seed : Fenugreek, Ajwain, Cumin, Coriander, Fennel, Dill

Fruit : Cumin, Coriander, Fennel, Black pepper, Chilli, Dill

Flower : Saffron

Bud : Clove

Underground rhizume : Turmeric, Ginger, Onion, Garlic

Bark : Cinnamon, Tejpat

Leaf : Mentha, Coriander, Tejpat, Fenugreek

5. Based on taste and flavour

- **Taste:** Cardamom, Ginger, Coriander, Cumin, Garlic, Onion, Tamarind, Black pepper, Chilli
- **Flavour:** Clove, Cardamom, Coriander, Curry leaf, Cinnamon, Asafoetida, Garlic

v. Classification of flowers

1. Based on botanical relationship

S. No.	Comon name	Botanical name	Family	Colour
1.	Amaranthus	Amaranthus candatusa	Amaranthaceae	–
2.	Balsam	Impatiens balsamina	Balsaminaceae	–
3.	Cock's comb	Celosia spp.	Amaranthaceae	–
4.	Gaillardia	Gallardia pulchella	Compositae	Red
5.	Gompherena	Gomphrena globosa	Amaranthaceae	
6.	Kochia	Kochia scoparia var tricophylla	Chenopodiaceae	
7.	Portulaca	Portulaca grandiflora	Portulaceae	
8.	Sunflower	Helianthus annus	Compositae	
9.	Tithonia	Tithoinia speciosa	Compositae	
10.	Zinnia	Zinnia elegans	Compositae	
11.	Ageratum	A. houstonianum	Compositae	Blue
12.	Antirrhinum	A. mojus	Scrophulaiaceae	
13.	China aster	Callistephusw chinensis	Compositae	
14.	Calendula	C. officinalis	Compositae	Yellow
15.	Candy tuft	Iberis spp.	Cruciferae	White,Pink
16.	Cineraria	Senecio cruentus	Compositae	
17.	Clianthus	C. dampieri	Leguminoceae	
18.	Coreopsis	C. tinctoria	Compositae	Yellow
19.	Cosmos	C. bipinnatus	Compositae	
20.	Dahlia	D. variabilis	Compositae	
21.	Helichrysum	H. bracteatum	Compositae	
22.	Hollyhock	Althea rosea	Malvaceae	
23.	Larkspur	Delphinium hybridum	Ranunculaceae	
24.	Linaria	L. bipartite	Scruphulariaceae	
25.	Nasturtium	Tropaeolum majus	Tropaeolaceae	
26.	Nigella	N. domascena	Ranunculaceae	
27.	Pansy	Viola wittor ckiana	Violaceae	
28.	Petunia	P. hybrid	Solanaceae	
29.	Phlox	P. drummondii	polemoniaceae	

S. No.	Comon name	Botanical name	Family	Colour
30.	Salvia	S. splendens	Labitae	
31.	Rudbeckia	R. bicolour	Compositae	
32.	Statice	Limonium sinuatum	Plumbaginaceae	
33.	Stock	Mathiola incana	Cruciferae	
34.	Sweet Alyssum	A. maritimum	Cruciferae	
35.	Sweet Pea	Laythyrus odoratus	Leguminoceae	
36.	Sweet Sultan	Centaurea moschata	Compositae	
37.	Sweet William	Dianthus barbatus	Caryophyllaceae	
38.	Verbena	V. hybrid	Verbanaceae	

2. Based on season of growing

- **Summer:** Zinnia, Kochia, Portulaca, Tithonia, Gaillardia, Gomphrena, Sunflower, Cosmos, Coreopsis
- **Rainy:** Balsam, Cocks comb, Amaranthus, Gaillardia
- **Winter:** China aster, Sweet William, Sweet sultan, Phlox, Verbena, Candytuff, Petunia, Nigella

3. Based on colour of flower

- **White:** Allysum, China aster, Mathiola, Nigella, Phlox, Papavera, Zinnia, Stock, Dimorphothica
- **Blue/Lavender/ Purple:** Blue lark spur, Ageratum, Anchusa, Browallia, Clitoria, Delphinium, Petunia, Viola
- **Yellow/Orange:** Calendula, Dimorphothica, Zinnia, Marigold, Coreopsis, Helichrysum
- **Pink:** Candytuff, Acroclinum

4. Based on purpose on growing

- **Rockery:** Ageratum, Alyssum, Phlox, Portulaca, Linum, Nemesia, Saponaria, Ice plant, Nasturtium Verbena
- **Shady:** Salvia, Cineraria
- **Screening:** Hollyhock, Sweet pea
- **Peculiar shape:** Clianthus
- **Hanging basket:** Petunia, Portulaca, Verbena, Torenia, Begonia, Dwarf ageratum,
- **Fragrant flower:** Sweet alyssum, Sweet sultan, Sweet pea, Stock, Phlox, Carnation, Rose, Jasmine, Tuberose

- **Bedding:** Dahlia, Marigold, Phlox, Verbena, Carnation, Petunia, Ice plant, Candy tuff, Balsam, Portulaca
- **Pots:** Carnation, Antirrhinum, Petunia, Alocasia, Anthurium, Begonia, Dracaena
- **Dry flower:** Statice, Helichrysum, Acrolinum, Nigella, Lady's lace

5. Based on pollination

- **Self pollination:** Lupin, Sweet pea, Salvia
- **Often cross pollination:** Larkspur, Linaria,. Phlox, Pansy,
- **Based on nature of growth**
- **Annual:** Hollyhock, Sweet pea, Chrysanthemum, Carnation, Sweet alyssum, Dahlia, Marigold, Verbena, Phlox
- **Perennial:** Rose, Jasmine, Chrysanthemum

6. Based on mode of propagation

- **Bulb:** Lily, Narcissus, Tulip
- **Corm:** Gladiolus, Crocus
- **Rhizobium:** Canna, Iris
- **Tuber:** Dahlia

7. Based on photoperiodic response

- **Short day plants:** Salvia, Poinsettia, Primerose
- **Long day plants:** China aster, Calendula, Gardenia, Delphinium, Stock
- **Day neutral plants:** Carnation, Hibiscus
- **Intermediate day:** Coleus
- **Long short day:** Aloe
- **Short long day:** Campanula, White clover
- **Hardy annual:** Digitalis, Rudbeckia, Viola
- **Tender annual:** Oxalis

8. Based on time of seed germination

- **In night:** Nicotiana, Lobelia, Echium
- **In dark:** Nigella, Phlox, Amaranthus, Allium

9. Based on number of seed

- **Maximum seed per gram:** Petunia, Portulaca
- **Minimum seed per gram:** Sweet pea, Sunflower

10. Based on seed size

- **Fine seed:** Marigold, Gaillardia, Chi8na aster etc
- **Bold seed:** Hollyhock, Lupin, Nasturtium, Morning glory

5

Bearing and Unfruitfulness in Fruit Plant

Bearing: Bearing is connotation of flowering and fruiting.

Bearing habit: The position of flower bud with respect to vegetative growth of the plant after the cessation of juvenility. Different fruit plants have different habits.

Depending upon position of fruit bud, fruit trees may be categorized as under:

1. **Shoot flowering:** Terminal flowering: Banana, Pineapple, Mango, Litchi, Avocado

   Lateral flowering: Coconut, Papaya, Guava, Orange, Ber, Passion fruit, Bread fruit
2. **Stem /Branch bearing:** It also known as caulifluorous bearing habit. In this habit, flower and fruit appear directly from the main stem or branch. Example: Jackfruit, Cocoa, Durian,
3. **Spur bearing:** It is a shot stubby shoot of more than one year age which bears fruit bud in many fruit plants. Example: Apple, Pear, Peach, Plum, Cherry, Grape, Apricot etc

Inflorescence

Definition: Arrangement of flowers on the shoot is known as inflorescence. Flowers may appear singly or in cluster in terminal or axillary position of the shoot as simple or mixed bud.

Different kind of inflorescence:

a. **Racemose inflorescence:** It is divided into three groups such as

   i. **Raceme:** Blackberry, Raspberry, Blue berry, Wild cherry etc.

   ii. **Catkin:** Walnut, pecanut, Chestnut, Mulberry

   iii. **Corymb:** Pear

b. **Cymose inflorescence:** It is divided into two groups such as
   i. **Panicle:** Mango, Litchi, Loquat, Grape
   ii. **Fasicle:** Ber, Cherry, Plum, Sweet orange
c. **Others:** It is a special type of inflorescence, these are,
   i. **Spadix:** Arecanut, Banana, Coconut
   ii. **Hypanthodium:** Fig, Gular

Flower

Definition: Consist form of calyx, corolla, androecium and gynoecium/pistil is termed as flower.

Types of flower:

1. **Staminate flower:** In which only male flowers are found
   Example: Aonla, Date palm, Grape, Coconut, Cashewnut, Pomegranate, Litchi, Walnut, Papaya, Mango etc
1. **Pistilate flower:** In which only female flower are found
   Example: Aonla, Date palm, Grape, Coconut, Walnut, Papaya etc.
3. **Hermaphrodite flower:** In which both male and female flowers are found.
   Example: Mango, Papaya, Ber, Citrus, Guava etc.

Pollination

Definition: It is the process of transfer of pollen grain to the stigma of the flower is called pollination.

Type of pollination

- **Self pollination/Autogamy:** When pollen from anther is transferred to the stigma of same flower is known as self pollination.
- **Geitonagamy:** Pollination of one flower (Male) to another flower (Female) in same plant.
  Example: Orchids
- **Cross pollination/Aullogamy:** When pollen from anther is transferred to the stigma of the other flower located on different plant of the same cultivar or related species, is known as cross pollination.
- **Often cross pollination:** It is intermediate condition between self pollinated and cross pollinated species. In this case, cross pollination exceeds 5–30% and self pollination occurs 70–95%.

Transfer of pollen

Pollinators: Pollen grain reaches to the stigma of the flower by various vectors. These vectors are called pollinators. These vectors are Insect, Wind, Water, Bird and Mammals/Animals.

Entomophilous (Pollination by insect)	**Anemophilous** (Pollination by wind)	**Hydrophilous** (Pollination by water)	**Ornithophilous** (Pollination by Bird)	**Zoophilous** (Pollination by Mammals/ Animal)
Mango, Guava Ber Litchi, Citrus, Custard apple, Apple Pear, Peach Plum, Almond, Walnut, Cucurbits Cricifers	Coconut Cashewnut Date palm Papaya Jackfruit Sapota Pomegranate Chestnut	Lily Giantt water lily	Banana Pineaplle	Elephant, Monkey, Squirrels etc are responsible for this pollination.

- Mango is pollionated by House fly *(Musca domestica)*
- Fig is pollinated by Wasp
- Oil palm is pollinated by Weevil

Factors favour for self pollination

1. **Bisexuality:** Male and female part must be present in the same flower.
   Example: Grape
2. **Cleistogamy:** Condition in which flowers do not open.
   Example: Grape, Papaya, Sapota, Lettuce
3. **Chasmogamy:** Condition in which flower open after pollination
   Example: Tomato, Capsicum
4. **Homogamy:** Maturity of the time of male and female flowers is same.
   Example: Apricot, Citrus, Peach, Phalsa, Dwarf coconut
5. **Manoecy:** When male and female flower are present in the same plant, this situation is called monoecy and the flowers are known as monoecious.
   Example: Banana, Jackfruit, Coconut, Pecanut, Walnut, Cucurbits etc.

Factors favour for cross pollination

a. **Unisexuality:** Only male or female part present in the same flower. It may be Staminate or pistillate flower.
   Example: Papaya, Date palm, Muscadine grape etc

b. **Dioecy:** Male and Female flowers are present on different plants.
Example: Papaya, Date palm, Asparagus etc.

c. **Dichogamy:** Maturity of the male and female part of the flower is different. There are two types.

Protogyny: Female part (Pistile) mature first before male part (Stamens) or Female flower first appear than of male flower.
Example: Banana, Pomegranate, Fig, Plum, Avocado, Sapota, Annona, Strawberry, Cole crops etc

Protoandry: Male part (stamens) mature first before female part (Pistile) or male flower first appear than female flower
Example: Coconut, Walnut, Pecanut, Aonla, Annona muricata, Passion fruit, Onion, Carrot etc

d. **Duodichogamy:** A condition in which each plant produce two batches of male flower that are temporally separated by a batch of female flower, this condition is known as duodichogamy.
Example: Chestnut

e. **Heterodichogamy:** It is differs from normal dichogamy, in that it involves two mating types (protogyny and protoandry) that occur at a 1:1 ration in a population. Flowering phase of the two mating types are synchronized and reciprocal, which was considered to ensure between type outcrossing.
Example: Pecanut, Pistachionut

f. **Heterostyly:** Condition in which length of styles of the flower is differ from the stamens. It is of two types:

1. Distyly flower

2. Tristyly flower

1. **Distyly flower:** It have also two types of flower

Pin type flower: Style is longer than stamens.
Example: Pomegranate, Sapota, Litchi

Thrum type flower: Style is short than stamens.
Example: Almond, Carambola

2. **Tristyly flower:** Three different form of style are present in the flower.

Long styled, medium and short stamens
Medium styled, short and long stamens
Short styled, medium and long stamens

g. **Herkogamy:** Due to physical barriers like Waxy film on the stigma, pollen can not penetrate the stigmatic surface.

   Example: Lima bean

h. **Self–incompatibility:** Inability of pollen from a flower to fertilize the same flower or other flowers on the same plant. It is of two types:

   1. **Sporophytic self incompatibility:** It is governed by the genotype of pollen producing plant.

      Example: Mango, Aonla, Cocoa

   2. **Gametophytic self incompatibility:** It is governed by the genotype of pollen.

      Example: Ber, Loquat, Pineapple, Apple, Pear, Apricot Almond, Cherry

i. **Male sterility:** It is defined as an absence or non–functional pollen grain, while female gametes function normally. Types of male sterility:

   1. **Cytoplasmic male sterility (CMS):** It is governed by Cytoplasmic genes. *Example:* Carrot, Sweet pepper, Cucumber

   2. **Gametophytic male sterility (GMS):** It is governed by nuclear genes. *Example:* Tomato, Musk melon, Water melon, Cole crops

   3. **Cytoplasmic gametophytic self incompatibility:** It is governed by both cytoplasmic and nuclear genes.

      Example: Onion, Carrot, Radish, Beet, Tomato

   4. **Transgenic male sterility:** It is induced by the technique of genetic engineering. *Example:* Tomato

   5. **Chemical male sterility:** It is induced by the use of chemical. These chemicals are called Male gametocides. Example: Gibberrellins, MH, Sodium Methyl Arsenate.

Pollen Viability

Definition: Pollen viability is the ability of pollen to germinate over stigmatic surface effecting elongation of pollen tube sufficiently to fertilize egg cell.

Pollen viability test

Acetocarmine test: The pollen grain are placed over slide and 1–2% acetocarmine solution is placed over it. The pollens which are viable are stained and non-viable are fail to get stained.

Unfruitfulness

Definition: Fruit trees fail to bear fruits due to phylogenical, physiological, managemental, parasitical and climatological factors is known as unfruitfulness.

- **Phylogenical factors:** Sex form like monoecious, dioecious, hermaphrodite, Dichogamy, Duedichogamy, Self incompatibility etc.
- **Physiological factors:** Poor germination of pollen, pre mature or delayed pollination, slows growth of pollen tube, nutritional status of plants etc.
- **Managemental factors:** Proper training and pruning, rootstock, supply of fertilizers etc.
- **Parasitical factors:** Insect-pests, Diseases etc.
- **Climatological factors:** Temperature, Humidity, Rainfall, Frost, Cloud etc.

6

Nursery in Horticulture Crops

Nursery

Definition: It is a small area or place where seeds are sown for getting baby plant to transplant in the main field. These baby plants are known as seedlings.

Generally, growing rootstock in fruit plants and small seeded vegetables like tomato, brinjal, onion, cole–crops etc are needed to raising nursery and further transplanting.

There are two types of nursery;

- **Temporary nursery:** This nursery is raised by soil in open condition.
- **Permanent nursery:** This nursery is raised permanently walled and often provided with overhead covering against rain or frost.

Components of nursery

1. Selection of site
2. Seed
3. After care

1. Selection of site

- Site should be under open and protected condition
- Near the source of irrigation
- Site should be well drained
- Location should be connected with roads to have an easy access to market

2. Seed

- Seed is the backbone of crop.
- It should be healthy, sound, high yielding and true to type.
- Reliable source of seed availabilities are National Seed Corporation, State Seed Corporation, State Agriculture University, Farms and Governmental nurseries.

3. After care

- Uniform moistuire level should be maintained in the seed bed.
- Avoid water stagnation situation in the nursery bed
- Remove weed time to time
- Spray of fungicides to protect fungi diseases..

Seed treatment

Before sowing, seed and soil should be treated against seed and soil born diseases. Three types of seed treatment are used to control diseases:

1. Disinfestation
2. Disinfectants
3. Protectants

Soil drenching

- It is the technique of applied or spray of pesticides or fertilizers to the base of plants.
- It is inhibited the growth of soil born fungi such as Fusarium, Pythium, Phytophthora etc.
- In soil drenching, Thirum, Captan, Ceresan etc can be used.

Preparation of nursery beds

There are three types of nursery beds:

- **Flat nursery bed:** It is prepared during spring–summer season.
- **Raised nursery bed:** It is prepared during rainy season. Raised bed of 10–15 cm height from ground level is prepared. Size is kept according to availability of area.
- **Sunken nursery bed:** It is prepared during winter season. This bed is prepared 10 to 15 cm downward from the soil surface.

Essential operation in nursery raising

Thinning: Removal of excess seedling to facilitate aeration and better development is known as thinning.

Pricking: Transfer of young seedling from one pot/bed to another pot or bed, is known as prickling.

Hardening off: Before exposing the plants to full sunlight, withholding the irrigation for about 7 to 10 days so as to make the plant able to tolerate external growing condition.

Mulching: It is a thin extraneous layer of farm waste, residues, wood–chip, saw, dust, ash, polythene applied on the surface to conserve soil moisture. After sowing of seed, 5 cm thick layer of mulch is applied over the bed.

Growing media for raising nursery plants

Soil: Easy and chip material used as growing medium.

Compost: Decomposed and rotten material of farm waste.

Sand: It used for nutritional experiments to eliminate the biasness of the result as affected by base nutritional status of the growing medium.

Sphagnum moss:

- It is a bog grass plant of the genus Sphagnum. It has very good water retention capacity.
- It has a pH of 3.5–4.
- It contains some specific fungicide which prevents dumping off of seedling grown in it.

Perlite:

- It is a grey–white silicaceous material obtained after heating the crushed ore to about 760 °C.
- It is neutral in reaction with a pH of 6–8. It does not contain mineral nutrient.

Vermiculite

- It is a micaceous mineral obtained from mica ore after processing the ore at 109 °C.
- It is a hydrated magnesium–aluminum–iron silicate.
- It is neutral in reaction with good buffering property and insoluble in water.
- It has good cation exchange capacity and thus can hold nutrient and release it slowly and slowly.
- Vermiculite contains enough magnesium and potassium needed for plants.

Peat

- It is heterogeneous mixture of decomposed plant material (humus) that has accumulated in a water saturated environment and in the absence of oxygen.

There are three types of peat:

- **Moss peat:** It is least decomposed and derived from sphagnum or other mosses. It has high moisture holding capacity about 15 times to its dry weight, high acidity (3.2–4.5 pH) and contains little amount of nitrogen.

- **Reed sedge peat:** It consists of remains of grasses, reeds, sedge and other swamp plants. It holds 10 time water to its dry weight and its pH ranges from 4.0–7.5.
- **Peat humus:** It is highly decomposed material. It originates from hypnum moss or reed sedge peat. It has low water holding capacity and its pH range from 2.0–3.5.

Saw dust: It is decomposed material of timber. It has no nutrient content. It is fine and holds sufficient moisture for some period. It is an organic material and favours growth of fungus so its use is limited in propagation.

7

Protected Cultivation

Greenhouse

It is constructed by plastic, polythene, and fibreglass material having temperature control and ample light availability needed for propagating plants by seed, cutting and grafting.

Types of greenhouse

1. Based on shape and style: The commonly followed types of greenhouse based on shape are lean–to, even span, uneven span, ridge and furrow, saw tooth and quonset greenhouse.

Lean–to type greenhouse:

- It is limited to single or double–row plant benches with a total width of 7–12 feet.
- It is typically facing south side. It should face the best direction for adequate sun exposure.
- This design makes the best use of sunlight and minimizes the requirement of roof supports.
- It has the disadvantages: limited space, limited light, limited ventilation and temperature control.

Even span type greenhouse:

- It is attached to a house at one gable end. It can accommodate 2–3 rows of plant benches.
- The design has a better shape than a lean–to type for air circulation to maintain uniform temperatures during the winter heating season.
- A separate heating system is necessary unless the structure is very close to a heated building. It will house 2 side benches, 2 walks, and a wide center bench.
- The single span in general, varies from 5–9 m, whereas the length is around 24 m. The height varies from 2.5–4.3 m.

Uneven span type greenhouse

- This type of greenhouse is constructed on hilly terrain. The roofs are of unequal width; make the structure adaptable to the side slopes of hill.
- This type of greenhouses is not adaptable for automation.

Ridge and furrow type greenhouse

- This type of green house use two or more A–frame greenhouses connected to one another along the length of the eave.
- The snow loads must be taken into the frame specifications of these greenhouses since the snow cannot slide off the roofs as in case of individual free standing greenhouses, but melts away.
- In spite of snow loads, ridge and furrow greenhouses are effectively.

Saw tooth type Greenhouse

- These are also similar to ridge and furrow type greenhouses except that, there is provision for specific natural ventilation in this type.

Quonset greenhouse

- In this type of greenhouses polyethylene is used as a covering material.
- These greenhouses are connected either in free, standing style or arranged in an interlocking ridge and furrow.
- In the interlocking type, truss members overlap sufficiently to allow a bed of plants to grow between the overlapping portions of adjacent houses.
- A single large cultural space thus exists for a set of houses in this type, an arrangement that is better adapted to the automation and movement of labour.

2. Based on utility: Of the different utilities, artificial cooling and heating of the greenhouse are more expensive and elaborate. Hence based on the artificial cooling and heating. It is classified as greenhouse:

Greenhouses for active heating:

- During the night time, air temperature inside greenhouse decreases.
- To avoid the cold bite to plants due to freezing, some amount of heat has to be supplied.
- Various methods are adopted to reduce the heat losses, viz., using double layer polyethylene, thermo pane glasses (Two layers of factory sealed glass with dead air space) or to use heating systems, such as unit heaters, central heat, radiant heat and solar heating system.

Greenhouses for active cooling

- During summer season, it is desirable to reduce the temperatures of greenhouse than the ambient temperatures, for effective crop growth.
- Hence suitable modifications are made in the green house so that large volumes of cooled air are drawn into greenhouse.
- This greenhouse either consists of evaporative cooling pad with fan or fog cooling.
- This type of greenhouse is designed in such a way that it permits a roof opening of 40% and in some cases nearly 100%.

3. Based on construction: Based on construction, greenhouses can be broadly classified as wooden framed, pipe framed and truss framed structures.

Wooden framed structures

- In general, for the greenhouses with span 6–15 m, only wooden framed structures are used.
- Pine or Timber wood is commonly used as it is inexpensive and possesses the required strength.

Pipe framed structures

- Pipes are used for construction of greenhouses, when the clear span is around 12m.
- In general, the side posts, columns, cross ties and purlins are constructed using pipes. In this type, the trusses are not used.

Truss framed structures

- If the greenhouse span is greater than or equal to 15m, truss frames are used.
- Most of the glass houses are of truss frame type, as these frames are best suited for pre-fabrication.

4. Based on covering materials: Covering materials are the major and important component of the greenhouse structure. Covering materials such as polythene, glass have direct influence on the greenhouse effect inside the structure and they alter the air temperature inside the house.

Glass greenhouses

- Glass has the advantage of greater interior light intensity.
- This type of greenhouse has higher air infiltration rate which leads to lower interior humidity and better disease prevention.
- Lean–to type, even span, ridge and furrow type of designs are used for construction of glass greenhouse.

Plastic film greenhouses

- Plastic films including polyethylene, polyester and polyvinyl chloride are used as covering material in this type of greenhouses.
- The main disadvantage with plastic films is its short life. For example, the best quality ultraviolet (UV) stabilized film can last for four years only.
- Quonset design as well as gutter-connected design is suitable for using this covering material.

Rigid panel greenhouses

- Polyvinyl chloride rigid panels, fibre glass-reinforced plastic, acrylic and polycarbonate rigid panels are employed as the covering material in the quenset type frames or ridge and furrow type frame.
- High grade panels have long life even up to 20 years.
- The main disadvantage is that these panels tend to collect dust as well as to harbor algae, which results in darkening of the panels and subsequent reduction in the light transmission. There is significant danger of fire hazard.

Shading nets

- Shade nettings are designed to protect the crops and plants from UV radiation, but they also provide protection from climate conditions, such as temperature variation, intensive rain and winds.
- Better growth conditions can be achieved for the crop due to the controlled micro–climate conditions "created" in the covered area, with shade netting, which results in higher crop yields.
- All nettings are UV stabilized to fulfill expected lifetime at the area of exposure.
- They are characterized of high tear resistance, low weight for easy and quick installation with a 30–90% shade value range.

Lath house

- It is a structure erected primarily to create shade to raise tender plants and to protect the plants from high temperature and light intensity. Agro-nets of different shading intensities are used for erecting lath-house.
- By controlling light intensities, the lath-house reduces moisture stress and decrease the water requirement of plants

Hotbeds

- The standard size of hotbeds is 0.9 ×1.8 m^2.
- Red wood or cedar wood which is resistant to decay, is used for preparing hotbeds.
- The seedling starts growth and cutting root early in the season when hotbeds is used.
- In hotbeds heat is provided below the propagating medium by electric heating cables, hot water, steam pipes, hot air fumes or fermenting manure.
- For hotbeds of 1.8 × 1.8 m^2 about 18 meters of heating cable is required.
- The hotbeds are filled with 10–15 cm of a rooting or seed germination medium over the heating cables.

Cold frame

- Cold frame construction is similar to hotbeds except that no provision is made for supplying bottom heat.
- The standard glass 0.9 × 1.8 m^2 hotbeds are used as covering for the frame
- It is used for hardening for rooted cutting or young seedling before planting.
- Cold frames utilize only the heat of the sun retained by the transparent covering.

8

Planning and Layout of Orchard

Planning

- Generally 10% of the total area is left aside for building, roads, paths, tube-well, channels etc.
- Windbreak is very important aspect of orchard planning.
- Windbreak plants are planted in North–Wset direction.
- The market should be vicinity of orcharding site. It reduces transportation.
- The site of orchard should not be a wind or flood prone area.
- The soil should be neutral in reaction (pH 7).
- As per climate adaptability, fruit plants have been classified into three groups; tropical, sub–tropical and temperate types.

Layout

Square system

- The plants are planted in each corner of the square.
- Row to row and Plant to plant distance are same.

Rectangular system

- Plant to plant and row to row distance are not similar.
- Row to row distance is kept more than plant to plant distance

Hexagonal system

- Six trees are planted in each corner of equilateral triangle and making a hexagon.
- Seventh tree is planted in the centre of hexagon.
- 15% more plants are planted as compare to square system.

Quincunx system

- This system is similar to square system except one editional plant is planted in the centre of each square.
- The plants that are planted in the centre of each square is called " Filler plant".
- 81% more plants are planted as compare to square system.
- Papaya, Banana, Lime etc are important filler plants.

Contour system

- It is adopted in hilly area where land is undulated and soil erosion is great throat.
- Under this system, contour terrace is developed on the hill slop.
- The width of contour terrace is varies according the slop of the hills.

Cropping System

Cropping system, an important component of farming system. It represents a cropping pattern used on a farm and their interaction with farm resources, other farm enterprises and available technology, which determine their make up.

9

Training and Pruning

Training

- Training is related to shape and size of the plant.
- In this process, removal of part of the plant to develop a proper shape.
- It develops strong frame work of tree, balance between vegetative and reproductive growth and facilitate interception of sunrays to each and every part of trees.

Methods of training

Central leader system

- Main stem of tree is allowed to grow continuously.
- First branch is allowed to grow 45–50 cm height from ground level and other branches are allowed to grow on main stem at a distance of 15–20 cm.
- The tree attained **Robust shape**
- It is not suitable for high altitude and hot arid areas.

Open centre system

- When plant attains a height of 40–50 cm, top/terminal portion of main stem is removed.
- 4–5 branches well scattered, arranged and distributed all around the main stem are selected.
- The tree attained **Bowl shaped.**
- It is not suitable for high altitude and where severe frost is common.

Modified leader system

- It is intermediate stage of centre leader and open centre system.
- The main stem is allowed to grow for 4–5 years. After that, it is cut at a height of 120–150 cm from ground level.
- The first shoot is allowed 40–50 cm from the ground level.

- 4–5 branches located at a distance of 15–20 cm and placed all around the main stem are selected.
- It is suitable in almost all regions.

Other methods of training

Bush system

- Height of the plant is kept 2 meters.
- First shoot is allowed 25–30 cm from the ground level.
- Above first branch, 3–4 branches are allowed to grow at a distance of 15 to 20cm..
- Plant attains bush shape
- *Example:* Apple

Pyramid system

- Plant appears pyramid shape.
- Lower branches are longer and higher branches are gradually smaller
- The branches are allowed to grow on main stem at 20cm height from ground level.
- *Example:* Apple, Pear

Espalier system

- In this system, first row of wire is stretched at a height of 60–70 cm, second row at 130–140 cm and third row is stretched at a height of 200 cm from ground level.
- 3–6 branches are allowed to grow horizontally in both directions parallel to the ground.
- *Example:* Apple, Kiwi, Grape etc

Cordon system

- This system is also known as Single cordon, double cordon and triple cordon.
- The wires fixed to the ground using cement or concrete at 4–6 meters interval.
- Plants are planted at a distance of 1–1.5 m. The stem of the plant is tied with wire.
- *Example:* Grape, Peach, Plum etc

Tatura trellis system

- It is developed by David chalmers, Ban Van den and Leo van Heek during 1973 in Australia.

- The orientation of trellis is kept to north–south directions.
- The system favours high yield owing to optimum light interception and close planting.
- *Example:* Apple, Pear, Peach, Plum, Apricot, etc

Specific methods of training for grape vine

Head system

- Plant develops in bush shape.
- Plants are allowed to grow at a height of 75–90 cm.
- 5–6 side branches are allowed to grow on main stem.
- Side branches are pruned after one year during October in south and January in north india.
- It is suitable for less vigorous cultivars like Beauty seedless, Perlette, Delight etc

Kniffin system

- This is also known as 4–cane system.
- Two rows of wire are stretched at a height of 1–1.5 m from ground level.
- The vines are allowed to grow at a height of 1.5 m and after deheaded and 2 branches of the vines are trained to the wires parallel to the ground
- These vines develop 4 arms.
- It is suitable for medium vigorous cultivar like Early Muskat, Bhokari, Delight etc

Telephone system/Over head threllis system

- It is also known as 6–cane system.
- Poles are erected at a distance of 3.5–4.5 m
- 6 wires are stretched from one pole to another and the vines are trained over these wires.
- The vines are allowed to grow at a height of 1.5–1.6 m and then trained along with the wires.

Bower system

- The vines are trained on criss–cross network of wires.
- Poles, which are 2–2.5 m high, are fixed at a distance of 4.5–6 m.
- Wire stretched at distance of 60 cm and vines trained over these wires.
- 2 vigorous shoot in opposite direction are selected at the wire level for training as primary arms.

- On each primary arm, three laterals on either side are selected at 60cm distance to develop as secondary arms.
- Each secondary arm is allowed to have 8–10 tertiary arms. Tertiary branches bear fruiting cane.
- **Cost:** Benefit ratio of this system is 1:2.09

Pruning

- Removal of plant parts from the plant for the specific purpose, in favour of yield.

Methods of pruning

- **Heading back:** Removal of apical or terminal portion of the shoot leaving basal portion.
- **Thinning:** Removal of excessive part of the plant such as: flower, leaves, fruit etc.
- **Ringing/Girdling:** A circular ring (2.5–3 cm) is removed to accumulation of photosynthates in upward portion of the plant.
- **Notching:** Removing a wedge shaped bark (2.5–3 cm) **above a bud** to check the influence of hormone and encourages growth.
- **Nicking:** Removing a wedge shaped bark (2.5–3 cm) **below a bud** to accumulation of carbohydrates from the leaves to the bud and may result in the formation of fruit bud.

10

Propagation of Plants

Propagation

Definition: Multiplication of plant is termed as propagation.

Types of propagation

There are mainly two types of propagation

1. Sexual propagation
2. Asexual propagation

Sexual propagation

- Multiplication of plants by seed.
- Seeds create diversity. Diversity in plants is essential for genetic improvement of plant.
- Seed propagated plants are long lived, bushy appearance and have greater tolerance to adverse climate, soil, disease and insect endemic.
- Rootstock is raised by seed. Rootstocks are used in asexual propagation.
- Seed propagated plants are not true to types to the mother plants

Asexual propagation

- Multiplication of plants by vegetative parts of the plant such as; cutting, budding, grafting, layering, rhizomes, tuber etc.
- Asexual propagated plants are short lived.
- Asexual propagation produces true to types of to the mother plants.
- Repairing of damaged portion of plant by asexual propagation.
- Asexual propagation requires skilled person for budding, grafting and layering.
- Asexual propagation restricts diversity.

Methods of asexual propagation

- Cutting
- Budding

- Grafting
- Layering

Cutting

Definition: Separation of shoot/Leave/Root from the mother plant is known as cutting.

Process of cutting

- Cuttings have pencil thickness along with 2–3 buds.
- Length of the cutting is kept to 7–45 cm.
- In cutting, upper cut is given about 1–2 cm above the upper node in round shape while the lower cut is made slanting manner just below the node.
- Lower portion of cutting is planted in soil just because slanting cut covers more area of under the soil for rooting as compare to round cut.
- The upper cut is covered by Bordex past for preventing fungal or other damages and lower portion should be treated with IBA solution at 2000 ppm for better rooting.

Types of cutting

- Stem cutting
- Root cutting
- Leaf cutting

Stem cutting: A portion of stem is taken for propagation.

There are four types of stem cutting.

- Hard wood cutting
- Semi hard wood cutting
- Soft wood cutting
- Herbaceous cutting

Parameters	Hard wood cutting	Semi hard wood cutting	Soft wood cutting	Herbaceous cutting
Shoot taken	1 year old	4–9 month old	2–3 month old	1–2 month old
Shoot length	10–45 cm	7–20 cm	10–15 cm	7–15 cm
Cutting time	Nov–Feb	July–Aug	July–Aug	July–Aug
Number of buds	Atleast 3–4	Atleast 2–3	Atleast 2–3	Atleast 2–3
Example	Pomegranate, Karonda, Grape, Fig, Rose etc	Mango, Guava, Lemon, etc	Tea	Ornamental plants

- **Root cutting:** A portion of root is taken for propagation.

For root cutting, root is 2–3 cm thickness
Length of root is 10–15 cm
Root cutting prepared

- In North India December
- In South India July–Aug

Example: Apple, Pear, Guava etc

- **Leaf cutting:** A portion of leaves or leave is taken for propagation.

Example: Begonia, Bryophyllum, Tea and ornamental plants

Budding

Definition: A process of connecting **bud**, which is separated from mother plant and rootstock in a manner and grow a successful plant is termed as budding.

- **Mother plant:** A plant which gives bud or scion for the propagation. This plant is called mother plant.
- **Scion or Cion bud:** The bud which develops branches, flowers and fruit is termed as scion bud.
- **Rootstock or stock:** The portion over which bud is united which provides supportive stem and root system to the budded scion is termed as rootstock.
- **Cambium cell:** It is a responsible cell to connecting the scion or scion bud to the rootstock.
- **Millen effect:** A effect of bud on the rootstock and effect of rootstock on the scion or scion bud, which is responsible for connecting each other is known as Millen effect.

Budding process

- Remove leaves from selected scion or budded scion before 10 days of budding
- Bud of 2.5–3 cm length is taken out from scion
- Similar size incision is made on rootstock
- The bud insert in the incision of rootstock
- After inserting bud, union is wrapped by polythene tape for few days or month
- After completion of union, removed polythene tape
- Remove upper portion of rootstock

Types of budding

- Shield budding
- Patch budding
- Forket budding
- Ring budding
- Chip budding

Shield budding

- Boat shaped bud is taken from scion shoot
- It is also known as T-budding

Example: Rose, Apple, Pear, Peach, Citrus etc.

Patch budding

- Patch shaped or square or rectangular shaped bud is used for budding
- It is useful for thick bark plants

Example: Aonla, Mango, Jackfruit etc

Forket budding

- Patch shaped or square or rectangular shaped bud is taken out from scion shoot
- Incision on rootstock, the vertical flap of the bark is left intact with lower portion of the bark

Example: Rubber, Mango, Cashewnut etc.

Ring budding

- Ring shaped bud is used for budding
- No wrapping is required in this budding process

Example: Ber, Peach, Mango etc

Chip budding

- This method is used when there is lack of sap flow and bud does not taken out easily from the bark

Example: Mango, Grape, Citrus etc

Grafting

Definition: A process of connecting **scion or shoot**, which is separated from mother plant and rootstock in a manner and grows a successful plant, is termed as budding.

Process of grafting

- Remove leaves from selected scion before 10 days of grafting
- The Scion of 2–3 buds having pencil thickness
- The Scion of 8–15 cm length is taken out from mother plant
- Similar size incision is made on rootstock
- The scion insert in the incision of rootstock
- After inserting scion, union is wrapped by polythene tape for 3–4 weeks
- After completion of union, removed polythene tape
- Remove upper portion of rootstock
- The rootstock of 1–2 year age having pencil thickness

Types of grafting

- Veneer grafting
- Tongue grafting
- Whip grafting
- Cleft grafting
- Wedge grafting
- Bridge grafting
- Epicotyl grafting
- Soft wood grafting

Veneer grafting

- V–shaped cut is made on scion and similar size incision in rootstock

Example: Mango

Tongue grafting

- Double slanting cut is made on both rootstock and scion for interlock each other

Example: Apple, Pear, Sapota, Walnut etc

Whip grafting

- 1 year old rootstock is used for propagation

Example: Walnut, Apple, Pear etc

Cleft grafting

- It is useful in small height plants

Example: Custard apple, Mango, Grape etc

Wedge grafting

- V– wedge shaped cut of about 5 cm length is made on scion and rootstock

Example: Wood apple, Mango, Jackfruit etc.

Bridge grafting

- This method is useful for repairing of damaged portion of the plant

Example: Apple, Pear, Peach, plum, Walnut etc

Epicotyl grafting

- It is also known as **stone grafting**
- Specific method of mango plant
- Mango seeds are sown in nursery bed
- Seeds are **germinate 15–20 days** after sowing
- **7–10 days of seedling** are used as rootstock
- Seedling is deheaded at a height of 10 cm from ground level

Soft wood grafting

- It is a type of *in–situ* grafting.

Example: Cashewnut, Mango etc

Inarching

- It is a attached method of grafting
- Scion is detached after completion of union.

Example: Sapota, Mango, Apple etc.

Top working

- This method is used for converting an undesirable plant to desirable type
- 2.5–20 cm are consider ideal for top working

Layering

Definition: A ground touching portion of plant emerge out adventitious root while it remain attached to mother plant and then separate from mother plant, is known layering.

Process of layering

- 1 year old shoot is used for layering
- Used 2000–5000 ppm IBA solution
- Selected shoot bent downward in the soil and tied with the help of rope and covered with soil

- After 4–5 month, root emerge out from stayed shoot in the soil
- Separate from mother plant

Types of layering

- Simple layering
- Serpentine or compound layering
- Mound layering or stooling
- Trench layering
- Tip layering Air layering

Simple layering

Example: Guava, Apple, Pear etc

Serpentine or compound layering

Example: Muscadine grape

Mound layering or Stooling

- Height of the mound is about 15–20 cm

Example: Apple, Pear, Berries etc

Trench layering

- Base is covered with 5–10 cm layer of soil

Example: Apple, Pear, Cherry etc.

Tip layering

- It is a natural method of reproduction of blackberries and raspberries

Air layering

- It is also known as Chinese layering, Pot layering, Marcottage or Gootee.

Example: Guava, Cashewnut, Litchi, Lime etc.

Other parts of the plant which are used for propagation

Runner

A runner is the portion of the stem which develops from the axil of the leaves and grows horizontally and forms a new plant at the nodes where it comes in contact of soil.
Example: Strawberry, Dendrobium, Chlorophytum etc

Suckers

- Sucker is a aerial shoot that develops from an adventitious bud on a underground shoot or root and grows vertically.
- Sucker can be grown below the bud union on rootstock

Example: Banana, Pineapple, Date palm etc.

Stolen

- It is a modified stem which grows horizontally to the ground above the surface of the soil.

Example: Bermuda grass, Mint etc

Bulb

- It is an underground modified stem.
- Bulb produces small underground bulbs which are known as **bulblets**.
- Bulblets which are produced in the aerial portion of the stem are termed as **bulbils.**

Example: Onion, Garlic,

Offsets

- The bulblets when grow to full size are termed as offset.

Example: Date palm

Corm

- It is a swollen solid underground modified stem.
- It has distinct nodes and internodes.
- It enclosed by dry leaves

Example: Gladiolus

Rhizome

- It is a modified underground stem which grow horizontally just below the ground surface.
- It has nodes and internodes.

Example: Blue berry, Iris etc

Tuber

- A tuber is swollen underground modified stem.
- It has several eyes over the surface of tuber.
- *Example:* Potao, Jerusalem artichoke etc

Tuberous root

- It is a modified root which is thickened.

Example: Sweet potato, Cassava, Dahlia etc

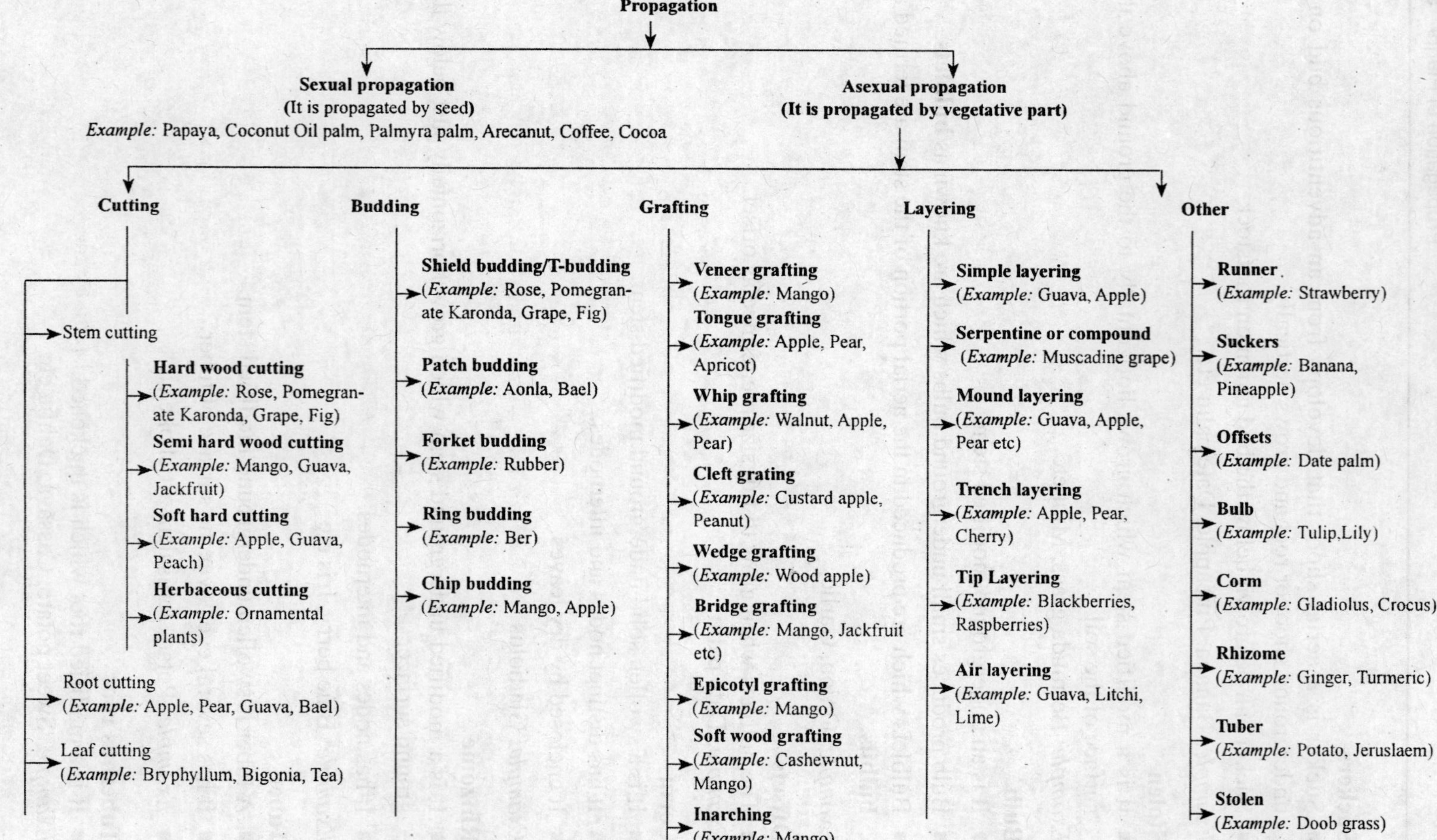
Propagation
Sexual propagation
(It is propagated by seed)
Example: Papaya, Coconut Oil palm, Palmyra palm, Arecanut, Coffee, Cocoa
Asexual propagation
(It is propagated by vegetative part)
Cutting
Budding
Grafting
Layering
Other
Stem cutting
Hard wood cutting
(Example: Rose, Pomegranate Karonda, Grape, Fig)
Semi hard wood cutting
(Example: Mango, Guava, Jackfruit)
Soft hard cutting
(Example: Apple, Guava, Peach)
Herbaceous cutting
(Example: Ornamental plants)
Root cutting
(Example: Apple, Pear, Guava, Bael)
Leaf cutting
(Example: Bryphyllum, Bigonia, Tea)
Shield budding/T-budding
(Example: Rose, Pomegranate Karonda, Grape, Fig)
Patch budding
(Example: Aonla, Bael)
Forket budding
(Example: Rubber)
Ring budding
(Example: Ber)
Chip budding
(Example: Mango, Apple)
Veneer grafting
(Example: Mango)
Tongue grafting
(Example: Apple, Pear, Apricot)
Whip grafting
(Example: Walnut, Apple, Pear)
Cleft grating
(Example: Custard apple, Peanut)
Wedge grafting
(Example: Wood apple)
Bridge grafting
(Example: Mango, Jackfruit etc)
Epicotyl grafting
(Example: Mango)
Soft wood grafting
(Example: Cashewnut, Mango)
Inarching
(Example: Mango)
Simple layering
(Example: Guava, Apple)
Serpentine or compound
(Example: Muscadine grape)
Mound layering
(Example: Guava, Apple, Pear etc)
Trench layering
(Example: Apple, Pear, Cherry)
Tip Layering
(Example: Blackberries, Raspberries)
Air layering
(Example: Guava, Litchi, Lime)
Runner
(Example: Strawberry)
Suckers
(Example: Banana, Pineapple)
Offsets
(Example: Date palm)
Bulb
(Example: Tulip,Lily)
Corm
(Example: Gladiolus, Crocus)
Rhizome
(Example: Ginger, Turmeric)
Tuber
(Example: Potato, Jeruslaem)
Stolen
(Example: Doob grass)

11

Nutrition of Horticultural Crops

Nutrient

Definition: Those elements are required for plant metabolism in more or less quantity, is known as nutrients. Plants have 30 types of elements but 17 elements out of 30 are essential for plant growth and development. These elements are called **Essential nutrients.**

Criteria of essentiality of plant nutrients theory: It is given by **Arnon and Stout (1939).** This theory stated that plant can not be completed their life cycle without the deficiency or complete absence of a single nutrient among the essential nutrients

Low of minimum: It is given by **Justus Von Leibing (1840)**. According to this low, the growth of the plants is limited by the plant ntruient present in smaller quantity, all other being in adequate amounts. This has been re–stated as *Barrel concept.*

Allen and Arnon (1955) laid out following criteria for categorising nutrients essentiality to plants:

1. Complete or partial lack of the element in question must make normal plant growth impossible
2. Deficiency symptoms must be reversibly by the addition of the elements in question
3. The element must play specific role in the plant metabolic symptom

Classification of nutrients

1. Based on essentiality

Essential plant nutrients: There are 17 type of elements for required of plant :

- **Structure/Basic elements: C, H, O**
- **Macro nutrients:** It requires more than 1 ppm by the plants. There are also two types

1. Primary elements: N, P, K
2. Secondary elements: Ca, Mg, S

- **Micro nutrients/Trace/Oligo/Spurme nutrients:** It requires less than 1 ppm by the plants.

  Fe, Zn, B, Cu, Mn, Mo, Cl, Ni
- **Beneficial nutrients:** Na, Al, Co, V
- **Functional nutrients:** 21 (17 essential+ 4 beneficial nutrients)
- **Ultra micro nutrients:** Mo, Co

2. Based on Mobility in soil
- **Highly Mobile elements:** $NO_{3-}, SO_4^{2-}, BO_3^{3-}, Mn^{2+}, Cl^-$
- **Less mobile elements:** $NH^{4+}, K^+, Ca^{2+}, Mg^{2+}, Cu^{2+}$
- **Non mobile elements:** $H_2PO_4^-, HPO_4^{2-}, Zn^{2+}$

3. Based on mobility in plant
- **Highly mobile:** N,P, K
- **Moderate mobile:** Zn
- **Less mobile:** S, Fe, Mn, Cu, Mo, Cl
- **Immobile:** Ca, B

4. Based on symptoms of part of the plant
- **Bud:** B, Cu
- **New leaves:** Mg, S, Mn, Fe, Cu
- **Old leaves:** N,P, K, Mo
- **New and old leaves:** Zn

Role of nutrients in plant

Carbon (C): Plant takes carbon from the air in the form of carbon dioxide (CO_2). Carbon is main element of all organic compounds.

Hydrogen (H): Hydrogen is the main component of water. It is obtained from the soil in the form of water.

Oxygen (O_2): It is also obtained from the soil in the form of water. It works as a electron accepter in aerobic respiration.

Nitrogen (N)

Function
- It is an essential component of protein, protoplasm, carbohydrates, enzymes, chlorophyll etc
- It is necessary for vegetative growth of the plants.

Deficiency

- Chlorosis/yellowing of leaves in plants
- Plant stunning
- Buttoning in cauliflower

Excessive

- Lodging in plant
- Late maturity condition can be developed in plants
- Increasing attack of insect and diseases

Phosphorus (P)

Function

- It is also known as **"Life saving elements"** or **"Key of life"**
- It is necessary for root development of the plants
- It is a energy transformation element in plant in the form of ADP and ATP
- Essential constituent for nucleic acid and phytin

Deficiency

- Root growth will be checked.
- Yellowing of stem in plant

Potassium (K)

Function

- It provides resistant in plants
- It regulates stomata closing and opening
- It increases resistance against insect and diseases in plants
- Develop shining in stem and tuber of sugarcane and potato respectively
- It prevent undesirable lodging of plant due to encourage strong stem or tuber
- Potassium is a luxury consumption element

Deficiency

- Necrotic area (Scorching and burning) developed on leaves tip and margin
- Margin of leaves may roll inward toward the upper surface
- "Greenback" disorder of tomato caused by K deficiency

Calcium (Ca)

Function

- It is constituent of cell–wall and cell membrane
- It is necessary for mitotic

Deficiency

- Distortion of young leaves and hooking of leaf tip
- Root become short, study and brown
- Blossom end rot disease in tomato, Bitter pit in apple, Cavity spot in carrot etc

Magnesium (Mg)

Function

- It is main component of chlorophyll
- It helps process of photosynthesis
- It is necessary for the activity of CO_2 fixation enzymes

Deficiency

- Interveinal chlorosis of the leaves
- Smoked leaves in banana

Sulphur (S)

Function

- It is responsible element for pungency in cruciferae, Aliaceae family
- It is a constituent of Cystine, cysteine, methionine, Biotin, Thiamine
- It act as stabilize protein structure

Deficiency

- Tea yellow disease of tea
- Chlorosis of the young leaves
- Increased accumulation of starch, sucrose and soluble nitrogen

Iron (Fe)

Function

- It is Required for chlorophyll synthesis, nitrogen fixation
- It is a component of various flavo proteins

Deficiency

- Total yellowing of leaves in grape
- Complete interveinal chlorosis in leaves

Boron (B)

Function

- It is essential for development of pollen tube in flowers
- It is involved in fertilization, DNA synthesis in meristems

Deficiency

- Leaves become coppery and brittle
- Lack of flower formation
- Heart rot in sugarbeet, Brown heart in sugarbeet, potato, celery Hollow heart in radish, stem cracking in knoll–khol, fruit cracking in tomato, Hen and chicken in grape etc.

Zinc (Zn)

Function

- It is involved in Auxin synthesis
- It promotes Starch formation, seed maturation and production
- It requires for biosynthesis of hormone

Deficiency

- Plant growth is stunted
- Mottled leaf of citrus
- Little leaf in cotton, Little leaf in brinjal and mango
- Distortion of shape and appearance of leaves and clustering of leaves on short branches known as rosette

Manganese (Mn)

Function

- It is an essential element in respiration
- It is involved in oxidation of IAA

Deficiency

- Chlorotic and necrotic spots in the intervienal areas of the leaves
- Marsh spots of pea, Speckled yellowing of sugarbeet

Molybdenum (Mo)

- **Function**
- It is responsible for phosphorus metabolism
- It is involved in nitrification process
- It required for sweetness in carrot and radish

Deficiency

- Whiptail disease in cauliflower
- Mottling of leaves
- Necrosis in leaves margin and infolding of the leaves

Copper (Cu)

Function

- It is involved in photosynthesis, protein and carbohydrate metabolism

Deficiency

- Necrosis of the young leaves
- Defoliation of the foliage
- Gummosis (Exanthema) of fruit trees, Die–back in citrus, Reclamation disease
- **(White tip)** in Graminae family, Little leaf in citrus etc

Chlorine (Cl^-)

Function

- It is necessary for shoot tip and root growth
- Plant used as a co-factor in the photosynthetic liberation of oxygen
- It reduce the quality of fruit like; Mango, Tomato etc

Cobalt (Co)

Function

- It is component of vit-B_{12}
- It is essential for formation of leghaemoglobin
- It is also known as **Animal protein factor**

Sodium (Na)

Function

- **Na** is important constituent of CAM plants
- **Na** is essential element of **Osmo-regulation**

Vanadium (V)

Function

- It is relatively obscure, V has been shown to have a role in plant nutrient
- Optimum application rate is 0.05 pound per acre, otherwise it is harmful for plant
- It stimulates biological N-fixation of bacteria (Azotobacteria, Rhizobium etc.
- It has an important role in the food chain (Essential in animal and humans)

Silicon (Si)

Function

- Plant takes silicon in the form of monosilicic acid
- It essential for rice and maize

Important indicator plant of nutrient deficiency

S. No.	Indicator plants	Nutrient
1.	Cauliflower	B, Mo
2.	Sugarbeet	B, Mn, Na
3.	Sunflower and Celery	B
4.	Potato	K, Mg
5.	Apple	K, Ca, Mg, B
6.	Beans	K

Some important points

- Nickel (Ni) is included 17th element in **1987**
- **"Criteria of essentiality of plant nutrients"** is given by- **Arnon & Stout**
- **(1939)**
- **"Low of Minimum"** is given by-**Justus Von Liebing (1840)**
- Functional nutrients is proposed by **D.J. Nicholas (1963)**
- Non-metalic nutrient is **B**
- Nutrient, available in both anion and cation form is **N (NH^{4+}, NO^{3-})**
- Arnon refined the criteria of essentiality of plant nutrients in **1954**
- Immobile nutrient in plant-**Ca & B**
- Energy exchange nutrient in plant-**H & O**
- **Assimilation:** Metabolic transformation of inorganic nutrient into organic plant constituent is known as **assimilation.**
- **C, H** and **O** constitute 96.5% portion of the plant on dry weight.
- Sharing of C, H and O individual in plant: C-10.5%, H–10%, O–76%

12

Soil Fertility Management

Soil fertility

- Soil serves as a source of nutrient required for the growth and development of plant. This characteristic of soil is called soil fertility.

Management practices

- Improved organic matter and soil moisture in soil, favours the growth of micro-organism beneficial for maintaining fertility of the soil.

Manures

- It is an organic waste material of plant and animal origin. It is used improvement of soil fertility. There are major 2 types of manure
  1. Bulky organic manures
  2. Concentrated organic manures

1. Bulky organic manures

- It contains little amount of nutrients in high quantity.
- *Example:* **FYM, Compost, Vermicompost, Vermiwash, Sewage and sludge, Poultry manure, Green manure, Sheep and Goat manure**

2. Concentrated organic manures

- Rich in nutrients than bulky manures
- It is applied in less quantity than bulky manure
- *Example:* **Oilcakes, Fish mamure, blood meal, bone meal** etc

S. No.	ORGANIC MANURE	$N_{2\%}$	$P_2O_5\%$	$K_2O\%$
	BULKY ORGANIC MANURES			
1.	Cattle dung	0.40	0.20	0.17
2.	Poultry manure	3.03	0.63	1.40
3.	Farmyard manure	0.50	0.25	0.50
4.	Rural compost	0.75	0.20	0.50
5.	Urban compost	1.75	1.00	1.50
6.	Vermicompost	3.00	1.00	1.50

S. No.	Concentrated organic manure			
1.	Castor cake	4.37	1.85	1.39
2.	Coconut cake	3.00	1.80	1.90
3.	Neem cake	5.22	1.08	1.48
4.	Blood meal	12.00	2.00	1.00
5.	Groundnut cake	7.30	1.50	1.30
6.	Pressmud	2.10	4.40	0.80
7.	Safflower cake	7.9	2.2	1.9

Nitrogen fixation in soil by green manure

S. No.	Name of crop	N fixation in soil (Kg/ha)
1.	Sunhemp	134
2.	Dhaincha	133
3.	Phillipesara	102
4.	Sesbania rostrata	96
5.	Cluster bean	91
6.	Cowpea	74

Fertilizers

It is a chemical substance which is manufactured artificially. Fertilizer is rich in nutrients. Generally, fertilizers are inorganic nature but Urea **(NH_2-CO-NH_2)** and **Calcium cynamide (CaCN)** are organic nature.

Classification of fertilizers

1. **Based on availability of nutrient**
   (a) Simple/Straight fertilizer: Urea, SSP
   (b) Compound/Complex fertilizer:
   Binary fertilizer: DAP (Diammonium phosphate), Potassium nitrate etc
   Tertiary fertilizer: CAN (Calcium ammonium nitrate), ammonium potassium phosphate etc
   (c) Mixed fertilizer: IFFCO-2 (12:32:16) etc

2. **Based on amount of nutrient**
   (a) Low analysis fertilizer: Less than 25% of primary nutrients
   Example: Ammonium sulphate, SSP etc
   (b) High analysis fertilizer: More than 25% of primary nutrients.
   Example: Muriat of potash, Potassium sulphate, Urea etc

Types of fertilizers

Nitrogenous fertilizer

- There are also 4 types of nitrogenous fertilizer
- **Nitrate fertilizer (NO_3^-):** Calcium nitrate, Sodium nitrate
- **Amide fertilizer:** Urea, Neem coated urea
- **Ammonical fertilizer:** Ammonium sulphate, Ammonium phosphate, Ammonium nitrate, Ammonium chloride
- **Ammonium–nitrate fertilizer:** Calcium ammonium nitrate, Ammonium nitrate, Ammonium sulphate nitrate.

Phosphoric Fertilizer

There are 3 types of phosphoric fertilizers

1. Water soluble phosphoric fertilizer:
   Formula is $[Ca^{2+}(H_2PO_4^-)_2]$
   It takes easily to the plants. *Example:* $H_2PO_4^-$
   Example: SSP, DSP, TSP, DAP, MAP etc
2. Citric acid soluble phosphoric fertilizer:
   Formula is $[Ca^{2+}(HPO_4^{2-})_2]$
   These fertilizers are used in acidic soil.
   Example: Dicalcium phosphate, Basic slag
3. Non-soluble fertilizer:
   Formula is $\mathbf{[Ca^{3+}(PO_4^{3-})_2]}[Ca^{3+}(PO_4^{3-})_2]$
   These fertilizers are not useful for plants
   Example: Rock phosphate, Bone meal etc

Potassic fertilizer

There are three types of potassic fertilizers

1. **Chloride potassic fertilizer:** Muriat of potash (KCL).
2. **Sulphate potassic fertilizer:** Potassium sulphate etc.
3. **Nitrate potassic fertilizer:** Potassium nitrate, Sodium potassium nitrate etc.

Methods of fertilizer

Broadcasting:

Fertilizer in solid state or granular or dust are spread uniformly over the entire field. Leaching loss may be more.

Disadvantages

- Some of the elements like phosphorous and potash do not readily move in the soil. Therefore, surface application may not be available to the trees especially in drier tracks.
- Leads to accumulation of potassium in surface soil beyond detrimental levels causing injury to plants.
- Surface application always stimulates weed growth.

Band placement

- Application of fertilizer on the sides of rows.
- Fertilizer in solid and liquid forms can be applied.
- Quantity of fertilizer may be economised.

Ring placement

- Commonly followed in fruit trees.
- Fertilizers are applied in a ring encircling the trunk of the trees extending the entire canopy.
- It is more labours intensive and costly.

Top dressing

- It is applied in standing crop

Contact placement

- Seeds and fertilizers are applied simultaneously at the time of sowing. To avoid salt injury, seeds and fertilizers are applied at different depths.

Pellet placement

- Fertilizers are applied in pellet form. For making pellet, soil and fertilizer are mixed in the ratio of ratio 1:10 and made into a dough.

Row placement

- It consists of placing the fertilizer along the rows of crops

Localized placement

- Fertilizers are close to the seeds or plants

Foliar application

- Fertilizers are applied in liquid form as foliar sprays.
- They are easily absorbed by leaves.
- Fertilizers are applied in a very low concentration tolerable to the leaves.
- Recommended when the nutrients are required in small quantity.

Starter solution

- Liquid form of fertilizer application.
- Seedlings and propagules are kept emerged up to their root system for varying duration in starter solution.
- The starter solution is prepared either by dissolving concentrated fertilizer mixture at a concentration not exceeding 1%.

Fertigation

- Application of fertilizers in irrigation water in either open or closed systems.
- Nitrogen and sulphur are the principal nutrients applied.

Advantages

- Nutrients especially nitrogen can be applied in several split doses at the time of greatest need of the plant.
- Nutrient is mixed with water and applied directly near the root zone, as such higher use efficiency.

Save cost of labour

S. No.	Fertilizer	Composition%		
		N	P_2O_5	K_2o
1.	Sodium nitrate	16	–	–
2.	Calcium nitrate	15.5	–	–
3.	Potassium nitrate	13.8	–	–
4.	Anhydrous ammonia	82	–	–
5.	Calcium ammonium nitrate	25		
6.	Ammonium sulphate	20		
7.	Ammonium sulphate nitrate	26		
8.	Urea	46	–	–
9.	SSP	–	16	–
10.	Double SP	–	32	–
11.	Triple SP	–	46–48	
12.	Ammonium phosphate		20	
13.	Mono ammonium phosphate		48	
14.	Ammonium phosphate sulphate		20	
15.	Basic slag		14–18	
16.	Bone meal		23–30	
17.	Dicalcium phosphate		34–39	
18.	Rock phosphate		20–40	
19.	Raw bone meal		20–25	
20.	Steamed bone meal		22	
21.	Potassium chloride (MOP)			60
22.	Potassium sulphate			48–50

S. No.	Fertilizer	Composition%		
		N	P_2O_5	K_2o
23.	Potassium nitrate	13		44
24.	Potassium magnesium sulphate			22

Problems in Soil

S. No.	Soil	pH	ESP	EC (ds/m)	Toxicity	Control (Application of)
1.	Acid	4–6.5	–	–	Al, Mn	Lime
2.	Saline	7–8.5	< 15%	> 4	Na, B	Gypsum
3.	Saline–Alkaline soil	8.5	> 15%	> 4	Na, Cl, B	Gypsum
4.	Alkali	8.5–10	> 15%	< 4	Na, B	Gypsum, Ca

Some important points

1. Black soil is included in Vertisol. It is rich in Montmorolinite minerals.
2. Red soil is rich in Kaolinite clay.
3. Soil order: (12 soil order)
   a. **Vertisol:** Black soil
   b. **Alfisol:** Red soil
   c. **Ultisol:** Laterite soil
   d. **Oxisol:** Acidic soil
   e. **Entisol:** Alluvial soil (New Released soil order)
   f. **Spodosol:** Sandy and Loam soil
   g. **Mollisol:** Grassland soils
   h. **Histosol:** Peat land, Fens and Bogs
   i. **Andisol:** Black soil
   j. **Inceptisol:** Similar to cristal but look of clay and nutrient
   k. **Gelisol:** Arctic and Anterectic regions soil
   l. **Aridisol:** Hot and cold desserts soil
4. Minerals on the earth: **Feldspars (48%) > Quartz (36%) > Mica (10%)**
5. Acid rocks: Quartz, Granite, Gneiss, Rhyolite etc.
6. Basic rocks: Basalt, Augite, Limestone etc.
7. **Salination:** Accumulation of soluble salt in soil
8. **Solonization:** Accumulation of high exchangeable Na+ ions and increases pH above 8.5
9. **Solodization:** Removal of Na+ ions from the soil
10. **Pedoturbation:** Process of mixing the soil
11. **Podozolization:** Leaching sesquioxide from 'A' horizon to 'B' horizon

12. **Laterization:** Sesquioxide extent 70–80% in soil, is called laterization
13. **Gleization:** Formation of Glei (blue, grey or green clay) in lower surface of soil profile
14. **Solum profile:** ‘A’ + ‘B’ horizon
15. **Regolith profile:** ‘A’ + ‘B’ + ‘C’ horizon
16. Weight of furrow slice: 2.25×10^6 kg/ha
17. Heavy clay soil weight less than an equal volume of the light sandy soil
18. Individual soil aggregates is known as: Peds
19. Size of clay particles: < 0.002 mm
20. Particle density (PD) of the soil: 2.60–2.75 g/cm^3
21. Bulk density (BD) of the soil: 1.33 g/cm^3
22. Solid space = BD/PD × 100
23. Pore space = 100 - Solid space
24. Sesquioxide clay: mixture of Fe + Al ions
25. 1:1 type silicate clay: Kaolinite, Nacrite, Dickite
26. 2:1 type silicate clay:

    Expanding type: Montmorilonite, Vermiculite

    Non–expanding type: Micas (Muscovite, Biotite), Illite
27. 2:1:1 or 2:2 type clay: Chloritye, Brucite
28. Organic matter content in Indian soil: 0.5%
29. Organic matter = Organic carbon × 1.724
30. 1.724 is called **Bemlen factor**
31. **Muck soil:** Having highly decomposed organic matter soil
32. **Peat soil:** Having partially decomposed organic matter and acidic nature with 3.9 pH
33. For nitrification process: Temperature: 30–35 °C

    pH: 6.5–7.5
34. CN ratio:

    Microbes: 4–9:1

    Arable soil: 8–15:1

    Legumes and Farm manure: 20–30:1

    Sawdust: 400:1

13

Water Management

Water

- Water constitutes about 35–95% of the different portion of the plants. The leaves of the plant contain 35–95% water, Roots 60–90% and Fleshy fruit contain 70–90% water.
- Water is one of the most important inputs essential for the production of crops.
- Plants need it continuously during their life and in huge quantities.
- It profoundly influences photosynthesis, respiration, absorption, translocation and utilization of mineral nutrients etc.
- Soil needs the application of water to:
  - Remove stress condition.
  - Release nutrients in the soil solution for absorption by plants.
  - Preparation of land for raising crops.
  - To maintain the temperature and humidity of the soil micro–climate and the activity of soil microbes at optimum level.

Types of groundwater

There are three types of groundwater

1. Hygroscopic water
2. Gravitational water
3. Capillary water

1. Hygroscopic water

- It held mostly by soil colloids in 4–5mm micron layer
- It is available on surface tension of 31 and above atmospheric pressure
- It is obtained by heating the soil at the temperature of 100–110 °C for 8–10 hrs.
-]It is not available for plants
- pF value of hygroscopic water is 7

2. Gravitational water

- It is held by tension of less than 1/3 or 0.33 atm
- It is also known as Drainage water, Free water etc
- It presents in macro pores
- It is also not available for plants
- pF value of gravitational water is 4.2

3. Capillary water

- It present in capillaries of soil
- It is held by tension of 1/3 (0.33) to 31 atm but plant do not take this water above the 15 atm.
- It is available for plants
- It is held between field capacity and hygroscopic coefficient in micro pores
- pF value of capillary water is 2.5

Movement of water in soil

There are three types of water move in soil

1. Seepage
2. Infiltration
3. Percolation

1. **Seepage:** Water moves horizontally in the soil.
2. **Infiltration:** Water moves downward from the different layer of the soil. It occurs in unsaturated condition
3. **Percolation:** Water moves downward from the different soil horizons by the macro pores. It occurs in saturated soil

Irrigation

Definition: Irrigation is the artificial application of water for the purpose of supplying moisture essential to plant growth.

System of irrigation

There are three basic system of irrigation are applied in the field:

1. Surface irrigation
2. Sub–surface irrigation
3. Overhead or aerial or micro irrigation

1. Surface irrigation

Flooding system

- When the land is flat, letting in water from one end floods the entire area.
- It is the easiest method but in this method there is wastage of water and leads to soil erosion also.
- It encourages growth of weeds and spread of diseases like gummosis in citrus and collar rot in papaya.

Check–Basin system

- In between two rows of tree, an irrigation channel is prepared.
- The channel is then jointed through square or rectangular shaped beds

Furrow system

- In orchards, two furrows on each side of the rows are generally made.
- It is suited to such lands, which have a moderate slope to the extent of 1–2% if the water is to run freely and reach the ends of the furrows.

Ring system

- In this system, a ring is formed close and around the tree and water is let into the basin.
- The size of the ring will increase as the tree grows.

Basin system

- Basin is prepared according to the size of the tree.
- Basins are connected with each other irrigation channel.

Pitcher system

- This system is especially used in arid region.
- The pitcher filled with water is buried in the periphery of individual tree where feeding roots are confined.
- The water is released slowly and slowly with the micro–pores available in the wall of pitcher.
- 4–5 pitchers per plant would be sufficient.

Funnel system

- In this system, a funnel of about 1 litre capacity is fixed along with the side of the plant.
- The water is applied in the funnel and it goes directly to the feeding roots.
- This system is useful for newly planted plants whose water requirement is less.

Border strip method

- Field is divided into number of strips by bunds of around 15cm height.
- Length of strip ranges from 30–50 cm while width is 3–5 m.
- The slop ranges from 0.1–1%.
- This method gives highest water use efficiency than other surface irrigation system.

Surge method

- It is also known as **"On and off system"** of irrigation.
- In this system, intermittent application of water to the field surface under gravity flow.

2. Sub–surface irrigation

- This system consists of conducting water in number of furrows or ditches underground in perforated pipelines until sufficient water is taken into the soil so as to retain the water table near the root zone.
- Where irrigation water or the sub–soil contains appreciable amount of salt, sub–soil irrigation is usually not advisable.
- Land must be carefully levelled for successful subsoil irrigation so that raising the water table will wet all parts of the field equally.

3. Over–headed or aerial or micro irrigation

Sprinkled irrigation

- Water is applied by sprinkler with delivery rate of more than 1000 litre/hrs
- It operates at the pressure of > 2.5 bar and through water as spray upto the distance of >10
- Water flows in the pipe line at the rate of 15 pond/inch^2
- Nozzles round at rate of 1–2 round/min
- Saving of water from 25–50% and land 10–20%
- Suitable for undulating land and steep sloppy
- Suitable for saline soils to leach salts
- Irrigation area is increased by 1–2 times with the same amount of the water

Disadvantages

- High initial cost
- Difficult to work in windy location
- High energy is required (0.5 to >10 kg/cm^2)
- Trouble from clogging of nozzle

- Interference in pollination process
- Requirement of more labours while removing or resetting.

Drip/trickle irrigation

- It is discovered in Israel
- Discharge rate of water per drippers/emitters is 1–4 litre/hrs
- Water flows in the main pipeline at the pressure of < 2.5 bar
- Diameter of main pipeline is 3.5–4cm while sub–pipeline is 1.5–2 cm
- Saving of water from 50–70%
- Water use efficiency is 80–90%
- Minimize soil erosion, percolation and runoff losses
- No land leaving is necessary
- Less disease and weed infestation
- It is usually practise in green houses and glass houses.

Disadvantages

- High initial cost
- Clogging of emitters
- Laterals can be damaged by rodents and other animals
- Salt accumulation near the plants due to lack of sufficient moisture for leaching
- Inadequate root development

Water requirement of important fruit crops

S. No.	Crop name	Water requirement (mm)
1.	Mango	890–1015
2.	Guava	700–1000
3.	Banana	2200–1200
4.	Citrus	900–1200
5.	Grape	500–1200
6.	Pineapple	700–1000
7.	Papaya	700–1000

Water requirement of important vegetable crops

S. No.	Crop name	Water requirement (mm)
1.	Potato	500–700
2.	Pea	350–500
3.	Onion	350–550
4.	Bean	300–500

S. No.	Crop name	Water requirement (mm)
5.	Cabbage	380–500
6.	Sugarbeet	550–750
7.	Tomato	500–700
8.	Brinjal	500–700

Measurement of irrigation water

- In crop production, measurement of irrigation water is made in terms of unit of volume or unit of depth.
- In terms of volume, quantity of water is expressed as litre, cubic meters etc.
- In term of depth, quantity of water is expressed as hectare-centimetre or hectare-metre, acre inch etc

There are two methods on the basis of measurement units.

1. Unit of depth or still water: These units are also two types

(a) Hectare centimetre

(b) Acre inch

(a) **Hectare centimetre:** 1 cm of water hold in 1 hectare of area is called one hectare centimetre.

1 hectare centimetre = 100 m^3

1 m^3 = 1000 litre

Means 1 hectare centimetre = 1 lakh litre (100 × 1000 litre)

(b) **Acre inch:** 1 inch of water hold in 1 acre op area is called one acre inch.

1 acre inch = 3630 fit^3

1 fit^3 = 6.25 gallon

1 gallon = 10 pond

1 acre inch = 3630 × 6.25 gallon

1 acre inch = 3630 × 6.25 × 10 pond

1 acre inch = 3630 × 62.5 pond

2. **Unit of volume or running water:** These units are also two types:

(a) Cumec

(b) Cusec

(a) Cumec: When water discharge in the field at the rate of $1m^3/sec$ is called 1 cumec.

1 Cumec = 1 m^3/sec

1 m^3/sec = 1000 litre/sec

1 Cumec = 1000 litre/sec

(b) Cusec: When water discharge in the field at the rate of 1 fit^3/sec is called 1 cusec.

1 Cusec = 1 fit^3/sec

1 Cusec = 6.25 gallon

1 Cusec = 62.5 pond

Other method of measurement of irrigation water

Volumetric method:

$$\text{Discharge rate (litre/sec)} \quad \frac{\text{Volume of container (litre)}}{\text{Time required to fill (sec)}}$$

Velocity area method:

(a) Float method: $Q = A \times V$

Where, Q-Discharge rate in m^3/s

Cross section of all area of channel in m^3

V- Velocity of flow in m/sec

(b) Water meters

Water measuring device

Orifices : It may operate under free flow or submerged flow conditions

Weirs: It measures the flow in an irrigation channel or discharge of well or channel outlet

Parshall flume or Venturi flume: It is the most measuring device which measures water flow in open conduit.

Tracer method

$$Qt = ad$$

Where, Q-Size of stream or discharge (litre/sec) or (ha.cm.hrs)

t- The time of application of water (sec or hr.)

a- Area (m^2 or ha.)

d- Depth in cm

Scheduling of irrigation

When to irrigate?

- The time when a plant needs irrigation can only be judged by a keen observing eye.
- The plants need water when their new leaves begin to show a wilting appearance. A little before the trees show the sign of wilting.
- The shedding of broad leaves in orchard shows distress symptoms.

How much to irrigate?

- If water supply is limited, only a light irrigation can be given at a time with higher frequency of irrigation.
- If water is available in plenty, the irrigation may be heavy with longer intervals between successive irrigations.
- However, inadequate irrigation reduces the growth and fruiting of the trees while, over irrigation serves no useful purpose and it may even prove to be harmful.
- It may create water logging, the nutrients may get leached and fruits may become watery and develop poor quality.
- Plants which have suffered from drought should not be given liberal doses of irrigations all at once. That may result in the splitting of fruits and even the splitting of bark of the branches and trunk.

Approaches of scheduling of irrigation

1. Soil moisture depletion approaches
2. Climatological approaches
3. Plant approaches

1. Soil moisture depletion approaches:

(a) **Estimate soil moisture percentage:**

$$\text{Moisture percent} = \frac{W_m - W_d}{W_d} \times 100$$

Where, W_m - Weight of wet soil

W_d - weight of dry soil

Note: if soil moisture percent is obtained less than 50% then irrigation should be done.

(b) **Neutron moisture meter:** This is the best method for estimation of chnges in soil moisture. It measures of number of H^+ present in volume of soil.

(c) **Tensiometer:** It is used for measure soil moisture surface tension. It works at 0.85 bar. It is not suitable for dry soil.

(d) **Pressure plat apparatus:** It is used for laboratory measurement of soil potential. Suitable for measuring soil moisture tension is 0–15 bars.

(e) **Electric resistance/Gypsum block/Bouyouneous meter method:** In this method, White stone bridge is used.

- In field capacity, value of electric resistance is obtained 400–600 ohm
- In permanent wilting point, value is obtained 50,000–75000 ohm.
- It is not suitable for saline soil
- It is used for measuring soil moisture tension up to 0–15 bars

2. Climatological approaches

- It is also known as **Book Keeping Method.**
- In this method IW/CPE ratio method, USWB-Class A pan evaporimeter measurement methods are used.

3. Plant approaches

- Indicator plant, Relative water content, Leaf water potential, Plant temperature, Water diffusion resistant etc method are used

Quality of irrigation water

Quality of irrigation water is judge based on total salt content, SAR (Sodium Adsorption ratio) and Boron content. The quality of irrigation water is mostly expressed on the basis of total salt concentration in water, relative N a concentration to other cations, bicarbonate content and boron concentration.

Sodium adsorption ration

It is the ratio of soil extract and irrigation water used to designate the relative the relative activity of sodium ion in exchange reaction with soil. The ionic concentration is expressed in milliquivalents per litre.

Classification of irrigation water based on SAR

Class	Sodium Hazard	SAR
S_1	Low	< 10
S_2	Medium	10–18
S_3	High	18–26
S_4	Very high	26–31

Classification of irrigation based on EC

Class	Water quality	EC (m.mhos/cm)	Salt concent-ration (g/l)	Remark
C_1	Low salinity water	0–250	< 0.16	Safe
C_2	Medium salinity water	250–750	0.16–0.5	Nees leaching
C_3	High salinity water	750–2250	0.5–1.5	Not suitable
C_4	Very high salinity water	2250–5000	1.5–3.0	Not suitable

Classification of irrigation based on Boron

Class	Boron content	Quality
B_1	< 3	Normal water
B_2	3–4	Low boron water
B_3	4–5	Medium boron water
B_4	5–10	Boron water
B_5	>10	High boron water

Water drainage

Drainage is situation of removal of excess water (gravitational water) from the field. It aims at maintenance of soil moisture within the range required for optimum crop growth.

Method of drainage

1. Surface drainage system
2. Underground drainage system

1. Surface drainage system

There are three types of surface drains

(a) Temporary drains: 10–15 cm depth drainage

(b) Permanent drains: It is constructed by bricks and stones.

(c) Cut-out drains: A channel is constructed between canal and field to check the direct flow of water from canal to field. This channel is called cut–out. Size of the cut–out is kept 1–1.5 m width and 1 m depth.

Note:

- Each channel is made in the size of 30 m length with 5 cm slope
- Length of the channel in sandy soil, 40–50 m and in heavy soil, 20–25 m should be kept.

2. Under surface drainage system: there are also 5 types of drains

(a) Stones drains

- It is constructed by "V" shape bricks or stone.
- The distance of two drains is kept 5–10 m

(b) Tiles drains

- It include perforated pipes
- <2% slope
- 30–45 cm or 1–1.5 fit and 7–10 cm diameters tiles are used.
- The distance of two drains is kept 4–9 m

(c) Mole drains:

- Suitable for clay soils
- It is made by mould bold plough
- Diameter of drains is kept 8–15 cm

(d) Pole drains

- It is made by wood sticks

(e) Pipe drains

- In these drains, 10 cm diameter pipe is used.

(f) Deep open drains:

- Water collected by seepage

(g) Burried drains

- Drainage channel is made below the ground surface and filled with tiles, fibres or plastics.

System of making drains or drainage channel

- **Herringbone system:** In this system, main channel is made on middle side of the field means laterals are provided in both side of the main channel.
- **Gridiron system:** Main channel is made on one side of the field means laterals are provided only one side of the main irrigation channel.

Some important definitions

Field capacity: The stable soil moisture content after 2–3 days of irrigation and drainage of gravitational water is called field capacity.

- It is a upper limit of water availability to plants
- The tension at field capacity is 1/3 or 0.33 bar
- Max field capacity is obtained at 0.01 atm soil tension.
- It is determined with the help of pressure plat apparatus and tensiometer.

Permanent wilting point: Soil moisture content at which plants can be no longer obtains enough moisture to meet their requirement unless water is added to the soil.

- It is given by **Briggs and Shantz** in 1912
- It is the lower limit of water availability to the plants
- Soil moisture tension is 15 bar or 15 atm
- pF value on PWP is 4.18

Available water: It is the portion of capillary water held between Field capacity to permanent wilting point. Soil moisture tension ranges from 1/3 to 15 bars.

- Concept given by **Veihmayer and Hendricson** 1981
- P^F value is given **Schoefild** (1935)
- Generally 5 cm of irrigation water is applied to most of field crops.
- Normally, Irrigation water (IW) and Cumulative pan evaporation (CPE) ration of 0.75–0.8.

14

Weed Management

Weed

Definition: "Weed is an unwanted plant growing where it is not desired." – Jethro Tull

Commonly noticed weed species in fruit orchard:

- There are more than 30,000 species of weeds distributed world over, out of which 18,000 are noxious and cause serious losses.
- Around 250 species are causing serious economic losses.
- **Monocot weeds (Narrow leaf/Grasses):** Cyprus, Cynodon, Poagrass, Rye grass, Quackgrass etc.
- **Dicot weeds (Broad leaf weeds):** *Dandelion, Chenopodium* spp., Parthenium, *Solanum, Euphrobia* spp., Ground ivy etc

Characteristics of weed

- Prolific seed production: Amaranthus spp.- 1,96,000 seeds/plant, Chenopodium sp. 72,000 seeds/plan.
- Dormancy in seed: Chenopodium sp.- 20–25 years, Phalaris minor- 4–5 years.
- Competitiveness and A gressiveness: High and fast growth rate, having higher leaf area.
- Vegetative propogated: Propogated by rhizomes, bulbs, tubers, stolens, suckers etc.
- Mophological similarities: Phalaris minor in wheat and Echinochloa sp. in rice
- Deep root system: Roots of Convolvulus sp. has up to 20 feet deep roots, whereas Cyperus rotundus has 5–7 feet deep.
- Early seed setting and early maturity.
- Evasiveness

Classification of weeds

1. Based of life Cycle

Annual weeds: They complete their life cycle within one year or one season.

- Kharif: Eleusine, Echinochloa, Celosia, Cyperus
- Rabi : Argemone, Phalaris, Chenopodium, Euphorbia, Solanum sp.

Binnial weeds: They complete their lify cycle two season or year.

- *Example:* Dacus carota, Cirsium vulgare, Alternanthera pungens, Eichornia intybus etc.

Perrenial weeds: They appear in the field through year.

- *Example:* Cyperus rotundus, Convolvolus, Cynodon sp., Saccharum spontanium, Zyziphus rotundifolia etc.

2. Basis of Site of Predominance

Obligate weeds: Such weeds are grown in cultivated field, e.g. Anagallis, Chenopodium

Facultative weeds: Grown both in wild and cultivated field, e.g. Argemone, Euphobia

3. Basis of Parasitic Nature

Parasitic Nature	Weed	Host Crop/Plant
Semi root	Striga spp.	Sugarcane
Semi stem	Loranthus spp.	Mango
Total root	Orabanchi spp.	Brinjal, Tobacco
Total stem	Cuscuta spp.	Lucerne

4. Basis of Morphological Characteristics

- **Grasses:** All graminaceous weeds, e.g. Avena, Cynodon, Echinochloa spp.
- **Sedges:** All weeds belong to Cyperaceae family, e.g. Cyperus spp.
- **Broad leaf :** All dicot weeds, e.g. Chenopodium, Camellina etc

Other Basis

(a) **Relative weeds:** Rice in wheat field.

(b) **Absolute weeds:** Cyperus rotundus

(c) **Rogue weeds:** The off type crop varieties

(d) **Mimicry weeds:** Phalaris in wheat field, wild rice in rice field

(e) **Noxious weeds:** Parthenium sp. (difficult to control)

(f) **Objectionable weeds:** Convolvulus arvensis and P halaris in wheat and wild rice in rice field.

(g) **Associated weeds:** P halaris minor and Avena fatua in wheat, E chinochloa spp. in rice

Classification of herbicides

1. Based on Selectivity of Herbicides

- **Selective herbicides:** It kills certain kind of specific weed without causing any significant injury to others.

  Example: 2, 4–D, Simazine, Atrazin, Butachlor, Pendimethalin Fluchloralin, Fenoxaprop, Isoproturon etc.
- **Non–selective herbicides:** It kills all the plants that come in contact.

  Example: Diquat, Paraquat, Pendimethalin etc.

2. Time of Application of Herbicides

- **Fallow application:** It is applied before more or 10 days of sowing. It is applied for problematic weeds with higher dose.
- **Pre–plant incorporation:** Applied 1–3 days before sowing/planting

  Example: Fluchloralin, Alachlor etc.
- **Pre–emergenc:** 1–4 days after sowing

  Example: Simazine, Atrazin, Butachlor Pendimethalin, Alachlore, Chlorimuron etc.
- **Post–emergence:** It is applied 30–40 DAS

  Example: 2, 4–D , Diquat, Paraquat, Isoproturon, Dalapan Sulfosulfuron, Fenoxaprop ethyl.

3. Based on nature of herbicides

- **Systemic herbicides/Translocated herbicides:** They are absorbed by leaves, stems or roots of treated plants. Herbicides are translocated through either phloem or xylem.

  Example: Atrazine, Simazine, Diuron, Alachlor.
- **Contact herbicides:** Kill all the plants that come in contact.

  Example: Paraquat, Diquate, Glyphosate (destroy green tissue only).

Methods of weed control in orchards: Broadly classified as:

1. Cultural methods
2. Biological methods
3. Chemical methods
4. Integrated weed control
5. Soil solarisation

Losses caused by weeds (Harmful effects)

1. Weeds compete with fruit crops for nutrients, moisture, air and light.
2. They increase the cost of production.
3. Reduction in crop yield.
4. They impair the quality of crop.
5. Weeds harbour pests and diseases.
6. They bring problems in irrigation, drainage etc.
7. Weeds reduce human efficiency through allergism and poisoning.

Cultural or mechanical control includes:

1. Hand weeding
2. Tillage operation
3. Growing of intercrops
4. Use of mulching

Guidelines for use of herbicides

1. Use correct recommended concentration.
2. Sprayers should be properly calibrated; nozzles should be directed towards the target weeds away from the fruit tree trunk.
3. Young weeds are killed easily than older ones or established ones.
4. Application should be avoided during raining or windy situations.
5. Wetting agent should be added to facilitate spreading of herbicide more uniformly on leaf surface.
6. If the leaves of fruit trees are accidentally sprayed the sprayed portion should be immediately be cut off.

Note: The efficiency of weedicide is good, when it is used on weeds with new sprout/growth.

Integrated weed management

This is a weed management system that suppresses weeds by combining two or more weed control methods. IWM seems to be best suited for control of weeds in tropics or in fruit orchards.

Practices

1. Deep ploughing during summer.
2. Repeated tillage and hand weeding/use of chemicals.
3. Intercultivation/cover cropping, intercropping etc.
4. Organic mulching in basins.
5. Use of herbicides—2–3 times per year.

6. Use of bioagents whenever possible.
7. Proper regulation of irrigation.
8. Use of drip irrigation.

Chemical groups

Chemical Groups		Associated Herbicides
Sulphonyl ureas	:	Sulpho sulfuron, Chlorimuron– ethyl, Meta sulfuron–ethyl
Aliphatic	:	TCA, Dalapan
Amide	:	Alachlor, Butachlor and Propanil
Bipyridiums	:	Paraquat, Diquat
Dinitroanilines	:	Fluchloralin, Pendimethalin
Chloro phenoxy compound	:	2, 4–D, 2,4,5–T, 2,4–5T etc.
Triazines	:	Atazine, Simazine
Ureas	:	Monuron, Diuron, Isoproturon
Dipheyl ether	:	Nitrophen, Oxyflorefen
Phenoxy phenoxy alkanoic acid	:	Clodinofop, Fenoxa prop–ethyl
Thiocarbamate	:	Benthiocarb
Organophosphorus	:	Glyphosate, Anilophos
Imidazolines	:	Imazethapyr, Imazapic

Trade name of different herbicides

Chemical Name		Trade Name
Acifluorfen	:	Blazer
Acrolein	:	Aqualin, Weedazol
Anilophos	:	Azalin
Atrazine	:	Atratof, Anilogaurd
Alachlor	:	Lasso, Lazo
Butachlor	:	Machete, Delachlor
Benthiocarb	:	Saturn
Chlorimuron–ethyl	:	Classic, Kloben
Chlosulfuron	:	Glean
Chlorimuron 10 per cent + Metasulfuron–methyl 10 per cent	:	Almix
Diuron	:	Cormex
Diquat	:	Reglone, Dextrone
Dalapan	:	Tafapan, Radapan
Ethoxy sulfuron	:	Sunrise
Fluchloralin	:	Basalin
Fenoxa prop–ethyl	:	Puma super, Whip super, Rice star
Glyphosate	:	Roundup
Linuron	:	Afalan
Metalachlor	:	Dual
Metribuzine	:	Sencor
Nitrofen	:	Toke E–25
Oxiflurofen	:	Goal

Oxadiazone : Ronstar
Paraquate : Gramoxone
Pendimethalin : Stomp
Propanil : Stam F–34
Simazine : Tafasine
Sulfosulfuron : Leader
2, 4–D : Plantgard, Weedmar
2, 4–DB : Butoxone

Biological control of weeds

S. No.	Weeds	Bio–agent	Remark
1.	Lantana camara	Crosidosema lantani Agromyza lantanae Thecla echion	Totricid moth Seed fly
2.	Opuntia spp.(Cactus)	Cactoblastic cactorum Dactylopius opuntiae	Moth borer Cochinial insect
3.	Cyperus rotundus	Bactra varutana	Shoot boring moth
4.	Eichornia crassipes	Rhizoctonia solani	A fungus
5.	Orabanchi spp.	Sclerotia spp.	A fungus
6.	Xanthium stramarium	Nupserha vextor	A beetle
7.	Aquatic weeds	Chinese grass carp (T.idella)	
8.	Cuscuta spp. (Dodder)	Melangromyza cuscutae	Insect
9.	Parhenium hysterophorus	Diacrisia oblique	Insect

Commercialized Bio-herbicides

S. No.	Product	Content	Target Weeds Controlled
1.	DEVINE	Phytophthora palmivora	Strangle vine
2.	BIPOLARIS	Bipolaris sorghicola	Johnson grass
3.	COLLEGO	Colletrotrichum gloesporiodes	Saccharum spontanium
4.	TRIPOSE	Shrimp	Echinochloa spp. in rice
5.	DR. BIO SEDGE	Puccinia coriculata	Cyperus exculentus
6.	LUBOE-2	Colletrotrichum gloesporiodes	Cuscuta reflexa
7.	VELGO	Colletrotrichum coccoids	Volvet leaf in soybean
8.	BIOMAL	Colletrotrichum gloesporiodes	Cassia obtusifolia
9.	ABG 500 B	Cercospora rodmanii	Abutilon theopharsti

Toxicity Category of Herbicides

Toxicity Category	Acute Toxicity LD 50 (mg/kg)	Colour of Triangle
Extremely toxic	0–50	Bright Red
Highly toxic:	51–500	Bright Yellow
Moderate toxic	501–5000	Bright Blue
Slightly toxic	> 5000	Bright Green

Some important points

- Solvinia malesta is the world's worst weed.
- Herbicidal selectivity-refers to the killing of target plant species in a mixed population without harming or only slightly affecting another plants.
- Phalaris minor come in India in 1960.
- Agropyron reopens is a soil binding grass.
- Eichornia cressipes is known as 'weeds of fisherm
- 2, 4–D was discovered in 1940 and 1st time used in 1946.
- Herbigation – Application of herbicide along with irrigation eg. Benthiocarb in paddy.
- Lay by application -It is the application of herbicide after the last cultivation of crops i.e. earthing up in sugarcane.
- Herbicides move or absorbed faster in young plants than in old ones.
- Mexican poppy (Argemon mexicana, weed) has Censer mechanism.
- All type of dormancy mechanisms (Innate, Induced and Enforced) exist in wil oat.
- For control of aquatic weeds, 2, 4–D and Copper sulphate is used.
- Highest yield reduction through weeds is found in sugarbeet.
- A poplast herbicides absorb through roots, while S ymplast herbicides through shoots and foliage.
- Allelopathy effect is given by Molish (1937).
- Critical period of crop weed competition may be defied as "the shortest time span during the crop growth, when weeding results in the highest economic returns". The crop benefit obtained by weeding during this period is almost similar to that about by the full season weed free conditions.
- Herbicides are not used in fodder crops.
- Mode of action of herbicides indicates that how the herbicide kills or inhibits growth of plants.
- Atrazine is non selective when it is applied @ 10 kg/ha and selective, when applied @ 1 kg/ha.
- Paraquat is the contect, non–selective and zero persistent herbicide in soils.
- Glutathio-S-transferase is responsible for selectivity of-Triazines
- Triazine herbicides are said as notorious herbicide because of-L ong residua toxicity
- Triazines tolerate broad leafy weed biotype-Chenopodium album

- Herbicides have low residual toxicity-Diquat, Paraquate
- Herbicides have high residual toxicity-Diuron, Atrazine
- Propanil has to be applied to rice crop at 2–3 leaf stage

15

Plant Growth Regulators

Plant growth

Definition: The quantitative increase in plant body such as increase in the length of stem and root, the number of leaves etc., is referred to as plant growth.

Plant development

Definition: The qualitative changes such as germination of seed, formation of leaves, flowers and fruits, falling of leaves and fruits is referred as developement.

Phytohormones

Definition: These are the organic substance or hormones produced by plants which in low concentrations regulate plant physiological process. It is synthesized in one part of plant and translocated to other parts. These are endogenous substance means naturally occurring in the plant.

Plant growth regulators

Definition: These are chemically or organic compounds. It regulates plant growth and development. It works similar to the phytohormones but synthetic in nature.

Types of plant growth regulators

There are five types of plant growth regulators:

1. Auxins
2. Gibberelline
3. Cytokinin
4. Abscisic acid
5. Ethylene

1. Auxins

- Precursor of auxins is **Tryptophan**
- It was proposed by **Charles Darwin (1880)**
- Auxins is a Greek word which means " Increase"

- The chemical isolation and characterization was done by Kogi et al. (1934).
- Auxins are the first identified hormones of which IAA seems to be the major naturally occurring endogenous Auxin in plants and crops.
- "Avena–curvature Test" is given by **Went (1928).**
- In Avena curvature test, Agar block is used.
- Auxins have polar movement *i.e.* apex to downward.
- **Site of Synthesis:** Shoot tip, Young leaves of apical portion of the plant.

Role of auxins

Apical dominance

- Cell division and enlargement
- Tissue culture, Shoot multiplications, callus growth , root multiplication
- Breaking dormancy
- Shortening internodes: Apple trees (NAA) dwarf branch fruit.
- Rooting of cutting: 2000 ppm–IBA
- Prevent lodging: NAA develop woody and erect stem.
- Prevent abscission
- Parthenocarpic fruit: Grapes, Banana and Orange (IAA).
- Flower initiations: Pineapple uniform flowering and fruit ripening (NAA) and delay flowering (2, 4–D).
- Weed control: 2, 4-D 2,4 5-T etc

2. Gibberellin

- Precursor of gibberellins is **Mevalonic acid**
- It was discovered by **Kurusava in 1926.**
- It was extracted from the fungus "Giberella fujikurai (Fusarium moniliformae).
- **West and Phinney** are discovered GA_3 in 1956.
- **Site of synthesis:** Young leaves, roots, immature shoots

Role of gibberellin

- Berry enlargement
- Effecting cell elongation or cell division or both.
- Enhance metabolic activity: Mobilization of reserved food material, promote growth and height, increase root activity.
- Shoot elongation: GA_3 spray increases height of seedlings.
- Delay senescence: Increase photosynthetic and protein synthesis so decrease abscission.

- Increase cambial growth and differentiation:
- Induce flower and fruit set
- Dwarf plant **(genetically)** to normal height
- Promote flowering in Long Day Plants: Substitute for long day condition and cold treatment (vernalization).
- Induce parthenocarpy in grapes
- Thinning of leaves or flowers or fruits
- Breaking dormancy and leaf expansion.

3. Cytokinin

- Precursor of Cytokinin is **Dimethylallyl pyrophosphate**
- It is also known as **Phytokinin**
- It was proposed by **Skoog and Miller in 1950**
- Skoog and Miller was discovered **Kinetin**
- Skoog isolated a substance from maize in 1964– **Zeatin**
- **Zeatin** is a natural hormons but **Kinetin** is a synthetic
- **Site of synthesis:** young fruit, young leaves, root tip etc

Role of Cytokinin

- Cell division, elongation and enlargement
- Tissue culture morphogenesis
- Induction of flowering and fruit development
- Parthenocarpy
- Apical dominance overcoming
- Breaking dormancy
- Delay senescence and retention of chlorophyll

4. Ethylene

- Precursor of ethylene is **Methionine β–alanine or isoamyl alchohol**
- **R. Gane in 1934** reported that plant synthesize ethylene
- **Crocker in 1935** considered ethylene as a plant hormone
- **In 1969,** ethylene accepted as a plant growth regulators or hormones by recognize committee
- It is the only **gaseous hormone**
- Chemical structure of ethylene is $CH_2 = CH_3$
- **Site of synthesis:** old leaves and fruits

Role of ethylene

- Stimulates fruit ripening
- Induce shoot and root growth
- Differentiation of shoot and root
- Stimulates leaf and fruit abscission
- Induction of femaleness in dioecious flower
- Inhibit elongation and lateral bud growth
- Breaking dormancy: by Ethylene chlohydrin

5. Abscisic acid (ABA)

- Precursor of abscisic acid is **Violaxanthin, C_{40} (Carotenoids)**
- In 1961, Liu and Carns was discovered abscisi-1
- **Ohkuma** was discovered ABA or abscisin-11 in **1965**
- **Site of synthesis:** old leaves

Role of abscisic acid

- Induce abscission
- Induction and maintenance of dormancy
- Stomatal closing
- Helps during water stress

Growth retardants

Definition: Plant growth retardants are defined as synthetic organic chemicals that reduce the growth of the plants. Growth retardants treated plants appear normal though their stems are shortened. They do not effect the formation of leaves, flowers and fruits.

Example: AMO–1618, Phosphon-D, Cycocel, Chloromequat, MH and Alar etc

Methods of application

Growth regulators can be applied in different ways like:

1. Spraying method
2. Injection of solution into internal tissues
3. Root feeding method
4. Powder form
5. Dipping of cuttings in solution
6. Soaking in dilute aqueous solution

16

Mulching

Mulching

Definition: It is the practice of covering the soil with loose extraneous matter is known as mulching.

Types of mulching

There are two types of mulching:

1. Organic mulching
2. In–organic mulching

1. **Organic mulching**: In this mulching the open soil is put under loose cover of straw, hay, crop residue, leaves, saw dust etc.
2. **In–organic mulching:** In this mulching the open soil is put under plastic, film, metal foil, sand, stone etc.

Advantages

- Conservation of soil moisture moisture
- Suppressing weed growth
- Regulating soil temperature
- Protection from sun and wind.
- Improves soil structure.
- Reduces soil temperature fluctuations.
- Increases soil organic matter level.
- Controls erosion.
- Improves water infiltration rate.
- Improves nutrient availability through better soil condition micro flora.
- Avoids competition for nutrient and moisture with main crop.

Disadvantages

- Low growing plants are suppressed by mulches
- Warm moist condition favours spread of disease and pest

- Use of polythene mulch creates anerobic condition. Under such condition, plants experience oxygen starvation and its severity may prove lethal
- Dry mulches may invite fire hazard
- Roots grow shallow due to the effect through soil temperature and moisture
- Transportation.

Some of the recommendations made for different crops

S. No.	Crop	Mulch material
1.	Banana	Polythene, Straw mulch, Banana trash and Sugarcane trash
2.	Mango	Straw mulch especially effective against spongy tissue
3.	Pomegranate	Sugarcane trash, Paddy husk and Groundnut husk
4.	Ber	Sugarcane trash, Wheat straw, Black polythene, Trash of Sachrarum munja and Local grasses
5.	Sapota	200 gauge black polythene
6.	Grape	Black polythene
7.	Acid lime	Dry leaf mulch
8.	Strawberry	Black polythene, Cut grasses and Pine needles
9.	Guava	Organic mulches
10.	Lemon	Dry grasses and Black polythene
11.	Coorg mandarin	Dry leaf mulch and Weed scraping
12.	Sweet lime	Dry grasses
13.	Date palm	Local weed bui (Aerva persica)
14.	Pineapple	Black polythene, Saw dust and Dry leaves
15.	Apple	Oak leaves, Black alkathene and Conifer leave

17

Biofertilizers

Biofertilizers

Definition: Biofertilizers are defined as preparations containing living cells or latent cells of efficient strains of micro–organisms that help crop plant's uptake of nutrient by their interaction in the rhizosphere when applied through seed or soil. They accelerate certain microbial process in the soil which augments the extent of availability of nutrient in a form easily assimilated by plants.

Types of biofertilizers

There are some types of biofertilizers:

1. Nitrogen fixing biofertilizers
2. Phosphorus solubilizing biofertilizers
3. Phosphorus mobilizing biuofertilizers
4. Biofertilizers for micro–nutrients
5. Plant growth promoting rhizobacteria

1. Nitrogen fixing biofertilizers: Atmospheric nitrogen is fixed by two types of micro–organism

(a) Symbiotic nitrogen fixation
(b) Asymbiotic nitrogen fixation
(c) Associative symbiotic

(a) Symbiotic nitrogen fixation

- The symbiotic relationship between legumes and Rhizobium bacteria seems to be species– specific.
- Only bacteria are not capable for fix nitrogen.
- **Rhizobium bacteria** are a soil habitat bacterium, which can able to colonize the legume roots and fixes the atmospheric nitrogen symbiotically.
- The rhizobia penetrate into the root and it causes root nodul.
- The nodules have the red pigment called leghaemoglobin. It is an oxygen carrier.

- Leghaemoglobin provides oxygen to bacteria
- Nitrogen fixation process is an anaerobic process
- Nitrogenase loses activity is an aerobic process
- First stable product in nitrogen fixation process is Ammonia (NH_3)
- Nitrosomonas Bacteria convert ammonia to nitrite
- Nitrobacter bacteria convert the nitrite to nitrate
- Conversion of ammonia to nitrite and nitrate is called nitrification
- **Symbiotic micro–organism rhizobium** fixes 37–101 kg N_2 per hectare

(b) Asymbiotic nitrogen fixation

- The fixation of N by free living bacteria is termed as asymbiotic nitrogen fixation.
- It is classified into three groups:
- **Aerobic bacteria:** Azotobacter, Beijerinckia, Derxia, Mycobacterium
- **Anaerobic bacteria:** Clostridium, Chlorobium and Cromatium
- **Facultative anaerobic bacteria**

(c) Associative symbiotic

- **Azospirilum lipoferum** is perform associative symbiotic relation with the graminaceous plants. It is a gram negative bacteria.

2. Phosphorus solubilising biofertilizers/PSM (Phosphorus solubilising mycorrhiza)

- About 95–99% of total soil phosphorus is insoluble and thus not absorbed by the plants
- Pseudomonas bacteria, Bacillus and fungi like Penicillium and Aspergillus, posses the ability to bring insoluble phosphate in soil into soluble form.

3. Phosphorus mobilizing biofertilizers

Mycorrhiza: It is the symbiotic relationship between plant roots and fungus. There are two types of micorrhizal fungus:

- **Ectotrophic or Ectomycorrhiza**
- **Endotrophic or Endomycorrhiza**

- Mycorrhizal plants incresse the surface area of the root for better absorption of nutrient from soil especially when the soil is deficient in phosphorus.
- **VAM** (Vasicular–arbuscular mycorrhiza) is the class of endotrophic.
- The **VAM** fungi are intracellular obligate endosymbionts.
- The VAM fungal association with plant roots can help plants to overcome water stress by stomatal regulation in citrus.

4. Biofertilizers for micro–nutrients

- The transfer of nutrient mainly **P, Zn** and **S** from soil to the cells of the root cortex.
- Intracellular obligate fungal endosymbionts of the genera Glomus, Sclerocysts, Endogene which posses vesicle for storage of nutrients and arbuscles for funnelling these nutrients into the root system.
- Micro-organisms are capable of degrading silicates and aluminium silicate.

5. Plant growth promoting rhizobacteria

- The group of bacteria that colonize roots or rhizosphere soil band beneficial to crops are refferred to as plant growth promoting rhizobacteria.
- The PGPR inoculants currently commercialized that seems to promote growth through at least one mechanism:
  - Suppression of plant diseases: is termed as Bioprotectants
  - Improved nutrient acquisition: is termed as Biofertilizers
  - Phytohormon production: is termed as Biostimulants

S. No.	Group	Example
N fixing bacteria		
1	Symbiotic	Rhizobium, Frankia, Anabena azola
2	Non–symbiotic	Azotobacter, clostridium, Anabena Nostoc, Beijerinckia, Derxia
3	Associative symbiotic	Azospirillum
P solubilising biofertilizers		
1	Bacteria	Pseudomonas, Bacillus
2	Fungus	Penicillium, Aspergillus
P mobilizing biofertilizers		
1	VAM/Endomycorrhiza	Glomus ssp., Gigaspora ssp., Sclerocysts ssp. Endogene
2	Ectomycorrhiza	Luccaria ssp., Boletus, Amanita etc
3	Ericoid mycorrhiza	Pezizella ericae
4	Orchid mycorrhiza	Rhizoctonia solani
Biofertilizers for micro–nutrients		
1	Zn and Silicate solubilizers	Bacillus ssp
Plant growth promoting biofertilizers		
1	Pseudomanas	Pseudomonas fluorescens

Rhizobium ssp in different crops

Host group	Rhizobium ssp	Crop	N fix kg/ha
Pea group	R. leguminosarum	Pea, Lentil	62–132
Soybean group	R. japonicum	Soybean	57–105
Alfa group	R. melliloti, R. Medicago, R. Trigonella	Mellilotus	
Beans group	R. phaseoli	Rajma (Phaseoli)	80–110
Clover group	R. trifoli	Bersim	130
Cowpea group	R. ssp	Moong, Red gram, Cow-pea, Groudnut	57–105
Cicer group	R. ssp	Bengal gram	75–117
Lupiini group	R. lupine orinthopus	Lupinus	70–90

Biofertilizer in vegetable cultivation

- **Azotobacter:** Okra, Brinjal, Chilli, Cauliflower etc
- **Phosphate solubilising:** Brinjal, Cauliflower
- The application of Azotobacter along with organic matter and fertilizer ensures good germination, growth and production.
- The application of Azospirillum at the rate of 2 kg per hectare as basal in combination with 75% recommended nitrogen gave very high yield.
- **Seed treatment:** About 200g of biofertilizer is sufficient for 10 to 14 kg seed. One packet of biofertilizer weighing 200g is poured in 400ml of water and it is mixed thoroughly. The seeds are then spread on the ground in the shade for drying for 10–15 min.
- **Cutting/Set treatment:** 1 kg of culture is mixed in 50–60 litre of water and suspension is prepared. The planting materials are dipped in suspension for 10 to 15 min.
- **Seedling treatment:** 1 kg of culture is dissolved in 10 litre of water. The roots of seedling are dipped in suspension for 15–20 min. The seedling are then transplanted immediately.
- **Soil application:** 5–7 kg of biofertilizers is mixed in 100–150 kg of soil. The soil is broadcast evenly on one hectare of land.

Section 'B'
Fruit and Plantation Crops

MANGO

(*Mangifera indica*, *Anacardiaceae*; 2n=40, Origin; Indo-Burma)

- India contributes 56% of total mango production in the world
- Highest productivity in the world– Venezuela
- Pollination: House fly (*Musca domestica*)
- The flower is hermaphroditic with male and female flowers in the same flower panicle.
- Inflorescence-Panicle
- Hybridization work was started by **Burns and Prayag** in 1911 at Pune in MH.
- **Caging technique** of breeding was used in Mango by **Dr. R. N. Singh.**
- In mango, only 0.1% flower develops fruit to maturity.
- The optimum temperature range for its growth and development is 24°C to 27°C.
- It can tolerate up to 48°C during fruit development with regular irrigations, which improve fruit size, quality and maturity.
- For flower bud differentiation, suitable temp is13°C–19°C.
- Mangoes are highly susceptible to low temperature injury/Chilling injury.
- Mango stores in 9°C–12°C.
- Vapour heat treatment (VHT) is recommended for disinfection of mango against fruit flies (bactocera frauenfeldi) and stone weevil (sternochetus mangiferae).
- Optimum PH is 5.5–7.0.
- It cannot tolerate saline conditions.
- Mango is commercially propagated by Veneer grafting , Inarching, Epicotyle grafting
- Best time for grafting is June to Sept/Oct.
- Polyembryonic seedlings (3–4 seedlings/seed) are best in providing uniform root stocks.
- Mango can withstand deficiency of P but not K.
- Flower bud formation takes place 2–3 months prior to flowering.
- Flowering occurs from November–December to February–March depending upon region and variety and continues for about 2–3 weeks.
- Flowers are polygamous-sex ratio can be improved by application of NAA 200 ppm at flower bud initiation stage.

- Fruit drop is a natural phenomenon and is very high in mango especially during the first four weeks.
- Mango plant normally takes 90–120 days from fruit set to fruit maturity.
- Mango grafted plants come to bearing in about 2–3 years.
- Average yield is 8 tones/ha and may vary according to variety and locality.
- Waxing 3% with hot water treatment improves storage life mangoes can be stored at 5–14°c and 90% RH for about 2–7 weeks depending upon the variety

Physiological disorder

- **Malformation:** It was first observed in 1891 in Bihar.
  - Malformation is serious disorder in North India than in South India. It may result in loss of about 50–60% crop.
  - Krishnabhog, Collecter, Langra, Neelum are tolerant to mango malformation.
- **Flower/Fruit drop:** To overcome this problem Spray of 2 4–D 10 ppm is done.
- **Biennial bearing:** It controlled by Smudging and chemical regulation like application of paclobutrazol (5–10gm/tree), spraying 1–2% KNO_3, 6–8% $CaNO_3$, etc.
- **Black tip:** It was observed by **Woodhose** in **1909**. Due to polluted atmosphere with smoke, carbon monoxide (CO), carbon dioxide (CO_2), sulphur dioxide (SO_2), acetylene.
  - Spraying with Borax @ 0.6% from fruit set at 10–15 days intervals controls black tip.
- **Clustering (Jhumka):** Clustering of fruits without growth at the tip of the panicale caused by adverse weather (low temperature) condition during February–March leads to this disorder.
- **Spongy tissue:** It was first observed by **Cheema and Dhani** in **1934**. Fruit appears normal extremely but contains yellowish, sour spongy tissue inside high temperature, convertive heat and exposing to sunlight after harvest are supposed to be the causes.
- **Soft nose:** It is caused by calcium deficiency, causing breakdown of flesh towards the apex of the fruit before ripening leads to softness of the tissues.

Rootstock

- **Poly–embryonic rootstock:** Rumani, Olour, Bappakai, Chandrakaran, Goa, Kurukkan, Solan, Mulgoa, Bellary, Villiacolumban, Nileshwar dwarf

- **Introduced polyembryonic rootstock:** Apricot, Strawberry, Saigon, Simmonds, Sabre, Combodiana, Carabao, Pico, Terpentine
- **Salt resistant rootstock:** Kurukkan, Moovandan, Nekkare

Use of rootstock

- Rumani is used for dwarfing effect in Dashehari
- Olour is used for dwarfing effect in Langra and Himsagar
- Villiacolumban is used for dwarfing effect in Alphonso

Varieties

North-Indian Vars: Alternate bearing, Mono-embryonic, Self incompatibility

South-India vars: Regular bearing, Poly-embryonic

Regular bearing varieties: Neelum, Gulabkhas, Himasagar, Totapari, Pairi

Exotic coloured vars.: Tommy Atkins, Zilette, Haden, Sensation, Julie

- **Alphonso:** Export variety. Susceptible to spongy tissue.
- **Banganpalli:** Recently GI variety of India. Popular in Andra Pradesh.
- **Bombay green:** Early variety. Highest Vit–C. It is called Malda in UP and Sehroli in Delhi.
- **Fazli:** Late maturity variety.
- **Chausa:** Sweetest variety among all the varieties.
- **Dashehari:** Popular in North–India. High fruit retention variety.
- **Langra:** It has turpentine flavour. **Highest number of perfect flowers**. Most prone to fruit drop
- **Kesar:** Good processing quality
- **Niranjan:** Off season variety
- **Neelum:** Most popular variety. Best combiner and take 2 crop per year.
- **Rosica:** Mutant variety
- **Madhulica:** Most precocious variety
- **Malbhog:** Susceptible for water logged condition
- **Malgoa:** Mono-embryonic in North-India and Poly-embryonic in South-India
- **Lal sindhuri:** Powdery mildew resistant variety
- **Rumani:** Apple shaped variety. **Lowest number of perfect flower.**
- **Xavier:** Highest TSS variety (24.8 Brix)
- **Akshay:** Selection from Dashehari

Hybrid

S. No.	Varieties	Parents	Remarks
1.	**Ambica**	Amrapali × Janardan pasand	Regular bearer, Export variety
2.	**Amrapali**	Dashehari × Neelum	Dwarf variety, Suitable for HDP (2.5 × 2.5 m^2)
3.	**Ratna**	Neelum × Alphonso	Regular bearer, Free from spongy tissue
4.	**Sindhu**	Ratna × Alphonso	Seedless var. 3% seed of total fruit weight
5.	**Arka puneet**	Alphonso × Baganpalli	Free from spongy tissue
6.	**Arka Aruna**	Baganpalli × Alphonso	Dwarf, Free from spongy tissue
7.	**Arka Anmol**	Alphonso × Janardan apsand	Free from spongy tissue
8.	**Arka Neelkiran**	Alphonso × Neelum	Free from spongy tissue
9.	**Manjeera**	Rumani × Neelum	
10.	**Prabha sankar**	Bombay × Kalapady	
11.	**Pusa Arunima**	Amrapali × Sensation	
12.	**Sai Sugartha**	Totapari × Kesar	Free from malformation, Regular bearer

- **Self incompatible varieties:** Dashehari, Langra, Chausa, Bombay green
- **Mulgoa** is mother of all coloured cultivars of mango.
- **Villiacolumban** is Allo–octaploid (2n= 80) variety.
- Good varieties of mango have TSS of 20%.
- Maturuity indices for harvesting on the based on specific gravity
  - Alphonso– 1–1.01
  - Dashehari– 1.0
- In Epicotyle grafting, 7–10 days old seedlings are used.
- Mango seed viability: 1 month (30 days).
- Highest Vit-A (4800 IU) among all the fruit crops.

BANANA

(*Musa paradisiaca*; *Musaceae*, 2n = 22, 33, 44, Origin; South East Asia)

- Banana fruit is botanically known as berry.
- India's share is 32% of the total fruit production.
- This is the only tropical fruit which is exported in large quantities and is leading fruit in the international trade.
- It is used as staple fruit in most of the African countries.
- It is popularly known as —Kalpataru (a plant with virtue).
- The central core of the banana plant is known as pseudo stem.
- Various processed products like banana chips, toffee, puree, powder, flour, vinegar, jam, jelly and wine can be prepared from the fruit.
- Banana is rich source of energy (350–550 kilo joules/100g) and is a good source of minerals and vitamins.
- Banana contains 73% moisture, 25–30% carbohydrates, 1.4% protein, 0.3% fat.
- Ripe banana contains 27% sugar
- India has the second largest diversity of indigenous bananas in the world.
- India has more than 300 germplasms, out of 600 reported worldwide.
- Edible Banana has arisen as a result of natural crosses between two wild progenitors viz,. Musa. paradisiaca and Musa. balbisiana.
- It can grow in slightly alkaline soils.
- Banana is moisture loving plant.
- It cannot tolerate water stagnation condition.
- Artificial ripening hormone is used in banana crop: Calcium carbide (CaC_2)
- It is grown up to an altitude of 1200 m from mean sea level.
- The temperature range is 20–30°C for getting good yield.
- Heavy storms, frost, low temperature or extremely high temperature are detrimental to plant growth which leads to abnormal or malformed condition.
- The family musaceae has two genera viz., Ensete and Musa with about 50 species.
  - **Ensete:** It is an old genus, which probably originated in Asia and spread to Africa. It has about 6–7 species, of which Ensete and Ventricosa has been reported to be grown as a food crop.

- **Musa:** It is having 40–45 species, all the varieties under these species are under cultivation. The genus Musa is divided into following sections:
- **Eumusa (2n=22):** This is the largest section with 13–15 species, all are cultivated forms; Pseudostem, produces 10–25 nodes of flowers and covered with dull brown colour bracts, gives the edible cultivated parthenocarpic banana and are derived from 2 wild species:
  1. Musa accuminata (A)
  2. Musa balbisiana (B)
- **Callimusa (2n = 10):** It is having 5–6 species. Parthenocarpy is absent.
- **Australimusa (2n = 20):** These fruits are parthenocarpic and predominantly female sterile; The fruiting bunch is erect and contains a red sap, the skin is orange in colour when ripe. *Example: Musa textilis* (Manila hemp).
- **Rhodochlamys (2n = 22):** It is having 5–7 species, pseudostem less than 3m height with erect inflorescence, parthenocarpy absent eg–*Musa ornate* & *Musa velutina* are sometimes grown as ornamental plants.
- **Incertae sedis:** ($x = 7$; $2n = 14$) – It is the largest among the Musaceae family.

- Triploid cultivars are mostly used for consumed.
- The basic haploid numbers is 11.
- Simmonds and Shephered (1995) have distinguished the major morphological charecters of M. acuminate and M. balbisiana.
- Genetic classification of banana was given by Simmond and Shephered.
- The best known bananas all over the world belong to the pure acuminata (AAA) group.
- The clones which are having both the parents are associated with the greater drought tolerance and resistance to diseases. *Example:* AB, AAB, ABB, AA or AAA.
- Banana is commercially propagated by Sward suckers or rhizome or tissue culture plants.
- The weight of sward suckers is 500–750g and their age is 3–4 month.
- Sexual propagation is not possible due to Parthenocarpic nature of fruits.
- Banana produces two types of suckers. 1. Water suckers. 2. Sword suckers.
- Banana takes 12–13 months to yield and gives bigger bunches.
- Sword suckers are closely associated with the mother plant and therefore develop strong thick rhizome of their own.
- Cut rhizomes called "Bits" or "Peppers" may also be used as a planting material.

- Banana can be planted throughout the year but June–July is the most common season of planting.
- The pit size of 60 cm^3 should be kept at 1.8 × 1.8 m or 2 × 2 m (Tall varieties) adopting square system.
- Due to tissue culture, increase yields about 10–20 per cent more than suckers.
- In HDP (High Density planting), the cultivar Robusta and Dwarf Cavendish spaced at 1.5 × 1.5 m accommodates 4444 plants/ha is recommended by IIHR was recorded highest yield.
- Banana requires high amount of water ranging from 1800–2500 mm annually.
- About 40–45 irrigations are required from planting to harvest.
- Planting method:
  - Furrow method– used in GJ and MH
  - Trench method– used in TN
- Male flower flowers of banana are resistant to panama wilt disease but susceptible to bunchy top disease.
- Temperature above 36–38°C causes scorching effect with increased transpiration.
- Banana is calcifuges crop. Their calorific value is 67–137/100g
- In TN, banana is specially grown for leaves production
- Finger tip disease is serious in HDP.
- Two spray of KH_2PO_4 at fruit development stage increase the bunch weight.
- For getting maximum yield a minimum of 10–12 leaves are required to be retained on the mother plant
- Hybridization work was started in Central Banana Research Station
- Banana improvement work was started in the year 1949 in TN
- Seedlessness of banana is controlled by spray of 2 4–D at the rate 25 ppm.
- During the life cycle, the plant produces 30–40 leaves @ 4 leaves/month depending on variety.
- The last leaf produced at shooting which is small in size is called **flag leaf.**
- Spraying of NAA at 100 ppm after 5 and 7 months of planting markedly increases fruit size and yield.
- Spraying of 2–4 D@ 20 ppm increased the quality of fruits.
- Application of GA3 at 50 mg/l resulted in maximum yield and required less number of days for fruit maturity in Giant Governor Banana

- Under favorable conditions, banana starts flowering in 9–12 months and Fruits matures in about 4–5 months depending upon varieties, climate etc.
- Banana are harvested at 3/4th (75–80%) maturity stage for distant markets or for chips making purpose while, for local markets are harvested at full maturity.
- Bunches are harvested by leaving 2 fit of peduncle on the bunch.
- Tall cultivars usually yield 15–20 tones/ha.
- Cavendish group varieties yield about 40t/ha,
- Hill banana/cooking varieties yield about 11–15 tones/ha.
- Banana can be stored at about 13°C with the Relative Humidity of 85–95% for 3 weeks and is ripened in a week at 16.5–21°C.
- Banana aphid–vector of the virus disease bunchy top.
- Salt water treatment reduces duration banana fruits.

Diseases

Panama wilt

- Caused by Fusarium oxysporium.
- It is the most severe and important disease of banana.
- **Rasthali and Gross Michel** are highly susceptible cultivar while **Basarai** is immune.
- It is serious in poorly drained soil.
- Resistant varieties are Poovan, Robusta & Dwarf Cavendish.

Leaf spot/Sigatoka

- Caused by Cercospora musicola.
- This disease was observed in 1913.
- The Gros Michel and Cavendish group are all (AAA) highly susceptible to sigatoka, While, all ABB clones are resistant.

Banana bunchy top virus (BBTV)

- It was first observed in **1891** in **Fiji.**
- It is transmitted by aphid (Pentalonia nigronervosa).
- The dwarf banana cultivars are very susceptible.
- The leaves are bunched together like a rosette at the top, the margins are wavy and slightly rolled upward.

Important culture practices

- **Desuckring:** It is done by cutting the pseudostem of sucker at the ground level followed by application of kerosene/2–4, D @ 0.5 percent, be allowed to grow for ratoon crop.
- **Earthinp up:** To prevent uprooting of plant by wind soil is mounded around the pseudostem during rainy season.
- **Proping:** Support to the plant when it is at bunching stage.
- **Denavelling:** Removal of male buds after the last set of fruit. It increases the bunch weight/fruit weight and quality of fruits also.
- **Thracing:** A process of removal of old, dry, diseased and senescent leaves this could reduce the disease and facilitate better light, temperature and air.
- **Bunch coveringh:** Bagging of bunch with perforated polythene cover or dried leaves to protect against cold, sun scorching, attack of thrips and other scrapping insects, during bunch maturity stage.
- **Mattocking:** It is the process of cutting the pseudostem after harvesting of bunches.

Varieties

- **AA-**Anaikomban, Matti, Kadali, Tongat.
- **AB-**Ney poovan (Elakki bale), Kunnan, Nathu Poovan. Thaen kunnan, Adakka Kunnan.

  Lady finger
- **AAB-**Poovan, Rasthali, Pachanadan/Kaali/Galibale, Nendra paditha, Rajapuri,

  Virupakshi/Sirumalai, Nendran/Rajeli, Chinali, Hill banana
- **AAA-**Dwarf Cavendish/Basrai, Giant Cavendish, Robusta, Gross michel, Grand naine,

  William, Nagabale, Chenkadali/Red banana, Chakkarakeli, Amrit sagar. Lal velchi
- **ABB-**Nalla Bontha, Monthan/Kanchkela, Keribontha, Peyan, Karpuravalli, Sugandhi.
- **AAAA-**Bodles Altafort, IC–2.
- **ABBB-**Klue Taparod
- **AABB-**Kalamagol
- **AAAB-**Atan, Gold finger (FHIA).

Characteristics of important Banana varieties

- FHIA–1: Belong to pome group. Resistant to wilt and sigatoka leaf spot.
- Bodles altafort: Synthetic variety.
- Klue teparod: Natural tetraploid.
- Rajapuri: Resistant to cold
- Moongli: Mutant of Nendran
- Nendran: Good for making banana chips.
- Grand naine: Tall mutant of dwarf Cavendish. It requires propping.
- Poovan: Fruit cracking are the major disorder.
- Hill banana: Suitable for Jam making.
- Pey kunnan: Tolerance to biotic and abiotic stress. Good for making baby food, Juice, wine.

CITRUS

(*Citrus* spp.; Rutaceae; 2n=18, Origin– South East Asia)

- Citrus is the leading tree fruit crop in the world. In India, citrus ranks second in area sharing 12.8% the total area under fruit crops with 9.6% share in production.
- Under citrus group, mandarins are the most important, occupying 50% of the total area under citrus followed by sweet orange and limes.
- Citrus is micro–nutrient loving plant.
- Seeds of citrus don't have dormancy so they should be sown immediately after extraction.
- Blooming (Bahar): Three time in a year:

1. Ambe bahar: February–March
2. Mrig bahar: June–July
3. Haste bahar: October–November

- Mrig bahar is preffered.
- Poly–embrynic nature: Mandarine, Sweet orange, Acid lime, Grape fruit
- Mono–embrynic: Citron, Pummelo, Tahati lime
- Rangpur lime: Rootstock for Mandarine and Sweet orange.
- Adajamir (Citrus assamensis) rootstock is resistant to nematodes.
- Citrus have special kind of skin reffered as 'Leather rind'.
- Ultra dwarf rootstock of citrus is **Fly dragon.**
- Fruits of citrus are ripen 9 month after planting.
- Trifoliate orange: Resistant to Phytophthora and nematodes.
- Best time for pruning: Late winter or early spring.
- Single stem method is used for training.
- Pits of 60 cm^3 are dug and filled with soil + FYM + Carbofuron and Manures.
- Planting is normally done during monsoon season at spacing of 6m × 6m.
- **Limolin:** The glycoside which is responsible for bitter taste of citrus fruit juice.
- Degreening of citrus fruit is done by CaC_2
- Preharvest fruit drop is common in citrus fruit. It is due to:

  (a) Physiological disorder

  (b) Pathological factors

- Fruit drop is controlled by 2 4–D @ 20 ppm.
- Double ring method is suitable for irrigation.
- Stopping irrigation 1 or 2 months prior to flowering is beneficial to the crop, till the tree withers and drops half of its leaves.
- Classification of citrus was given by Tanaka and Swingle.
- Swingle (1948) recognized only 16 species under the genus Citrus.
- Swingle divided the genus Citrus into subgenera viz;
  (a) Eucitrus having 10 species
  (b) Papeda having 6 species
- Tanaka (1954) described as many as 144 species.
- Tanaka divided the genus Citrus into two subgenera viz;
  (a) Archicitrus having 98 species
  (b) Metacitrus with 46 species
- Grape fruit is also known as Forbidden fruit, breakfast food.
- Citron is also known as– Persian apple.
- Optimum temperature range from 16 to 20°C within a range of 17–40°C.
- Annual rainfall of 500–775mm is optimum.

Mandarine group

- Madarine occupies 50% area under citrus spp.
- Average temperatures for growth and development 10°C–35°C and an annual rainfall of 100–1200 cms.
- Nagpur mandarin was introduced in India in **1894** by **Shriji Raja Bhosle.**
- **Nagpure:** It is the finest mandarine in the world.
- **Coorg:** Commercia variety of South–India.
- **Satsuma:** Commercial variety of Japan.
- **Emperor** and **Fuetrelles:** Introduction from Australia
- **Satwal:** Introduction from Nepal.
- **Kinnow:** It was introduced in **1959**. It is developed by **H.B. Frost** in USA in **1935.**
- Kinnow can be grown in high density planting by using the cultivar —Troyer Citrange as a root stock by spacing the plants at 1.8 × 1.8 m^2 (3000 plants/ha) .
- **Kinnow = King × Willo leaf (C.nobilis × C.deliciosa)**
- Kinnow cultivar requires light chilling for good yields.

- Mandarin starts bearing from 4 years but commercially yields can be obtained from 10–12 years.
- Yield may vary from 500–1000 fruits/plant.
- Dipping the fruits in 50 ppm ethrel develops golden yellow colour in 5 days.
- Mandarins can be stored for many months at 8–10°C and 85–90% RH. Under room temperature, they can be stored well for 3–4 weeks.
- Granulation occurs more in young vigorous trees than old trees. It can be reduced by spraying lime, reducing irrigations and application of 2, 4–D (12ppm) or $Znso_4$+ $Cuso_4$ mixture (0.5%).
- Fruit drop can be controlled by proper cultural management and treating with 2, 4–D (10ppm) or NAA (5ppm) or 2, 4, 5–T (5ppm) and Aureofungin 20 ppm to check any fungal diseases.

S. No.	Species	Origin	Varieties	Remark
1.	Citrus reticulata	China	Nagpur, Coorg, Khasi, Ponkan	Polyembryonic
2.	C. unshu	Japan	Satsuma, Owari, Kara, Silver hill.	Seedless
3.	C. deliciosa	Mediterranean	Willow leaf, Kinnow, Blinda	Polyembryonic
4.	C. nobilis	Indo-China	Kunembo, King	Natural Tangor, Polyembryonic

Acid lime group

Acid lime or sour lime/Kagzi lime (C. aurantifolia)

- Native-India
- Polyembryonic, cotyledons whitish.
- Kagzi lime-susceptible to **tristeza and canker.**
- Acid lime is tropical plant
- It is highly susceptible to tristeza virus.
- Citrus canker is serious disease of acid lime.
- **Citrus pennivesiculata (Gajanimma)** is most promising rootstock followed by rough lemon for acd lime
- **Varieties:**

  Pramalini-cankar tolerant, **Chakradhar**-Seedless, **Vikram, PKM–1**

  Sai Sarbati-Tolerant to tristeza and cankar, **Jai Devi**-Pleasant aroma

  Selection 49: tolerant to canker, tristiza and leaf miner. It is also a prolific bearer.

- Acid lime is obtained yield 2000–5000 fruits/plant.
- It can be stored for 6–8 weeks at 8.3 to 10°C and 85.9% RH
- Citrus cankar in acid limes caused by **Xanthomonas compestris** (gram negative bacterium).

Lemon (C. limon)

- Native-Malaya
- India's rank 5th among major lime and lemon producing country in the world.
- Lemons are divided into 4 groups:1. Eureka 2. Lisbon 3. Anamalous 4. Sweet lemon
- Varieties: Eureka, Lisbon, Villafrance, Lucknow seedless, Nepal oblong, Nepal round, Feminello and Monactiello, Bernia, Pant lemon-I-self incompatible variety.
- Lemons for 8–12 weeks at 7.2–8.6°C and 85–90% RH.
- **Rough lemon** (C. jambheri**)**-Indian origin, polyembryonic, cotyledons light green, popular rootstock, fairly tolerant to virus diseases.
- **Citron** (C. medica)-Indian origin-Monoembryonic, Persisting style.
- **Kharna Khatta** (C. karna)-popular rootstock, cotyledons white.
- **Rangpur lime** (C. limonica)-hardy-popular rootstock, tolerant to tristeza and also salt.
- **Sweet lime** (C. limetoides)
  - **Native-India**
  - Self-incompatible
  - Non-acid juice
  - Resistant to greening
  - Varieties: Mitha chikna (thin rind), Mithotra (thick rind)
- **Tahati lime** (C. latifolia): Seedless triploid.

Orange group

Sweet orange (Citrus sinensis), **Sour orange** (C.aurantium).

- Native-China
- Sweet orange is susceptible for water logging and phytophthora rot.
- Deficiency of Zn and N is major nutritional problem of sweet orange.
- Best time for pruning is late winter to early spring.
- Most prone varieties for fruit drop are **Mosambi** and **Blood red**

- Sweet orange takes 9–12 months for maturity.
- Being non–climacteric should be harvested only after full maturity of the fruits.
- Yield is obtained from 500–2000 fruits/tree depending upon the variety, agro–climatic conditions and age of the tree.
- Fruits can be stored for 20 days at room temperature by dipping in 500 ppm Benlate or 0.1% carbendazim (Bavistin).
- Malta fruits can be stored for 2–3 months at 4.4°C
- Sathgudi stored for 4 months at 2°C
- Mosambi stored for 3 months at 5°C and 85–90% RH.
- Polyembryonic cultivars are:

1. Mosambi–Popular in MH and best rootstock is Rangpur lime,
2. Blood Red–popular in North–India and best rootstock is Karnakhata, Jattilhata,
3. Sathgudi– popular in Andhra Pradesh and best rootstock is Rough lemon,
4. Valencia–late variety,
5. Pineapple–Mid season variety
6. Hamelin–Early variety,
7. Washington Navel Orange,
8. Shamouti– introduced from Israel, Seedless variety
9. Succari–introduced from Egypt
10. Dobla Fina introduced from Spain
11. Mudkhed–bud mutant of Nagpur mandarin

Grape fruit and Pummelo group

Grape fruit (C. paradisica)
- Native-South China
- Polyembryonic. Leaves non–pubescent, fruits solitary.
- Varieties are: Poser, Star Ruby, Marsh, Duncan seedless, Thompson, Red blush, Triumph, Sharanpur special

Pumelo (C. grandis)
- Native–Malaysia
- Monoembryonic, Leaves pubescent in lower surface, fruits in clusters.
- Cultivars are: Kaopan-introduced from Thailand and Buntan.

Related genera

- **Ponicirus– Trifoliate orange**, fruits inedible, Polyembryonic rootstock.
- **Fortunella– Kumquat**– the species are margarita, japonica, errasiflora.
- **Hindsii**– Polyembryonic plants ornamental with small oval fruits.

Intergeneric hybrids

- Citrange–Trifoliate orange × C. sinensis.
- Citrandarin–P. trifoliata × C. reticulata (mandarin).
- Citrumelo–P.trifoliata × C. paradisi (grape fruit).
- Citermon–P. sp × C. aurantium
- Citrumquat–P. sp × C. japonicum × F. margarita (kumquat)

Intrageneric hybrids

- Tangor: C. reticulata × C. sinensis.
- Tangelo: C. reticulata × C. paradise.
- Lemonima: C. limon × C. aurantifolia
- Lemmonnage: C. limon × C .reticulata

GUAVA

(*Psidium guajava*, *Myrtaceae*: 2n=22, South America/Peru)

- It is also known as Amrud, Bihi, Poor man's apple.
- It ranks 4th in area and production after mango, banana and citrus.
- The fresh fruits are very rich in vitamin C (100–260 mg/100g pulp) at mature stage.
- Vit–A, B2, and minerals like Calcium, P, acidity 2.4%, carbohydrates 9–10%, TSS–13%.
- Fruits are rich in pectin. The best quality jelly can be prepared.
- Guava improvement work was started in 1907 at pune in MH.
- High density of planting reduces TSS, Sugar and ascorbic acid but increases titrable acidity.
- Soil like light sandy loam with the pH of 4.5– 8.2 is suitable.
- The optimum temperature is 23–28°C is suitable for its cultivation
- It can be grow up to 1500m above mean sea level.
- There are more than 150 species available in guava and some of the important species are:

- Psidium guajava– It is the commercially cultivated species, rest of them do produce fruits but small size, inferior quality and with high acid content.
- P. guineense – Guinea guava – has small fruit with poor quality.
- P. guajava var. aromaticum– small scented fruits.
- P. pomiferum – Fruits are round.
- P. pyriferum– Fruits are pear shaped.
- P. cattleianum– The strawberry guava with round red fruits.
- P. friedrichsthalianum– (**Chinese guava**) Dwarf rootstock and globose fruits having high acid content and resistant to guava wilt and nematode.

Guava Bahar:

S. No.	Bahar	Flowering	Fruiting
1.	Ambe	Feb–March	July–Sept
2.	Mrig	June–July	Nov–Jan
3.	Haste	Oct–Nov	Feb–April

- Mrig bahar produces best quality fruit.
- For the taking of Mrig bsahar, Crop regulation can be done.
- **Crop regulation**:
  - Taking one season crop or bahar (winter bahar) instead of another season crop or bahar (rainy bahar) is known as crop regulation.
  - In crop regulation, Root exposure in sun;light and withholding water and also deblosoming the rainy season by spray of 10% urea.
- Commercially guava is propagated by stooling /Air layering/Ground layering.
- 1 year old seedling is used as rootstock.
- Dwarfing rootstock: Anueploid–82
- Potassium nitrate also used at 1 per cent to prolong storage of seeds.
- The layers should be treated with IBA @ 2000–5,000 ppm for better rooting.
- Planting is done during monsoon at a spacing of 5m × 5m or 6m × 6m.
- Bronzing/Fatio disease: It is due to deficiency of Zn.
- Light annual pruning after harvesting to promote vegetative growth and flowering.
- Pollinator: Honey bees.
- Only 35–50% fruits are carried to maturity through initially 80–86% fruit sets.
- GA_3 @ 200ppm improves fruit setting.
- Fruits take 105–140 days to mature from fruit set.

- Guava is a climacteric fruit.
- The fruits are harvested throughout the year except during May and June.
- The tree reaches its peak bearing stage with in 15 to 16 years after planting.
- A mature tree yields about 90–150kg fruits or 10–15t/ha.
- Sardar (L–49) variety gives about 25t/hectare.
- It can be stored for 10 days at room temperature (18°–23°C)
- The shelf–life of guava can be extended up to 20 days at a temperature of 5°C with 75–85% RH.
- Fruit fly (Chaetodacus spp) – It is severe during rainy season crops
- Guava wilt (Fusarium spp) –It is most common in Alkali soil
- Anthracnose (Colletotrichum psidii)– It is severe during rainy season crops.

Varieties

- **L–49 (Lucknow–49):**
  - It is developed by Dr. Cheema in 1927 at pune.
  - It is developed by chance seedling from Allahabad Safeda.
  - It is very popular in Maharashtra and Andhra Pradesh. It is suitable for table purpose and yields about 25t /ha.
  - It is more susceptible to bronzing than Allahabad Safeda
- **Allahabad Safeda:** Popular in Uttar Pradesh. Fruit is white fleshed with good keeping quality.
- **Chittidar:** It has pinkish red dots of the pin head size on the surface of fruit.
- **Harijha:** Popular in Bihar
- **Hafsi:** Red fleshed variety
- **Behat coconut:** Seedless variety
- **Arka mridula:** Soft seeded variety. Seedling selection from Allahabad Safeda.
- **Allahabad round:** Parthenocarpy variety
- **Allahabad Surkha:** Uniform pink fruit with deep pink flesh.
- **Lalit:** Suitable for jelly making. 24% higher yield than Allahabad Safeda.
- **Shweta:** Highest TSS (140° Brix)
- **Hissar Surkh**

Hybrids

- **Arka Amulya** = Arka Safeda × Seedless

- **Kohir Safeda** = Kohir × Allahabad Safeda
- **Safed Jam** = Allahabad Safeda × Kohir
- **Other varieties**
- Apple Colour
- Nagpur seedless
- Saharanpur seedless

GRAPE

(*Vitis vinifera*; *Vitaceae*; 2n=38, Asia Minor)

- Asia minor– it is area of between Caspian & black sea
- Grape is an important sub–tropical fruit crop in India.
- The average productivity of grape in India is 16.95 t/ha.
- The genus vitis is sub–divided into two sub-Genera;
  1. Muscadinia: The Muscadina have 40 chromosomes.
  2. Euvitis: Euvitis have 38.
- Vitis vinifera is the most popular species of grapes grown in the world.
- **H.D.Olmo:** He was grape breeder. He was developed **Delight** and **Perlette** varieties.
- Table wine contains less than 14% alcohol.
- Muscat flavour of grape is– **Methyl Anthranilate.**
- **Tartaric acid** is commercially extracted from grapes.
- **Grape gourd–** It is a craft paper coated with Potassium metabisulphates (KMS) and plastic polymer.
- **Raising:** It is only processed product in India. It is developed by dipping berries ion soda oil containing ethyl oleate + K_2CO_3 and shade drying.
- The desert wines have more than 14 per cent alcohol.
- Optimum pH is 6.5–7.5.
- Optimum temperature range is 28–32°C.
- Skin of grape berry is covered with wax like layer which is called as **Cutin**
- **Fe** deficiency vis very common in black soil.
- **Mg** deficiency is universal in grape.
- **Calyptra:** a cape like structure of grape formed as a result of union of sepals and petals.

- Pink pigmentation is due to more than 20°C during ripening.
- **Cane:** A well mature and ripened shoot of the past season or that of the previous year which gives rise to shoots.
- **Shoot:** Young growth of green stem of the current season, which bears the grape in cluster
- **Spur:** It is cane pruned to 1–2 buds.
- **Fruiting spur:** A cane or well ripened shoot leaving 304 buds, producing a bunch after pruning.
- **Foundation spur or Renewal spur:** Foundation spur as it forms the base of the foundation wood on which next year's canes and fruiting spurs are formed or on which both growth of the year are borne.
- **Trunk:** Main stem of the plant.
- **Long spur:** A ripe shoot, has more than five buds. Normally it is 25–30 cm long with about 5–10 buds on it.
- **Medium spur:** It is a cane cut back keeping 3–5 buds.
- Characters of Vitis and Muscadinia grape

Characters	Vitis	Muscadinia
Shoots	Bark is longitudinally striate, fibrose	Tight bark, non–shedding, with prominent lenticels
Pith	Interrupted in nodes by a diaphragm	Without diaphragm
Tendril	Forked	Simple
Flower clusters	Elongated	Short, small
Berries	Adheringtothe cluster at maturity	Detach one by one they mature
Seeds	Pyriform with long or short beak	Oblong without beak

- Grape is propagated by hard wood stem cuttings.
- Grape can be propagated by chip budding.
- Rootstock:
  - Riparia Gloire, St. George, 1202– resistant to phylloxera
  - Dogridge, Salt creek, 1613, 1616, Telecki 5A– resistant to nematode and salt
  - Dogridge, 1616– resistant to nematode, salt and phylloxera
  - Dogridge, 110 R– Tolerant to drought and salinity
  - Salt creek– resistant to salt, nematode
  - Temple– resistant to Pierce's disease

- Pits can be of 1 m^3 and filled with mixture of soil and manure.
- One year old Seedling plants need to be planted.
- Spacing shoulb be kept from 1.2 to 5.0 m × 2.5 to 6.6m.
- Pandal system requires maximum spacing.
- Initial plants required staking.
- Best time for planting
  - Rooted cutting– Jan–Feb
  - Insitu planting– October
- Application of fertilizers should be done starting from 1st month after pruning, because the roots will active after the pruning only.
- Grape requires less water during fruit bud formation and more water during berry growth.
- Reduced irrigations during ripening improve the quality.
- Plant growth regulators
  - CCC (Cycocel) at 500ppm–increases fruitfulness (at five leaf stage after back pruning).
  - GA3 at 10ppm– will elongate the clusters (22–25 days after for pruning).
  - GA3 (60 ppm) –increases berry size (at bajra grain to red gram sized berries).
  - HCN– To hasten bud break at winter pruning.
  - NAA (50ppm)– To reduce post harvest fruit drop.
  - MH– For induction of male sterility.
- Girding the fruit bearing shoot also improves berry size.
- For production of one gram of grape fruit 16–26 cm^2 leaf area is requires.
- Training system adopted widely in India is the BOWER SYSTEMS.

Training system in grape

1. Head system
2. Kniffine or 4–cane system
3. Telephone/Overhead threlis/6–cane system
4. Bower system

- In India, bower system is mostly adopted.
- In bower system, **Cost: Benefit ratio** is : **1:2.09**
- Pruning is one of the most important operations in grape culture.
- Types of pruning:

- In North-India– December– January
- In South-India:
  1. Back Pruning/Foundation pruning-April
  2. Fore/forward/Fruit pruning-October
- Grape is a non climacteric fruit and has to be harvested at correct stage of maturity.
- Degree days from full bloom give a correct indication of maturity.
- Early cultivars require about 1600–2000 degree days and late cultivars about 3000 or more.
- Ethrel (250ppm) can be used 5 weeks after anthesis, 4 weeks after berry set for colour or uniform colour development.
- Grape starts yielding from 2–3 years and continues for more than 20–25 years.
- Average yield will be about 25–30 tonnes/ha Balancing but higher yields of 60–75 ton/ha also possible with good management.
- Grapes can be stored for 7–12 weeks under 15–25% Co_2 and at 0–1°C.
- Fruiting areas of different varieties:
  - Bangalore Blue-3–5 buds,
  - Bhokri- 3–4 buds,
  - Anab-e-Shahi-6–8 buds,
  - Cheemasabebi-5–8 buds
  - Pusa seedless, Kishmish charmi and Gulabi-10–12 buds.
- Pruning intensity:
  - Lowest: 3–4 buds
  - Highest: 10–12 buds

Physiological disorder:

- **Blossom end rot:** Calcium deficiency.
- **Interveinal chlorosis:** Mn, Zn or Fe deficiency.
- **Stalk necrosis:** Calcium deficiency.
- **Bud, flower and berry drop:** girdling 10 days before full bloom, 500PPM ethrel at ripening NAA 100PPM at 10 days before ripening, Reducing irrigation during bloom, Benzyl adenine 200ppm, 4– CPA 20ppm–for thinning.
- **Bud killing:** Excessive nitrogen.
- **Hen & Chicken** – Due to boron (B) deficiency.

Varieties

- **Coloured seeded:** Bangalore blue, Gulabi(muscatel), Kishmish chorni.
- **Coloured seedless:** Beauty seedless, Sharad seedless.
- **White seeded:** Anab-e-shahi, Dilkhush
- **White seedless:** Perlette, Pusa seedless, Tas–A–Ganesh, Sonnaka, Manik chaman.
- **Cane pruned:** Gulabi, Pusa seedless, Kismis charni, Thompson seedless
- **Spur pruned:** Bangalore blue, Beauty seedless, Bhokari, Delight, Perlette

Hybrids

S. No.	Hybrids	Parents	Remark
1.	**Pusa Urvasi**	Hur × Beauty seedless	Tolerant to anthracnose
2.	**Pusa Navrang**	Madeline angavine × Ruby Red	Temnturier
3.	**Arkavati**	Blank champa × Thompson seedless	Seedless var.
4.	**Arka Neelmani**	Black champa × Thompson seedless	Good for Red wine
5.	**Arka Krishna**	Black champa × Queen of vineyard	Juice
6.	**Arka Hans**	Bangalore blue × Anab–A–Shahi	White wine
7.	**Arka shyam**	Bangalore blue × Black champa	Double cropping
8.	**Arka Trishna**	Bangalore blue × Convent large black	Wine
9.	**Arka Shweta**	Anab–A–shahi × Thompson seedless	Table
10.	**Arka Majestic**	Anab–A–shahi × Black champa	Table
11.	**Arka Chitrah**	Angoor khan × Anab–ashahi	Table

- Thompson seedless variety occupies 55% of the area with its clone.
- In bower system, Thompson seedless is grow at a spacing of 1.8 × 1.8 m^2
- In Trellies system, Thompson seedless is grow at a spacing of 1.8 × 3.0 m^2
- **Queen of vineyard, Pusa seedless** are used as male parents to transmit seedlessness in progeny.
- **Kishmish Beli:** Outstanding raising grape cultivar
- **Arka kanchan:** Late maturity variety

SAPOTA

(*Achrus sapota/Menikara sapota, Sapotaceae*; 2n=26, Tropical America)

- The latex from stems and immature fruits is used in the preparation of chewing gum.
- Optimum temperature ranges from 11°C to 34°C.
- High temperature above 41°C causes drying of stigmatic surface.
- Calcareous soil (pH 6–8) gives good crops of Sapota.
- Commercially propagated by Inarching on Rayan or khirni (Manilkara hexandra) rootstocks.
- Rootstocks used are:
  1. Rayan/Khirni (*Manilkara hexandra*)
  2. Adams apple (*M. kauki*)
  3. Mahua (*M.latifolia*)
  4. Mee Tree (*Bassia Longifolia*)
  5. Star apple (*Chrysophyllum cainito*)
  6. Miracular fruit (*Sideroxylon dulcifieum)*
- Best sowing time– July–August.
- Approach grafting (Inarching) time– (Jan–March).
- 1m^3 pits size is suitable for its proper growth and development.
- HDP (High density planting) with 5m × 5m spacing improves yield.
- Spraying SADH 100ppm gives good fruit set
- NAA 300ppm gives high fruit retention. Sprayings should be done twice before flowering and again at pea stage.
- No regular pruning is needed for Sapota.
- Grafted sapota starts bearing fruit 2nd or 3rd year but commercial yield can be obtained from 7th year onwards.
- It takes about 7–10 moths from fruit set to maturity.
- It normally produces fruit throughout the year.
- Maturity indices:
  - Milky latex on scratching will be reduced.
  - Brown scaly material gets reduced.

- Dried stigma at the tip of the fruit drops easily.
- Fruits Develop dull orange or potato colour

■ Harvesting time:

- In North-India-Jan–Feb and May–June
- In South-India-March–May and Sept–October.

■ The average yield is 15–20 ton/ha.

■ Fruits ripen after harvesting in about 4–13 days.

■ Ripening can be hastened by use of Ethrel @ 250–750 ppm.

■ Storage:

- Ripe fruits – 2°C–3°C with 85–90% RH for 6 weeks
- Firm fruits – 8 weeks at 3 to 5°C and 85–95% RH.

■ Varieties:

1. Kalipatti
2. Chhatri
3. Dhola Diwani
4. Bhuripatti
5. Jingar
6. Vanjeet
7. Pala
8. Kirthibarthi
9. Cricket ball
10. Oval
11. Vanivalasa
12. Calcatta Round
13. Baramasi
14. Pilli patti
15. Gavarayya
16. PKM–1
17. CO-2
18. Murrabba
19. Guthi

Hybrids

S. No.	Hybrids	Parents
1.	CO–1	Cricket ball × Oval
2.	CO–3	Cricket ball × Vavivalsa
3.	PKM–2	Guthi × Kirtibharti
4.	PKM–3	Kallipati × Cricket ball
5.	DSH–1	Kallipati × Cricket ball
6.	DSH–2	Kallipati × Cricket ball

PAPAYA

(*Carica papaya; Caricaceae*; 2n = 18, Origin–Mexico)

- It gives maximum yield per unit and income next to banana.
- It can be grown in kitchen garden, home garden or nutrition garden.
- It is also grown as a filler plant in a other fruit orchard like Mango, Sapota etc.
- The milky latex which is obtained from immature fruits is known as-Papain, which is a proteolytic enzyme.
- Enzyme present in dried latex-Pepsin
- Papain contain protein-72.2%
- Papain-used in preparation of drugs for treating intestinal cancer, tape worms, round worms and kidney disorders.
- In green parts of papaya, present in-**carpaine alkaloid.**
- It is also be used for extraction of oil from liver of Tuno fish.
- The yellowness of papaya due to-**Caricaxanthine.**
- **Tutti frutti**: It is a processed product. Papaya bits (immature) are first soaked in brine and boiled in sugar syrup and immersed in sugar syrup for 48–60 hours with permitted colour.
- It is susceptible to frost.
- It requires worm humid climate.
- The optimum range is 22–36°C; a day temperature of 35°C and 25°C night temperature are most suitable.
- It is a thermo-sensitive plant.
- Papaya grows well under well drained soil with a pH range of 6–7.
- Papaya is commercially propagated by seeds.
- Seeds are covered with mucilaginous substance is called– Sarcotesta/Aril.
- For better germination seeds should be rubbed with ash to remove Sarcotesta.
- Papaya seeds are very light weight *e.t* 1gm = 20 seeds of papaya.
- Storage temperature- 10°C for 45 days in an air tight container.
- Before sowing of papaya seeds, treating of seeds in 100ppm GA_3 solution to enhance germination percentage.
- In dioecious variety, 4 seeds per polybag should be sown.
- In hermaphrodite varieties, 2 seeds per polybags should be sown.

- Seed rate:

  Gynodioecious vars– 250–300 g/ha

  Dioecious vars– 400–500 g/ha
- All gynodioecious varieties produce 100% female flowers.
- Seeds germinate in 2–3 weeks after sowing.
- Transplanting– 6–7 weeks after sowing.
- The pit size of 1–1.5 fit^3.
- Planting is done during monsoon season.
- In dioecious varieties, 4 seedlings are transplanted/pit.
- In hermaphrodite varieties, 2 seedlings per pit are sufficient.
- Papaya starts flowering in 5–6 months after planting;
- Ratio in papaya orchard Male: female= 1:10
- Papaya is a polygamous plant. It is reported by Frankel and Galun, 1977.
- In general there are 3 important types of flowers.
  1. Staminate or male flower
  2. Pistilate/Female flower
  3. Hermophrodite flower
- Seedless fruits are developed from the pure female flowers which are not cross pollinated.
- Fruits mature within 5 months after flowering.
- Spraying of planofix @ 1ml/liter avoid flower and fruit drop problem.
- Fruit thinning is suggested to get good size and quality.
- Papaya comes to bearing with 10 months after planting.
- The economic life is only 3–4 years.
- Fruits are harvested when the fruit turn slight yellow in colour.
- Fruits ripen in about 5–6 days after harvesting.
- After harvesting the fruits are graded on the basis of their weight, size and colour.
- Fruits are highly perishable in nature.
- They can be stored for 1–3 weeks at a temperature of 9–13°C with 85–90% RH.
- The average yield is 30–80 tons/ha.

Papain extraction

- The immature fruits of 90–100 days old are used for extraction of milky latex.
- Giving 4–6 cuts of about 2mm depth.
- Latex is collected from 5–6 tapping and sieved the latex and dried in sun or in vacuum shelf dryer.
- The quality and grade of papain is determined by colour and enzyme activity (Tyrosine unit).
- Fruits set during July yield more papain.
- Always collect the papain in glass vessels or Aluminum trays.
- Use Potassium Metabisulphite (0.05 per cent) to extend the storage life of papain.
- Papain yield– About 450g/plant and 250–375 kg papain per hectare.
- CO– 5 and CO–2 varieties: Highest papain yielder varieties.

Species

- The genus Carica contains 48 species of which, only 3–4 species are important.

1. *Cariaca papaya*– It is a cultivated commercial species and polygamous in nature.
2. C. monoica – Monoecious and is suited for mild climate, found in Amazon basin.
3. C. candamarcensis – It is known as **mountain papaya** is suited to cold climate.
4. C. gracilis– Ornamental
5. C. pubescens– Mountain papaya

Varieties/cultivars

Gynodioecious varieties

1. **Pusa delicious:** High yielder
2. **Pusa majesty:** Plants resistant to virus diseases. The fruit with stand long distance transport.
3. **Coorg honey dew:** Selection from Honey dew at IIHR.
4. **Sunrise solo:** Solo 'because one man can easily consume one fruit. Pyriform and yellowish orange pulp and keeping quality is good.
5. **Taiwan:** Blood red colour variety. It is known as Red lady.
6. **Surya**

7. **CO–3**
8. **CO–7:** Multiple cross hybrid

Dioecious varieties

1. **Honey dew**
2. **Pusa gaint**
3. **Pusa dwarf:** Suitable for HDP and home garden.
4. **Pusa Nanha:** It is developed by gama radiation, suitable for High density planting.
5. **CO–:** Selection from variety Ranchi
6. **CO–2:** Very good for table and papain extraction.
7. **CO–4:** Tall plant with large fruits (1–1.5kg)
9. **CO–5:** Selection from Washington.
9. **CO–6:** Selection from pusa majesty. 890 kg of dry papain/ha. High papain (7.5–8 g/fruit)
10. **Washington:** Vigorous plant.

Hybrids

S. No.	Hybrids	Parents
1.	IIHR–39	Sunrise solo × Pink Flesh Sweet
2.	IIHR–57	Waimanello × Pink Flesh Sweet
3.	CO–3	CO–2 × Sunrise solo
4.	CO–4	Co–2 × Washington
5.	CO–7	CO–3 × Pusa delicious × Coorg honey dew

PINEAPPLE

(*Ananas comosus*; *Bromeliaceae*, 2n=30, Origin– Brazile)

- Pineapple is known as "Golden Queen"
- It is drought tolerant crop.
- It is non–climacteric fruit.
- Pineapple contains Sugar 13%, Acidity–0.6–1.0%.
- The fruit contains a protein digestive enzyme **Bromelin.**
- Pineapple Candy is prepared from fruit core.
- The optimum temperature is from 21°C–24°C.
- The high temperature favours fruit development, low temperature is harmful and does not improve colour of fruits.

- Fruit size is larger in heavy soil but flavor of the fruit is better when grown in light soil.
- It prefers soils which are acidic (pH 4.5–5.5).
- High Mg and Mn content are injurious to the crop.
- Pineapple is propagated by vegetative parts of pineapple *viz*., Suckers, Slips, Crowns
- The suckers arise from the axils of the leaves below the ground level.
- It bears flowering atleast 40 leaves stage.
- Flowering

  Slips: 15–18 months after sowing.
  Suckers: 20–22 month after sowing.
  Crown: 24–25 month after sowing.
- Propagating materials

  Slips: 250–400g
  Suckers: 500–750 gm
  Crown: 40–45cm
- The planting materials are treated with mercurial fungicide.
- The planting materials should not be stored more than 14 days.
- The suckers or slips are planted in 22.5 × 60 × 75 cm^3 or 25 × 60 × 90 cm^3 size of pits.
- Planting may be done in single or double row systems.
- In single row system, about 15,000 –20,000 plants/ha – yields about 20t/ha
- In double row system, (25 × 35 × 90cm) High Density Planting (HDP) is adopted. About 64,000 plants/ha– about 100– 120t/ha of fruit yield.
- Fe, Zn and Co deficiencies are common in pineapple.
- To induce good and uniform flowering, growth regulators are (NAA 100–200 ppm or Ethrel at 25 ppm combining with Urea (2%) and sodium carbonate @ 0.04%) applied at 35–40 functional leaves stage (1 year after planting).
- Fruit takes 41/2 (four and half)–51/2 months (five and half) from set to harvest (June –Aug)
- The fruits should be harvested along with 5–7 cm stalk on full maturity.
- Yield: Plant population of 35,000–40,000 per hectare is about 40–50 tonnes.
- The plant population of 43,000–50,000 per hectare normally varies between 50 and 60 tonnes.

- Storage temperature

  10–13°C for 20 days and above.

  Do not store at less than 8°C.
- Pre-harvest application of Ethrel @ 500 ppm induces uniform ripening and colour development, but fruits will be acidic and lack flavour

Physiological disorder

Sunscald: Due to expose of cells under the fruit skin in sunlight.

Fasciation and multiple crowns: Due to genetical factor as well as due to soil and environmental reasons. It is also due to excess Nitrogen.

Black heart/Internal browning: Due to low temperature or exogenous application of GA_3 can induce this disorder.

- A fruit exposed to high temperature (40°C) for 24 hours reduces black heart in cold stored pineapple.
- Pineapple wilt virus – It is transmitted by mealy bugs.

Varieties

- Smith (1979) established two genera:
  1. Ananas
  2. Pseudananas,

1. **Ananas**: It produce slips but not stolons and a fruit remains seedless. The genus Ananas has 8 species viz.,

(a) Ananas comosus: Large fruits and a short thick spike.

(b) A. monstrosus (Crownless)

(c) A. bracteatus

(d) A. fruitzmuelleri

(e) A. ananassoides

(f) A dwarf species

(g) A. parguazensis

(h) A. lucidus(Spineless)

2. **Pseudananas:** It produces elongated stolons and no slips. Only one species has been listed in Pseudananas– P. sagenarius

The varieties have been classified in to 5 groups.

1. Queen group: Conical fruits.

   Example: Queen, Mac gregor, Natal, Ripley and Alexandria.

2. Cayenne group: Cylindrical fruits
   Example: Cayenne, Baron, Rothschild, Smooth Guatemalan, Kew, Giant Kew and Typhone.
3. Abacaxi group: Concal fruits
   Example: Perola, Abakka, Sugar loaf, Papelon, Venezolana, Amarella.
4. Spanish group: Globose fruit.Resistant to mealy bugs.
   Example: Mauritius Red Spanish, Singapore Spanish, Green Selangor, Castilla, P.R.1–67.
5. Maipure Group:Fruits ovoid to cylindrical.
   Example: Maipure, Bumuguesa, Rondon, Perolera, monte lirio.

Cultivars: Kew, Giant kew, Queen, Mauritius, Jhaldheep (Sweet type) & Bakhat (Assam), Sour Lakhat (Nagaland) and Baruipur local (West Bengal).

POMEGRANATE

(*Punica granatum*; *Punicaceae*; 2n= 18, Origin: Iran)

- The tree is deciduous in temperate region, while it is evergreen in tropical and subtropical regions.
- Pomegranate develops multi–stems.
- Edible part: Juicy seed coat, also called the Aril.
- The juice is useful for patients suffering from **leprosy**.
- The dried seeds of pomegranate give important condiment called "Anardana"
- Tannin is obtained from fruit rind leaves stem & root bark.
- Wild type pomegranate is known as– Daru
- Anti–transpirant such as 10% Kaoline, 10^{-5}m phenyl mercuric acetate, 1.5% power oil and 1% liquid paraffin, increases its productivity.
- One pomegranate fruit supplies about 40% of an adult's daily Vit–C requirement.
- It requires hot & dry climate during fruit development and ripening.
- At high temperature, it cannot produce sweet fruits.
- It is drought tolerant crop.
- Suitable pH range of 5.5 – 7.5.
- It is propagated by hardwood stem cutting.
- Plants will be ready in 55–60 days after planting of cutting in the soil.
- Pits size is 60–75 cm^3 at a spacing of 5 m × 2 m.

- Planting time– monsoon season (June–July).
- Papaya can be taken as filler plant.
- In India, multi–stemmed training system is followed.
- It may be trained as multi–stemmed and single stemmed tree.
  - Multi-stemmed tree: 3–4 stems are retained. This will give a bushy frame work to the plant.
  - Single stemmed tree: Remove all the side shoots upto 2–3 feet and single stem is left.
- Bahar in pomegranate:

  There are 3 main seasons viz.,
  1. Ambe bahar: Flowering time– February –March
  2. Mrig–bahar: Flowering time– June–July.
  3. Hastha Bahar: Flowering time– September – October.
- In pomegranate, Ambe bahar is prefer to take fruits.
- Severe incidence of fruit cracking takes place in Mrig bahar.
- The tree starts bearing fruits from 3–4th year and continues for about 25–30 years.
- Pomegranate fruits become ready for harvesting in 5–7 months after flowering.
- Economic yield is obtained from 6th or 7th year onwards.
- The fully grown up tree of about 10 years old produces 80–120 fruits (16–20 Kgs)/tree.
- Anar fruit fly/fruit borer (*Virachola Isocrates):* serious pest of this crop.

Physiological disorder

Fruit cracking:

- It is common in pomegranate and is a serious disorder.
- It is due to the sudden irrigation during fruit development.
- In the young fruits, it could be due to **boron deficiency.**
- The cultivars like: Bedana Bosek, Jalore seedless and khog are comparatively tolerant to cracking.

Varieties

- **Paper shell:** Popular in South India.
- **Alandi or Vadki:** It is commonly grown in Maharastra and Gujarat. The seeds are very hard.

- **Ganesh:** It is a selection from "Alandi". It has soft seeds.
- **Jyothi:** It is selection from Basin seedless variety. Soft seeded variety.
- **Mridula:** It is a seedling selection from an open pollinated F2 population of a cross Ganesh and Gul– e–Shan red. Soft seeded veriety.
- **Jalore seedless:** It is a soft seeded variety developed and recommended by CAZRI, Jodhpur for arid regions.
- **Bhagawa (G–137):** Clonal selection from Ganesh. It is ruling variety.
- **P–26:** Seedling selection from Muscat.
- The other varieties popularly grown are:

Dholka, Kandhari, Kabul, Muscat, Jodhpur red, Muskati red, Spanish ruby, Madhugiri, Bassein seedless, Nabha,

Hybrid

Ruby: Ganesh × Kabul × Yercard. Released by IIHR, Bangalore. Soft seeded variety.

Amlidana: Ganesh × Nanha. Dwarf, released by IIHR.

Soft seeded varieties: Paper shell, Ganesh, Jyoti, Bassein seedless.

Hard seeded varieties: Alandi or Vadki, Kandhari

FIG

(*Ficus carica*; *Moracea*; 2n = 26; Origin, South East Asia.)

- Fig is a large shrub or low growing deciduous shrub.
- Fruit solitary, axillary, green or yellow, pear–shaped.
- The related genera with edible fruits are Artocarpus, Cudrania and Morus.
- Some important species are *Ficus glomerata*, *Ficus benghalensis*, *Ficus religiosa*, *Ficus elastica*, *Ficus hispida*, *Ficus roxburghii* etc.
- The fresh fruit contains 11.5% total sugars, traces of iron, vit.–A, vit.–C, Protein, Fat, Calcium, Riboflavin, Thiamine, etc.
- Latex of Fig is used to coagulate milk.
- Edible part– "Synconium" which consists of hollow receptacle with a narrow aperture called as "Ostiole" at tip and numerous small flowers lining the inner surface.
- The true fruit is tiny drupelets inside the cavity of the fused peduncle.
- **Caprification:** The process of pollination in fig is caprification.

Classification:

The fig is classified into 4 classes viz.

1. Common or Adriatic fig or Edible fig

- Pistilate parthenocorpic fruits.
- Hybrid: F. carica × Indigenous species.
- *Example:* Poona, Bellary, Gangam Marseilles, Trojano and Dottato of Italy, Brown Turkey, Frage, Conardia and Lepe of Spain.

2. Capri fig

- Capri fig is a primitive fig.
- It has functional staminate flowers.
- It bears non edible fruits.
- Flowers are pollinated by a wasp (Blastophage psenes).
- *Example:* Stanford, Cordelia, Samson and Brawley.

3. Smyrna fig:

- It is important in Europe and USA.
- It bears long stylled pistillate flower.
- Pollination by Caprification.
- *Example:* Kadota, Bianco Grasso, Calimyrna, Zidi, Taranimt and Nutty Flavour.

4. San pedro fig:

- It bears two crops.
  - Parthenocarpic crop: It is also called "Breba"
  - Pollinated crop:It requires pollination (Caprification).

  Example: Gentile, Blanguette, king, Dauphine, Lampeira, etc.
- Exotic cultivars: Deanna, Conadria and Exeel are reported to perform better.
- It withstands low temperature (12°C–9.5°C).
- Fruits ripen prematurely if the temperature exceeds 38°C.
- Optimum temperature for vegetative growth is 15.5–21°C.
- It is a deep rooted fruit plant.
- A good quality of fruit is obtained on heavy soils.
- Fig is mainly propagated by hardwood stem cutting.
- The rooted hardwood cuttings of 4 weeks old are used for planting.
- Planting time-August to September.

- The pit size of 60 cm^3 with the distance of 3 × 3 m to 8 × 8m.
- Multi-stemmed training system is mostly used in India.
- Notching is practiced for activating dormant.
- Application of HCN (Hydrogen Cyanamide) at 1.5–2.0% advanced the date of bud burst.
- Fig is drought tolerant crop.
- Excess of irrigation during ripening causes cracking of fruits.
- It responds to heavy manuring crop.
- In fig crop generally, three types of buds occur:
  1. **Flower buds**:These buds produce parthenocarpic fruits only.
  2. **Mixed buds**:These buds are conical shape. It produces normal fruits.
  3. **Vegetative buds**:These buds usually remain dormant and rarely produce shoots.
- Yield is obtained from 5th year onwards.
- The average yield is about 150–300 fruits /tree or about 8–12 tonnes /ha.
- Fig bears fruits twice in a year *viz.*, July – September and February – May.
- Harvesting time: – February–May.
- Storage temperature– 0°C with 90–95% RH for 4 weeks and CO_2: O_2 ratio of 3.3:5.5.
- Sulphur fumigation followed by drying is commonly done in fig.
- Parthenocarpy favours or inhibits in a given type by climatic condition of the place where it is growing.
- Fig mosaic – Viral disease transmitted by vector fig mites (*Aceria ficus*).

Disorders

Sun burn: Due to expose in sunlight. Light pruning to avoid exposure of main branches /trunk. White painting of main trunk and branches.

Fruit cracking /splitting: Sudden rain at the time of ripening or nutritional disorders. This can be minimized by maintaining proper soil moisture.

Varieties

- **Parthenocarpic varieties:** Black Ischia, Brown turkey and Poona
- Other varieties: **Merselies, Bangalore, Lucknow, Kabul, Dinkar.**

JACKFRUIT

(*Artocarpus heterophyllus; Moraceae*; 2n = 56, Origin:India)

- It is the largest edible fruit (20–40 kg).
- It is also called as **"poor man's fruits"**.
- It is a Good source of protein.
- The seedling of the Jack fruit may take 10 years to bear.
- Seeds are sown immediately after extraction.
- Cauliflorus bearing habit.
- It contains 20% of carbohydrate.
- They cannot tolerate cold and frost.
- Softwood grafting is commonly practiced.
- Patch budding 100% success provided there must be sufficient sap present in scion and root stock.
- Jack fruit is planted as a shade tree in coffee garden or as an avenue plant.
- Spacing is 10×10 m^2 is followed.
- Flowering time–December and continues up to March.
- It is monoecious plant.
- Inflorescence-Spike.
- Cross pollinated plant and pollination done by honey beers.
- A multiple types of fruit, known as sorosis develops following pollination and fertilization.
- Edible part- Perianth.
- The fruits take about 90–110 days after appearance of the spike.
- It is a climacteric fruit.
- Harvesting is done by cutting off the stalk carrying the fruits.
- Yields: 15 year old tree– 250 fruits/tree.
- The individual fruit may weight from 1.0 kg to about 20 kg.
- Storage: 5°C with 85–90% RH for 2–3 months and 1.0 week under room temperature.

Species

- The *A. hetrophyllus* previously known as *A. integnifolia*.
- *A. altilis* (Bread fruit) – small sized round fruit.
- *A.lakoocha* (Monkey Jack)– Small edible fruits.

- *A. hirsute* – It is a semi–wild edible species, native to India.
- *A. champeden* – Strong odour like Durian

Varieties

1. Gulabi (rose scented)
2. Champa
3. Hazari
4. Rudrakshi(small roundish fruits)
5. GKVK–1
6. Swarna
7. Gumless jack
8. Muttan Varica
9. Singapore or Ceylon Jack.

TAMARIND

(*Tamarindus indica*; *Leguminosae*, sub–family: Caesalpinae; 2n = 24; Origin: Tropical Africa)

- It is a good wind break.
- The tree is large 40–60 feet high.
- India is the only country to exploit tamarind extensively.
- The unripe fruits are rich source of tartaric acid.
- Seeds are rich in pectin.
- The bark and leaves are used for tanning purpose.
- Fruit is a pod.
- It contains of 55% pulp, 20.6% water, 3.1% protein, 0.4% fat, 70.8% carbohydratess, 3% fibre and 10% tartaric acid.
- Seeds have 63% starch, 16% protein.
- Tamarind is a hardy tree, which grows well under warm climatic conditions of tropics and subtropics.
- It is drought tolerant tree, but sensitive to frost.
- Fruit size and shape: Baily reported that 2 types of fruit on the basis of size and shape:
  1. East Indian type – having long pods with 6 – 12 seeds.
  2. West Indian type – having shorter pods with 1–3 seeds.

- Tamarind is propagated mainly by seeds.
- To raise seedlings for 1 hectare – 2.0 – 2.5 kg seeds is needed.
- Seedlings ready for planting in July – August.
- Plan spacing: 12 × 12 /15 × 15 m^2.
- Seedling tree of tamarind comes to bearing in 10 – 14 years after planting.
- Vegetatively propagated tree requires 7– 8 years.
- Flowering time–April – June.
- Productive life of tree remains up to 60–70 years.
- A fully developed tree can give about 200 – 250 kg fruits /year.
- The reddish pulp type – locally known as Raktichinch.
- Yogeshwari – A high yielding red type variety released by Marathwad Agriculture University, Parbhani, Maharashtra.

Varieties

Makham, Waan, Secthong, Manila sweet, Pratisthan, Urigam, Cumbum, PKM—1 for HDP, DTS – 1 and DTS – 2– Released by UAS, Dharwad, (Dharwad Tamarind Selection).

ANNONA (SUGAR APPLE/CUSTARD APPLE)

(*Annona Squamasa; Annonaceae*; 2n = 14; Origin: Tropical America/Peru)

- The edilble part of anona is areoles.
- It has about 120 species.
- Popular species of Annona:
  - Annona cherimola– Cherimoya/Lakshmanphal
  - *A. muricata*–Soursop/Mullu Ramphal/Mamphal
  - *A. reticulate*–Bullock's heart/Ramphal
  - *A. squamosa*– Custard apple/Sitaphal/Sweet Sop/Sugar apple
  - *A. glabra*–Pond apple/Hanumanphal/Monkey apple
  - *A. senegalensis*–wild soursop. The African species.
  - *A. atemoya*–A. squamosa × A. cherimola.
- It is a good source of Vit–A and C.
- Its calorific value ranges from 822–1050 K Cal/kg.

- **Acetogenins** are potential anticancer property compounds as they have cytotoxic effect.
- Ethanol extracts of cherimoya seeds are used as insecticides and antiparasitic properties.
- Suitable pH of 6.0 – 6.5 are ideal.
- Custard apple is a hardy plant. It prefers dry climate with mild winter.
- It is very sensitive to frost.
- Dormancy period: – November–January after harvesting.
- Moist climate is favorable for proper growth and development of fruits.
- The plant can tolerate extremes of heat but the yield goes down as shedding of flowers occurs more than 39°C temperature.
- It is commercially propagated by **cleft grafting.**
- Planting time – monsoon (June–July).
- About 6–12 months old seedlings are used as a rootstock.
- **Spacing:** Cherimoya – 6.0 × 4.0 to 8.0 × 6.0 m
  Custard apple– 3.0 × 3.0 to 5.0 × 5.0, 5.0 × 7.0 m
  Sour sop– 4.0 × 4.0 to 8.0 × 8.0m
  Bullock's heart – 5.0 × 5.0 m
- Light pruning helps in inducing better branching.
- Annona plants starts bearing from 3 years of planting.
- Yields starts from 5–6 years after planting.
- Increase in fruit set by application of NAA at 20 ppm during flowering for 3–4 times at 8– 10 days interval and spraying with GA3 at 50ppm.
- Harvesting time– In dry areas: October–November/December in dry region
  In humid areas: – August.
- It is a climacteric fruit.
- It gives yield about 100–150 fruits *i.e.*, about 8–10 tonnes/ha.
- The fruits are highly perishable and cannot be stored for long duration.
- Storage: 7 days by treating with 8% wax emulsion.

Varieties

- **Balanagar:** It is a popular variety of Andhra Pradesh.
- **Mammoth:** This is a high yielding variety. The fruit has a good keeping quality.
- **Red sitaphal:** The fruits are medium in size.

- **Barbados:** The fruits are of small to medium in size.
- **British Guinea:** This is high yielding variety.
- **Islander:** Large fruit (410g), TSS 26 percent with less seeded.
- **Mahaboobnagar**
- **Washington**

Hybrids

- Atemoya: *A. squamosa* × *A.cherimoya* – sweet pulp, with few seeds.
- Arka Sahan: Annona atemoya (Islander) × Annona squamosa (Mammoth)
- African pride: Cherimoya × Custard apple

BARBADAS CHERRY (WEST INDIAN CHERRY)

(*Malphigia puncifolia: Malphigiaceae;* Origin: Tropical America)

- It has high Vitamin–C (ascorbic acid) among all the fruit crops.
- It content Vit–C 10–33 g/kg edible pulp.
- It is also called "Pill of natures"
- The soil pH 5.0–6.5 is good for its cultivation.
- It is a tropical plant.
- It cannot withstand less than 5°C for longer period.
- Cherry Seeds lose their viability quickly, and to be sown immediately for good germination.
- It takes about 10–12 days for germination and 6–8 months old seedlings are used for transplanting.
- It is commercially propagated by air layering.
- Planting time– During rainy season.
- Hardwood cuttings treated with IBA @ 2500ppm give better rootin.
- Spacing: For general cultivation– 7 × 7m
  For hedge purpose– 3x3m
- Light pruning is necessary to encourage new growth.
- The flowering starts after two years of planting.
- Flowering time– Onset of monsoon (May to August).

- Flower–bud production appears 15–18 days after pruning.
- The fruiting starts from second year after planting.
- Fruit is highly susceptible to bruising.
- An average yield– 2 kg/plant, Obtained from 4 year old tree.

Species and varieties: The genus Malphigia mainly having 2 related species

1. Malphigia coccijera
2. Malphigia urense

The cultivated types are grouped into two:

1. **Acid types** – The vitamin C level is excess, these fruits are considered acceptable in many countries where fruit is used fresh or blended to fortify other juices low in Vit.C

Varieties: Maunawik, J.H. Beanmont, C.F. Rehnbong, F. Haley, Red jumbo.

2. **Sweet type:** These cultivars were developed for general home planting and for potential use in baby foods and products requiring minimum acidity.

Varieties: Manoa sweet, Tropical Ruby, Hawaiian Queen, Florida sweet

Other varieties: A–14, 12, B–6, 7,8,15 and 17 grown in Puerto Rico.

JAMUN

(*Syzygium cuminii*; Myrtaceae; 2n = 40, Origin: India)

- Jamun is also known as Java plum or Gulab jamun.
- The genus Syzygium is having about 400 – 500 species.
- Edible species:
  - ***S. Jambos*** **(Rose apple or Safed Jamun):** The tree is ornamental. Polyembryonic nature.
  - ***S. fruitecosum*** – The species are suitable for wind break.
  - ***S. Javanica*** **(Water apple):** This species is found in South India and West Bengal.
  - ***S. densiflora*** – It is used as a root stock for *S. cuminii*. It is resistant to termites.

- ***S. uniflora*** **(Surinam cherry or Pitanga cherry):** These species have bright red with aromatic flavor fruits.
- ***S. Zeylanica*** – Popular in Western Ghats of India.

- Jamun vinegar is good for curing stomach disorder.
- The Jamun seeds can be sown within 3–4 weeks.
- Germination of the seeds in 10–15 day.
- Seedlings are ready during February to March.
- Commercial propagation method of jamun is patch budding.
- Spacing: 10 × 10 m. for budding/grafts

  12 × 12 m. for seedlings.
- Flowers bearing: Seedling tree- 8 – 10 years.

  Grafted trees – 6–7 years.
- Flowering time– March to April.
- Anthesis and dehiscence occurs between 10 am to 12 noon.
- Stigma receptivity is maximum one day after anthesis.
- Pollinators–Honey bees, house flies etc
- There is a heavy drop of flowers and fruit (50–60%) at very young stage during 5–8 weeks after blooming.
- Reduced fruit drop problem–Two sprays of GA3 @ 60 ppm first at full bloom and second spray, 15 days after initial setting of fruit.
- There are 3 phases of fruit growth and development *i.e.*

  I phase–15 to 52 days after fruit set.

  II phase–52 to 58 days after fruit set. Having fast growth.

  III phase–58 to 60 days after fruit set.
- Yield:
  - Seedling tree: – 80 –100 kg fruits.
  - Vegetative propagated tree: – 60–70 kg.
- The fruits of Jamun are highly perishable in nature.
- It cannot be stored more than 3–4 days under ordinary conditions.
- Storage temperature– 9–10°C with 85–90% RH for 3 weeks.

Varieties/Cultivars

- Raj Jamun
- NDUA & T (Narendra Deva University of Agriculture & Technology, Faizabad)

- Paras (Released from GAU)
- PKV – 15, 4, 14 and 13
- Gokak
- KRC
- KJS – 20

WOOD APPLE

(*Feronia limonica*: *Rutaceae*; 2n=18, Origin: India and Ceylone)

- It is one of the hardy and drought tolerant crops.
- Rich source of riboflavin.
- The seed contain non–bitter, oil, high in unsaturated fatty acids.
- Leaves, bark, roots and fruit pulp are all used against snakebite.
- It can tolerate low temperature (0–15°C) as well as a temperature as high as 47–50°C.
- Flowering time–February–march.
- The flowers are mainly staminate and hermaphrodite.
- It is highly cross pollinated crop.
- Polyembryony present in wood apple seeds.
- Polyembryonic seedlings are vigorous in growth and true to type.
- Commercially it is propagated by Whip grafting.
- Softwood grafting is highly successful with eight to ten months old seedlings.
- Spacing– 8 × 8 or 10 × 10 m^2.
- The best time for planting is July–august.
- Central leader system is followed in wood apple.
- It does not require regular pruning.
- Fruits are available from October to March in the market.
- Yield: 200–250 fruits per annum.

Species and Cultivars

- It is a monotypic genus of the only species.
- **HB–10:** having large sized fruits with an average weight of 350 g and pulp of 222g.

BAEL

(*Aegle marmelos*; *Rutaceae*; 2n=18; Origin –India)

- Bael fruit is hard shelled berry
- It is drought tolerant fruit crop.
- Trifoliate aromatic leaves which are divided into three leaflets.
- Complete defoliation of leaves during the month of April (time of ripening of fruits).
- The new leaves and shoots appear at the end of April.
- Due to mucilaginous texture and numerous seeds in its pulp, it is not popular as a fresh fruit.
- Bael leaves are used for sacred offering to lord shiva.
- Fruit is a rich source of riboflavin (Vitamin B12) among all the fruit crops.
- Marmelosin – Active ingradient present in bael, it is extracted from bark.
- It can be grown in acidic, alkaline and stony soil.
- Suitable pH ranges from 5–10.
- Bael tree can withstand maximum temperature of 46.6°C and minimum of 6.6°C.
- Common method of propagation of bael is by seeds.
- Sown time– June to july
- Seedlings become ready for transplantation after a year.
- Commercially method of propagation is Patch budding.
- Rootstocks:
  - *Aegle fraglegabonensis*
  - *A. chevlieri*
  - *A. paniculata*
  - Swinglea glutinosa
- Pruning time– April–May and August.
- Flowering starts from the middle of May.
- Fruit setting starts from 3rd week of May and continues up to July.
- Fruiting occurs on one year old shoots.
- For uniform ripening it can be treated with the application of ethrel @1000–1500 ppm keeping the fruits at 30°C.
- Ripe bael fruits can be stored for 2 weeks at 27–32°C temperature.

- Fruits below 9°C temperature are greatly injured.
- Yield: In seedling bael: fruits start after 7–8 years of plantation.
  In budded tree: fruits start after 4–5 years of plantation.
  10–15 years tree gives: 200–400 fruits/year.

Species and Cultivars

- The genus consists of 2–3 species.
- **Etawah Kagzi:** It is mid season ripening cultivar and bears heavily.
- **Deoria large:** Fruits are largest among all the cultivars. Fruits have less mucilaginous substances.
- **Kagzi Gonda:** It is the best cultivar in UP having large sized fruit. It has excellent keeping quality of the fruits.
- **Mirzapuri:** Excellent keeping quality.

MANGOSTEEN

(*Garcinia mangostana; Guttiferae*; 2n = 88 /90; Origin-Malayan Peninsula)

- It is also known as Queen of fruit and Finest fruit of the world.
- Types of fruit– Berry
- Commercially propagation method– Seeds
- Transplanting stage– 2 leaves stage or 2 feet height.
- Planting time : May to November
- It is annually crop but in Nilgiris hill-take 2 crops– Aug–Oct and April–June.
- Shade tolerant tree.
- Red colour of rind : Cyanidin–3–glucoside
- Aroma due to Hexyl acetate
- Fruit requires 90–105 days to maturity after fruit set.
- Problem : Slow growth rate of tree and Lack of root hairs
- It cannot tolerate temperature below 5°C or above 38°C.
- Seed loose viability very quickly (Recalcitrant seed).
- Spacing– 7 × 7 m^2 to 10 × 10 m^2.
- Alternate bearing fruit plant.
- Yield– 500–1500 fruits/plantor 20–25 kg/tree (4–5t/ha).

- Storage temp–
  - Room temp: 2–3 weeks
  - 4–6°C with 85–90% RH– 50 days.

Species

The important species of genus Garcinia. spp are.

- G. mangostana: It is only cultivated species. Allopolyploid hybrid.
- [(G. mangostana = G hombroniana ($2n = 48$) × G. malaccensis ($2n=42$)].
- G. cowa
- G. schomburgkiana
- G. hanburyii: Gum resins used for aolouring.
- G. xanthochymus: fruits are edible, young shoots & mature fruits as vegetables.
- G. dulcis
- G. indica:Found in tropical forests of India.

Varieties

- **Jolo**

Physiological disorder

- **Gamboge:**The presence of yellow dried latex oozed from the latex vessels on the fruit skin is known as Gamboge, it may be scrapped off.
- **Fruit spliting**

BER

(*Zizyphus mauritiana*; *Rhamnaceae*, 2n=48, Origin–China)

- Ber is an ancient fruit crop of India.
- It is highly suitable for marginal land and hot arid region.
- It contains 20–28 per cent sugar.
- The powder and decoction prepared from the roots are effective in case of fever, ulcers and old wounds.
- The tree is a host plant for rearing of the lac insect.
- It can be grown in saline soils.
- It is extremely drought hardy.
- Gametophytic self incompatibility present.

- It prefers hot and dry climate for quality fruits and production.
- Ber commercially propagated by Ring budding.
- In dry areas, in–situ budding is highly successful.
- Spacing: 6 m × 6 m.
- Planting time:

  In South India– Monsoon period June–July
  In North India–August–September
- Training: Single stem training system is followed in initial stage.
- Final balancing and correction of frame work should be done in the third year.
- Pruning: A regular annual pruning in ber is very much necessary to induce a good and healthy growth.
- Thinning out of branches is necessary to avoid too much crowding which helps in reducing the incidence of pest and disease.
- The best time for pruning when it sheds its leaves and become dormant.
- Pruning time– May–June.
- For optimum yield and good quality fruits, 25% of one year old shoots should be headed back.
- Flowering starts from July and extended upto November.
- It is cross pollinated crop.
- Pollinators: Honey bees, Houseflies and Yellow wasp.
- Dwarf rootstock: Zizyphus nummulaia
- The fruit set ranges from 6.19–8.16%.
- Spraying of GA3, 2,4,5– T is found to improve the fruit set and reduces the fruit drop.
- Fruit growth of ber followed a double sigmoid curve.
- Ber plant growth in three distinct phases *i.e.*

  Early phase-45 days after fruit set (DAFS)
  Middle phase-45–90 DAFS
  Final phase-90 Days After Flowering to maturity (185 days).
- The growth patterns of fruits and seeds were similar.
- Picking is done manually and sorted in different groups as over – ripe fruits, unripe fruits, damaged fruits, etc., the correct matured fruits are graded as per size, i.e., large, medium and small and marked after proper packing.

- Harvesting time
  - South India-October– Navember
  - North India-Feb–April
- Yield: 80–200 kg per tree from 10–20 years old tree.
- Storage: 3°C and 85% RH for 30 days.

Species and Varieties

- The genus Zizyphus consists of 40 species in tropical and subtropical regions.
- Two species are mainly grown:
  1. Zizyphus jujuba (Cheneese ber)
  2. Z. mauritiana (Indian ber)
- Umran
  - Alwar in Rajasthan is known as Katha and Kotho in Maharashtra.
  - Other name of Umran; DetriGola, Narik, akrota, Seo. Laddu etc.
- Early varieties: Gola, Safeda, Sandur, Narnaul, Seo, Choncahl, Shamber, Badami, Manuki, Narma varnasi, Banarasi Gola, Delhi Gola
- Mid season varieties: Kaithli, Sanaur–5, Muria, Muria, Mahrara, Mehrun, Darokhi, Kharki, Banarasi
- Late varieties: Umran, Illichi, Pathini
- Extremly dry area: Gola, Seb
- Dry area: Umran, Illaichi
- Humid area: Mehrun

Special characteristics of varieties

- Sonnar–2: Powdery mildew resistant variety
- Dodhia: Fruit fly resistant
- Illaichi: 90% pllen sterility
- Umran: suitable for making chhuhara
- Goma kriti (Ganesh kirti): Selection from Umran

AONLA

(*Emblica officianalis /Phyllanthus emblica*; Euphorbiaceae; 2n=28;Origin–India)

- Aonla/Amla is also known as Indian goosberry.
- It is the second richest source of vitamin C content (500–750mg/100g pulp).
- It can be grown successfully in arid climate.
- It can withstand in the soils of higher pH and poor fertility wastelands.
- Bark, leaves and fruits are used for tanning.
- Fruits are rich source of pectin which is used for preparing jelly.
- Aonla fruit is also important ingredient of Chyawanprash which is an ancient well known ayurvedic medicine.
- Apart from chayavanaprash, it is also used for preparing of Triphala, amrit kalash, Trilax, Amla plex, Neutrale, Tylophora plus, etc.
- Aonla is commercially propagated by Patch budding.
- Budding time– July to august.
- Spacing– 10 × 10 m^2.
- It has no required special pruning and training.
- Flower bud differentiation in the first week of March.
- Flowers started opening from the last week of March.
- There is no self incompatibility in aonla due to high percentage of staminate flowers.
- In aonla male–female ratio is 307.9:1 and 197: 1
- Aonla seeds have dormancy for 3–4 months.
- Flowers open in the morning whereas dehiscence of pollen grain occurs in the evening.
- Pollination occurs through wind as well as by honeybees.
- Fruits become ready for harvesting by November–December.
- Fruits can be stored for 7–8 weeks with temperature at 32–35°F and RH of 85–90%.
- Yield:
  - 200 kg fruit yield can be obtained/year/tree.
  - The average yield is about 125 q/ha.
- Start bearing:
- Seedling plants- 10 years of plantation

- Budded or grafted trees- 6–7 years
- Physiological disorder: **Necrosis**

Varieties

Banarasi: Best cultivar for murraba. TSS–13%. Seed pulp ratio is 1:21.
Chakiya: it is a hardy cultivar with very heavy bearing habit. It is a good pollinizer.
Hathijhool (Francis): Late bearing tree and has poor keeping quality.
NA–4 I(Kanchan): Seedling selection from Chakiya.
NA–5 (Krishna): Seedling selection from Banarasi. An early maturing variety.
NA–6: Seedling selection from Chakiya.
NA–7(Amrit): Seedling selection from Francis.
NA–9(Neelum): Seedling selection from Banarasi. An early maturing variety.
NA–10

LITCHI

(*Litchi chinensis; Sapindaceae*; 2n = 30; Origin–China)

- The litchi fruits are available during May –June in northern India.
- Suitable temperature for its flowering and fruiting is 21°C– 38°C.
- Acidic soils produce good quality fruits.
- Mycorhizal association found in roots of litchi plant.
- Highest producing state of litchi in India–Bihar
- Highest producing country in the world–China followed by India.
- Red pigment in litchi fruit due to–Anthocyanin.
- The pH range is 5.5–7.0 with adequate soil depth.
- It is commercially propagated by Air layering (500ppm IBA).
- Modified central leader system of training is followed.
- Flowering:
  - The grafted or layered litchi tree– 3–4 years.
  - Seedlings tree take –8–12 years.
- Flowering starts from: Jan–Feb.
- Night temperature of 15–16°C for 2 months is essential to induce flowering and for vegetative growth.
- The ideal temperature is 30°C.
- Flowers are terminal and appear on current season wood.

- Litchi flowers are petalless.
- To control fruit drop NAA at 20–30ppm, GA3 at 20–50ppm or 2–4–D20 ppm, to be applied before flower opening.
- Girdling and centering also increases flowering.
- Litchi is non–climacteric fruit.
- Litchi pulp is out growth of the seed.
- Edible part of Litchi–Aril.
- The fruits are harvested during May and June.
- The maturity indices are flatness of tubercles.
- It takes about 55–60 days from flowering to harvest.
- The whole bunch is harvested manually.
- Yield: About 80–150 Kg of fruits/tree.
- Storage:
  - The fruits cannot be stored for more than 2–3 days under room temperature.
  - It can be stored for 5 weeks at a temperature of 1.6–7.2°C.
- Dipping of fruits in 250ppm ethrel improves the fruit colour.

Physiological disorder

Fruit cracking: It is due to B deficiency. To avoid fruit cracking: The field to be irrigated during fruit growth and in early summer. Spraying with 2, 4– D (10ppm), GA3 (20 ppm) and Boron (0.4 percent) spray reduces fruit cracking.

Species and varieties

- The family sapindaceae and and subfamily Nepheleae has about 125 genera and more than 1000 species.
- The genus Litchi has two species.
  - Litchi philippinesis– It is a wild type mostly used as root stock
  - Litchi chinensis– It is a commercial important species.

Varieties

Sahi	China	Purbi	Rose Scented	Kasba
Dehra Dun	Muzaffarpur	Saharanpur		
Rose scented	Bombay	Bedana	Elachi	Haak yip
Tai so	Wai chee	Brewster	Gee Kee	

- Table purpose varieties: Shahi, China, Elaichi, Early Bedana
- **Shahi**– Suitable for canning

DATE PALM

(*Phoenix dactylifera;Arecaceae*, 2n=26, Origin–West Asia)

- According to Arabians: "Foot in running water and its head in the fire of the sky"
- Date palm-Monocotyledon, Dioecious and Unbranched stem plant.
- 1kg of ripe dates = 3150 calories.
- Date palm tolerates high soil salinity (pH 9–10).
- Ideal temperature for flowering and fruiting–25–29°C.
- Inflorescence-Spadix.
- Type of fruit-One seeded berry.
- Propagation-Off shoots (10–25 kg weight).
- Planting time-July–august.
- 2–3 male plants are enough for pollinating of 100 female plants.
- Wild species–*Phoenix humilis*
- Metaxenia is a common problem in date palm.
- Leaf pruning is important culture practice.
- Leaf pruning time-June
- About 75–100 leaves are found optimum yield.
- Date stages:
  - Doka stage–Harvesting stage in India. It is useful for making Chhuhara. 70–80% moisture available in this stage.
  - Dang/Rutab stage– Harvesting for fresh eating (translucent and softening stage).
  - Tamar or Pind stage– Harvesting for storage purpose. It attains fully mature condition.
- Processed liquid product of date palm is known as– Dibis
- Liquor prepared from date palm is– "Arrack"
- Trailer mounted palm duster is used for pollination.
- Required heat units for full maturity–3300 units.
- Ethephon is an effective fruit thinning agent.
- Processed products of date palm–Chhuhara, Pind khajur, Dibis, Liquor, Jaggary, Toddy, Neera

- Yield
  - Rainfed area– 40–50 kg/palm
  - Irrigated area– 200 kg/palm

Varieties

- Early varieties: Halawy, Khunezi
- Mid season varieties: Khadraway, Medjool, Hayany, Barhee, Zahidi
- Soft seeded varieties (Invert sugar date): Khadraway, Medjool, Halawy, Barhee
- Semi dry date varieties (Canesugar date): Dayari, Deglet nor, Zahidi
- Dry date (Bread type date): Thoory
- Chhuhara making: Khadraway, Medjool, Sharan
- Fresh eating: Halawy, Barhee, Khalas, Sevi, Khunezi
- Pind khajur: Zahidi

AVOCADO

(*Persia Americana; Lauraceae*, 2n=24, Origin–Mexico)

- It is also known as 'Fruit of new world', Butter fruit, Alligator pear and 21st century fruit
- It is a evergreen tree and can grow about 80 feet height.
- Fruit type– Single seeded berry.
- It contains 24.26% Fat and 1% sugar.
- It's energy value is twice as much as Banana fruit.
- In India, it is grown as backyard tree.
- It have recalcitrant seed
- Inflorescence–Compound panicle of raceme.
- Viability of seeds– 2–3 weeks.
- Propagation method– Seed.
- Spacing– 5 × 5 m^2
- Cross pollination due to-PDSD (Protogynous diurnally synchronous dichogamy)
- PDSD was 1st reported by Bergh (1969)
- It is climacteric fruit.

- Harvesting time– August to September.
- Harvesting index– Oil colour
- Girdling is the important cultural operation.

Varieties

- Avocado is classified into 3 distinct races:
  1. Mexican: Gotfried, Duke, Pernod
  2. West Indian: Pollock, Simmonds, Black Prince, Fushsia, Peterson, Waldin.
  3. Guatemalan: Taylor, Linda, Queen, Benit
- **Mexican races:** It matures 6 months. It is suitable for low temperature condition. It contains 30% oil.
- **West Indian races:** It matures 5 months. It is tolerant to salinity. It contains 8–15% oil.
- **Guatemalan races:** It matures more than 12 months. It contains 3–10% oil.
- India varieties:
- **Green (Guatemalan type):** Oval shape fruit
- **Purple (West Indian type):** Pear shape fruit
- **Duke:** Resistant to root rot and cold hardeness.
- **Pollock:** Overcome salinity problem.
- **Hass:** World famous cultivar

Hybrid

- **Furete:** Mexican × Guatemalan, Resistant to cold.

Physiological disorder

- **Tipburn:** Due to Chloride toxicity.
- **Grey pulp**
- **Pulp spot**
- **Discolouration**
- **Fizzles**
- **Apoplexy**

KARONDA

(*Carrisa carandus; Apocynaceae*; 2n=22, Origin–India)

- It is commonly planted as a Hedge.
- It requires 2–3 picking.
- Fruits are richest source of Fe(Iron)
- It is a Xerophytic plant.
- Fruits have antiscorbutic properties.
- Fruits are mature for 100–110 days after fruit set.
- Yield-3–5 kg/plant.
- Storage temp.– 20–25°C for 2–3 days. SO_2 solution (2000 ppm) for 6 month.

Species

- Carrisa ovate– used for Jam preparation
- Carrisa edulis– used for Scented flower
- Carrisa grandiflora– It is a African spp. and also known as Natal plum

Varieties

- **Maroon**
- **Types of varieties:**

(a) Green fruited

(b) White fruited

(c) Dark purple fruited

KIWIFRUIT

(*Actinidia deliciosa; Actinidaceae*; 2n=58, Origin– China)

- It is also known as Chinese gooseberry.
- National fruit and symbol of New Zealand.
- It is deciduous vine.
- It was first planted in the Lal Bagh garden at Bangalore.
- Fruit skin is good source of antioxidant.
- It is commercially propagated by Hard wood cutting.
- Cuttings are treated with 2500 ppm IBA+NAA 2500 ppm for 20–30 second.
- It bears fruit 4–5 year.

- Kiwi seeds require stratification for breaking dormancy.
- Adopted planting method– T–bar and Pergola.
- After harvest, fruits divided into grade:
  - A–grade: 70 g fruit weight
  - B–grade: 40–70 g fruit weight
- Yield
  - Fruit: 50–100 kg/plant
  - Vine: 25 ton/ha (7 year plant)

LOQUAT

(*Eriobotrya japonica; Rosaceae*; 2n=34, Origin– China)

- First introduced name in India- Japanese medlar.
- It is the only evergreen fruit plant in Rosaceae family.
- Highest production country: Japan followed by China.
- It is rich source of Vit-A.
- Application of paclobutrazol (500 ppm) around the base of trunk is recommended for increased fruit size.
- Propagation method-Air layering.
- Planting time-June–July.
- Plant population-180–300 plants/ha.
- Self incompatibility present in loquat plant.
- Self unfruitfulness present in loquat varieties.
- Frost is the limiting factors for its cultivation.
- Yield: 16– 20 kg fruit/tree.
- It is available in market during March–May.
- Storage temperature
- At room temperature-4–6 days
- 11°C with 85–90% RH– 2 weeks

Varieties

- **Early vars:** Golden yellow, Improve yellow, Pale yellow, Large round, Thames pride.
- **Mid vars:** Fire ball, Large Agra, Mammoth, Matchless, Safeda.

- **Late vars:** California advance, Tanaka
- **Self incompatible vars:** Golden yellow, Improve golden yellow, Pale yellow, Large Agra
- **Best pollinizer vars:** Dolforma advance, California advance

MACADAMIA

(*Macadamia ternifolia*; *Proteaceae*; 2n=48, Origin–Australia)

- It is also known as **Australian nut** and **Queensland nut**.
- Edible part-Kernel (Resemble cashew).
- It contains 75% oil and 10% protein.
- Ideal temperature for its cultivation– 25°C.
- Propagation method– Wedge grafting
- Flowering time– December to January.
- Fruiting time– July to August.
- Yield– 80–90 kg/tree(18 year old plant)

Species and Varieties

- **M. integrifolia** (Smooth shell type): Kakea, Ikaika, Keauhou, Kau, Purvis, Makai, Mauka
- **M. tetraphylla** (Rough shell type): Greber, Renown, Anamour, Mammoth, Sewell, Probert–2

Hybrids

- Beaumout, Nelmak–1, Nelmak–2

MAHUA

(*Basia latifolia/B. longifolia*; *Sapotaceae*; 2n=24, Origin–India)

- Mahua seeds have no dormancy.
- Propagation method– Veneer grafting and Seeds
- Propagation time– July–August.
- Spacing– 9 × 9 m^2
- Seeds are germinated within 10–15 days after sowing.
- Each seed contains 2 kernel.

- Kernel contains 50% oil.
- Ripe fruit shed from tree– June–July
- One ton dry husk yield absolute alchohol.
- Mahua flowers rich in sugar 65–73%.
- Yield
  - Dry flowers– 100–150 kg/plant/year
  - Kernel– 60–80 kg/plant/year

Varieties

- NM–2, NM–4, NM–7, NM–8

OLIVE

(*Olea eumpaea; Oleaceae*, Origin-Mediterranean region)

- Ideal temperature for its cultivation: 15–21°C.
- Propagation– Seeds and Cuttings.
- Rooting temperature: 21–26°C with 70% RH.
- Planting time– June–July and Jan– Feb.
- Important practices: Staking and Mulching.
- N based fertilizers should not be applied to newly planted sampling until they are – 6–8 month old.
- Harvesting
- Early– Low quality and quantity
- Late– Acidity of oil

Varieties

- **Oil types:** Carolea, Caratina, Pendolina, Frontoio, Canino, Ascolanaterena, Aglandeau
- **Pickle types:** Ascolano, Mission, Grosseune, Picholine, Cornicobra

PASSION FRUIT

(*Passiflora edulis*; *Passifloraceae*; 2n=18 , Origin– Brazil)

- Rich source of vit–A
- It is also known as "Hen's egg fruit"
- It is commercially propagated by grafting method.
- Spacing– 2 × 3m^2.
- Fruiting time-Aug–Dec and March–April.
- Fruit set to harvesting duration-80–85 days.
- Yield
  - Purple varieties– 8–10 kg/vine
  - Kaveri– 16–20 kg/vine

Varieties

- **Purple varieties** (P. edulis**):** Susceptible for color rot, wilt and brown leaf spot
- **Yellow varieties** (P. edulis **vars** flavicarpa**):** Field tolerant
- **Noel's special:** It is self incompatible variety. Tolerant to Alternaria laef spot.

Hybrid

- **Kaveri=** Purple × Yellow. Resistant to color rot, wilt and brown leaf spot.

PERSIMON

(*Diospyrus kaki; Ebenaceae*; 2n=90, Origin–China)

- National fruit of **Japan**
- Rootstock:
  - Diospyrus letus : Self incompatible and susceptible for crown gall
  - Diospyrus virginiana : Susceptible to cephalosporium
- TSS at maturity stage of fruit: 14–17%
- Complete dormancy: 8–10°C for 888 hrs.
- Best quality fruit obtained in non astringent varieties at: 16–22°C.
- It is propagated by Seeds and Whip grafting.
- Seed germination: 2–3 weeks.
- Suitable temperature for seeds germination : 28°C

- Planting time : Jan–Feb
- For removing astringent in persimmon fruit: treated with 500 ppm ethophan for 2 min.
- Fuyu is the only non–astringent cultivar which grown in subtropical climate.
- Astrigent and Non–astrigent varieties are two types:
  - Pollination constant
  - Pollination variant

Varieties

- There are two types of persimmon varieties:
  1. Astringent
  2. Non–astringent

1. Astrigent

- It requires cool climate.
- Fruit contains 1–2 seeds
- Varieties: Hachiya, Nightingale, Triumph, Hiratanenashi

2. Non–astrigent

- It requires warm climate
- Fruit contains 4–5 seeds
- Varieties: Fuyu, Jiro, 20th century, Mastumoto

PHALSA

(*Grewia subinequalis; Tilliaceae*; 2n=36, Origin–India)

- Tolerant to drought.
- Bushy type fruit plant.
- Propagation : Seeds
- Planting time : July–August
- Germination of seed : 2 weeks
- Transplanting time : Jan–Feb
- Spacing : 2.5–3 × 3–4 m^2
- Rich source of Vit–A
- Fruits are born in current season's growth
- Tolerant temp : 45°C

- Pruning time : December to January
- Fe deficiency common in phālsa cultivation.
- Maturity indices : Colour
- Storage temp : 7°C for 7 days
- Harvesting indices: Deep red colour, May end.
- Yield: 2–4 kg fruit/plant.

CARAMBOLA

(*Averrhoa carambola*; *Oxalidaceae*; 2n=24, Origin–Indonesia)

- Cauliflorous bearing habit.
- Fruit cum ornamental tree.
- Fruit contains Oxalic acid. It is responsible for acidity.
- Root extract is used for poisoning.
- It has recalcitrant seeds.
- Spacing : 8 × 8 m^2
- *Averrhoa bilimbi* spp. Used for making pickle.

Varieties

- **Sour type:** 1% acid present Sweet type: 0.5% acid present
- **Golden star:** Introduce fron Hawaii
- **Icambola:** Introduced from Columbia
- **Tean Ma and Min Ma:** Introduced from Taiwan
- **Faung Tung:** Chinese sweet type variety.
- **Dah Pan**

APPLE

(*Malus domestica*; *Rosaceae*; 2n=32, Origin–Asia minor)

- Flower colour: White to Pink
- Stone cells are absent in flesh of apple.
- Most widely grown temperate fruit plant in the world.
- In India, apple covers 55% area and 75% production of total temperate fruits.
- Highest producing state: Jammu and Kashmir (J& K)

- 11–33% pollinizing trees recommended for proper cultivation.
- Apple bowl of india : Himachal Pradesh
- Optimum temperature for germination and fruit setting: 21–26.7°C
- Adverse affect in fruit setting when temperature goes to below –2.2°C.
- Suitable soil pH : 5.5– 6.5
- Stratification: 4–7°C for 60–90 days.
- Chilling temperature: 4–7°C for 1000 hrs.
- Terminal flowering present.
- Ancestor of cultivated apple : *Malus sylevestris*
- India spp. Of apple : *Malus baccata var. himalacia, M. sikkimmensis*
- Commercially propagation method: Tongue grafting.
- Common method of propagation: Stooling/Mound layering.
- One year old seedling stock are ready for grafting during: Feb–March
- Thomas Andrew Knight produced the 1st apple cultivar: Percentage
- Cultural practices: Ringing and Scoring.
- Apple varieties are self unfruitfulness due to presence of self incompatibility.
- Climacteric fruit.
- Maturity indices: Starch index (1–2)
- Alternate bearing present.
- Number of grades during marketing: – 6
- EMLA(East Mailling Long Ashton) series of rootstocks are resistant to virus.
- Wooly apple aphid *(Eriosoma langierum*) is the most devasting pest in the world.
- Predator of wooly apple aphid: *Amphilenus mali*
- San Jose Scale (*Quadraspidiotus perniciosus*) is the most serious pest of apple.
- Apple scab (Fungus– *Venturia inaequalis*) serious disease in the world.
- Fruit drop
  - Early drop: Due to lack of pollination, Fruit competition.
  - June drop: Due to moisture stress and environmental condition.
  - Preharvest drop: Due to accumulation of ABA, reduction of auxin and Increase Ethylene in fruit.
- NAA 10 ppm before expected fruit drop or 20–25 days before harvesting

checks the preharvesting fruit drop.

- Fermented beverage: Cidar
- Pruning: for maintaining vegetative growth and spur development.
- Spur type cultivars
  - 50–80% standard size
  - 20–50% yield potential
- Spur and standard colour mutant type cultivars observed: Delicious group.
- Delicious group of apple
  - It is cross pollinated
  - Self incompatible
- English group of apple
  - It is self pollinated
  - Used as a pollinizers
- High density planting
  - Low < 250 plants/ha
  - Moderate 250–500 plants/ha
  - High 500–1250 plants/ha
  - Ultra high >1250 plants/ha
  - Super high density/Meadow 20,000–70,000 plants/ha
- Storage temperature: –1.1 to 0°C with 85–90% RH for 4–8 month.

Rootstocks

- Seedling rootstock: Crab apple (*Malus baccata*), Indigenous rootstock.
- Clonal rootstock

1. Dwarf: M–9
2. Semi dwarf: M–4, M–7 and MM–106
3. Vigorous: Merton–793
4. Semi vigorous: MM–111
5. Ultra dwarf: M–27 (M–13 × M–9)
6. MM–104: Winter clonal hardy rootstock

Varieties

Pollinizer varieties

- **Early varieties:** Early shanburry, Tydemans early, Fenny, Irish peach.
- **Mid varieties:** Red delicious, Red gold, Red chief, Rome beauty, Top red,

Richared, Razakwar, Golden delicious, MacIntosh, Cortland, American mother

- **Late varieties:** Winter banana, Yellow newton, Lal Ambri, Granny smith, Rymer, Buckingham
- **Spur type varieties:** Star crimson, White spur, Red chief
- **Standard colour mutant:** Top red, Skyline supreme, Hardiman
- **Green English varieties:** Baldwin, Black bandavis, Pippins, Cox's– orange pippins
- **Low chilling varieties:** Michel, Schlomit, Anna, Tamma, Tropical beauty, Parlin's beauty
- **Scab resistant varieties:** Liberty, Freedom, Jonafree, Macfree, Florina, Firedous, Sir prize, Prima, Priscilla.
- **Triplois varieties:** Baldwin, Gravenstin, Winesap
- **Bitter pit susceptible vars:** Yellow newton, Golden delicious, Gravenstein
- **Internal browing susceptible vars:** Yellow newton

Hybrids

- **Lal Ambri:** Red delicious × Ambri
- **Amb red:** Red delicious × Ambri
- **Amb starking:** Starking delicious × Ambri
- **Ambroyal:** Royal delicious × Ambri
- **Amrich:** Rich–a–red × Ambri
- **Sunheri:** Ambri × Golden delicious
- **Akbar:** Ambri × Cox orange pippins
- **Chaubattia princes:** Red delicious × Early shanburry
- **Chaubattia anupam:** Red delicious × Early shanburry

Intergeneric hybrid

- **Pamapple:** Pear × Apple, Developed by Ellis Marks(1952)

Other important varieties

- Liberty is resistant to all fungal diseases.
- Golden delicious, Yellow newton, MacIntosh, Northern spy: Good seed viability.
- Red delicious popular in India.
- Golden delicious popular in USA and Europe.

- MacIntosh leading variety for Canada.
- Ambri and Rymer Indegenous variety.
- Northern spy: Resistant to wooly apple aphid.
- Ambri: Longest storage life
- MM series are resistant to wooly aphid.
- MM series released from John Innes Institute, England.
- **Prima:** 1st scab resistant variety.

PEAR

(*Pyrus communis*; *Rosaceae*; 2n=32, Origin–Europe)

- World largest producer country: Italy
- Flower colour: White
- Malic acid present in the fruit of pear.
- Type of inflorescence: corymbose
- Chilling requirement: 1200 hrs
    - Bartlest var: 1500 hrs
    - Pathernak var: 150 hrs
- Suitable temperature for its cultivation: 15.6–21°C.
- Tolerant temperature
    - At dormant: –26°C
    - At growing period: –45°C
- Highly fertile rich in due to causes: Pear psylla and Fire blight
- Seedling rootstock
    - Kainth/Mehal (*Pyrus pashia*): Vigorous rootstock
    - Shaira (*Pyrus serotina*)
- Clonal rootstock
    - Quince A: producing tree 50–60% of standard size
    - Quince C: dwarfing rootstock for pear
- Budding time: April to September
- Grafting time: December to January
- Filer plant in pear orchard: Peach
- Training method: Modified central leader system

- Commercial propagation method: Tongue grafting
- Most of the pear varieties are self fertile due to self incompatibility.
- Incompatibility is overcome by double grafting with Old Home or Beauty Hard.
- Old Home or Beauty Hard used as interstock between Bartlett and Quince.
- 180 cm soil depth is suitable for proper growth.
- Yield: 25–35 ton/ha
- Storage temperature: –0.6 to –1.6°C
- Europian pear is highly susceptible to fire blight than Oriental pear.
- Fire blight is a serious bacterial disease of pear: Bact (Erwinia amylovora).
- Pear decline is caused by MLOs which is transmitted by pear psylla.

Species

- Willo leaf pearl: pyrus salicifolia
- Europian/Common/Soft pear: Pyrus communis
- Japanese/Oriental/Hard: Pyrus pyrifolia (Country pear):Used in South India
- Resistant to fire blight: Pyrus calleryana

Varieties

- **Bartlett (Baggughosha):** Interspecific hybrid variety.
- **Flemish beauty:** free from grit cell, self fertile
- **Magnese:** free from grit cell
- **Anjou:** free from storage disorder.
- **Starkimson delicious:** red colour and flavoured
- **Winter Nellis**
- **Fertility**
- **Kiffer:** *P. communis* × *P. serotina*
- **Le–conte**: low chilling variety
- **Pathernakh (sand pear):** low chilling variety. Self pollinated.
- **Gola:** loe chilling variety.
- **China Pear**
- **Max Red Bartlett:** Bud mutant of Bartlett.
- **Punjab gold, Punjab nectar and Red blush:** PAU released varieties.

Physiological disorder

- **Cork break down/Brown Hear:** Storage disorder. Due to B deficiency.
- **Premature ripening:** when night temp is <7°C and Day temp is <21°C
- **Calyx end rot and Blossom blast:** B deficiency.
- **Hard end of pear:** due to unfavourable water condition.
- **Fruit cracking:** B deficiency.
- **Cork spot:** Ca deficiency.

PLUM

(*Prunus* domestic; *Rosaceae*; 2n=16/48; Origin–Asia and Europe)

- European plum: *Prunus domestic* (2n=16)
- Japanese plum: *Prunus solinicia* (2n=48)
- Chilling requirement
  - EU : 1000–1200 hrs
  - JP : 700– 1000hrs
- Propagation: Tongue grafting
- Flower colour: White
- Seeds of wild apricot: Zardalu
- Training–central modified leader system.
- Rootstock
  - Vigorous: Myrobalan–B, St. Julian–C, Myro–29–C
  - Dwarf: Pixy
- Common rootstock: Country peach
- Planting time: December to January
- Plums are graded into 3 grades.
- In plum heavy bearing is a problem.
- Plums are available in the market from second week of May (Titron) to third week of July (Jamari)
- Plums are stimulated bowl movement.
- Pollinator: Honey bee
- Deficiency of Boron in plum:
  - Leaves dark green and boat like.

- 0.1% boric acid.

- Flower thining: 200ppm ethophon/100ppm carbaryl
- Yield: 60–70 kg fruit/plant
- Storage: 0°C for 2–4 week with 85–90%

Varieties

- **European:** Golden drop, Yellow egg, Green gage, Grand duke, President, Prune, Diamond, Tragedy, Imperial books
- **Japanese:** Santa Rose, Satsuma, Beauty, mariposa, Kelsey, Frontier, Elephant hear
- **Early vars:** Methley, Kelsey, Santa Rose, Beauty, Settler, Cloth of gold
- **Mid vars:** Satsuma, Elephant heart, Frontier, Victoria, Burbank
- **Late vars:** Mariposa, Red ace, Late Yeloow, Grand Duke, Silver Wilkson
- **Other varieties:** Alu Kokhara, Alu Bukhara, Titron, Satluj purple
- **Hybrid variety:** Plum Coat/Pluot

ALMOND

(*Prunus communis, Rosaceae*; 2n= 16, Origin–Afganisthan)

- Chilling requirement: 800 hrs
- Almond can withstand temperature of –2.2 to –3°C
- Central modified system of training is adopted
- Almond tree become productive after 5 year
- Native to Middle East
- Almond contains: 49% oil, oleic acid 62%, linoleic acid 24% and palmitic acid 6%
- Rich source of vitamin–E

Varieties

- Sloe: Peach × Almond (self fertile)
- Drake – self fruitful variety
- Katha – self fruitful variety
- Dhebar – self fruitful variety
- Non–pareil – Most popular variety
- Makhdoom, Jordanolo, Merced, Texas (Mission), Peerless, Neplus ultra

APRICOT

(*Prunus Americana*; *Rosaceae*, 2n=16, Origin– China)

- It is also known as Brass/copper colour fruit
- **Moor park:** One of the best apricot for outdoor cultivation in small garden
- Origin: Eastern china
- Larger producer: Turkey
- Highly perishable fruit
- Wild apricot rootstock– Zardalu (Chuli)
- Chilling requirement: 300–900 hrs below 7°C for fruiting
- Peak water use period: April end – Mid june
- Summer temperature: 16.6 to 32.2°C
- Used for treatment of tumurs and ulcers
- High content of anti oxidant (carotenoids)

Varieties

New castle	Nugget
St. Ambrois	Farmingdale
Early	shipley
Royal	Alfred
Kaisha	Halman
Bebeco	Moorpark
Khante	Charmagz
Shakarpara	Chaubattria Alankar
Chaubattria Madhu	Chaubattria Kesari

WALNUT

(*Jaglans regia*, *Juglandaceae*; 2n=32, Origin–Indo–china)

- Nuts are harvested at PTB stage (when packing tissue turn brown)
- **Rootstock:** Paradox (J. hindsi × J.nigra)
- **J. nigra:** reduce the size of tree
- **In black line disease:** use J. regia rootstock
- **Trees:** Decideous 10–40 meters tall
- Temperature of 29–32°C near harvesting result in well filled kernels

- Hot summer with low humidity results in blanck nuts
- Sensitive to low temperature during spring and high temperature in summer
- Chilling requirement about 200 – 800 hrs
- Modified central leader system is most ideal for training
- Walnut contains Omega 3 fatty acid (good fats)
- Walnut have high antioxidant content (vitamin E) and fibre

Varieties

Lake English
Eureka
Wilson
Franquette
Gobind
Placentia
Chakrata
Roopa Karan

PECANUT

(*Carya illieonsis, Juglandaceae*; 2n=36, Origin–USA)

- Queen of nuts
- It requires warm climate
- It has biennial bearing
- Chilling requirement: 400 hrs at below 7°C
- Heterodichogamy is found in pecanut
- It contains 70% fat and good amount of phosphoric acid
- Suitable HDP varieties: Desirable and Cheyenne

Varieties

Mahan
Desirable
Nellis
Cheyenne
Burkett
Wichita
Stuart
Chicksaw
Western

STRAWBERRY

(*Fragaria ananasa, Rosaceae*; 2n= 56, Origin– Man made hybrid)

- It is a Man made hybrid crop
- Fragaria ananasa = F. chilonensis × F. Virginiana
- India strawberry spp. is *Fragaria visca* (Diploid)
- Wild Indian strawberry: F. moschata and F. versa

- Flower colour is white
- Edible part– Succulent thalamus
- All cultivated varieties of strawberry are Octaploid
- Mulching is important intercultural operation
- Propagation: Runner
- Excellent source of Vit–C
- Matted row system of training is commonly followed in India
- Highest producer country in the world – USA

Varieties

Chandler	Tioga Torrey	Selva	Belrubi	Fern
Pajaro	Premier	Red coat	Dilpasand	

CHERRY

(*Prunus avium*, *Rosaceae*; 2n= 16,
Origin– Europe and western Asia)

- Sweet cherry: Prunus avium
- Sour cherry: Prunus cerasus
- Wild cherry: Prunus puddum
- Sour cherry = P.avium × P. fruiticosa
- Duke cherry = P. avium × P. gudouini
- Botanically Paja rootstock spp. is *Prunus cerasoides*
- Chilling requirement: 2000–2700 hrs
- Cherry is first temperate fruit which come first in the market
- Red pigment in cherries: Keracyanin chloride (Anthocyanins)
- Flavour in cherries: Methyl anthrinilate or Methyl salicylate
- Highest chilling requirement among all the temperate fruit
- Heavy rainfall during flowering causes – Blossom wilt
- Heavy rainfall during ripening causes – fruit cracking
- " Kirschwascer" is distilled wine, making from fruit pulp of cherries
- Most commercial varieties of cherry are " self sterile"
- Modified leader system training method is used
- Seedling rootstock: **Paja, Mahaleb, Mazzard**

- Clonal rootstock: Colt, Mazzard F–12/1
- Donars varieties: Stela, Vista, Vic, Seneca, Vega

Varieties

Black heart	White heart	Napolean white	Stella
Lambert	Early rivers	Sunbrust	Compact stella
Summit	Sam	Pink early	Governors wood

PEACH

(*Prunus Persia*, *Rosaceae*; 2n = 16, Origin– China)

- Smooth skin peach: Nectarines (Single dominated gene mutation)
- Flower colour: Pink
- **Prunus Behmi:** Almond × Peach
- [In Almond, Sloe = Peach × Almond]
- Behmi (Prunus nira) is a rootstock
- Fruits have TSS about 8–13°C Brix
- Prunacin is the principle glycoside present in pulp of peach
- Peach has lowest chilling requirement among all the temperate fruit
- Tatura's trellies system of HDP is followed in peach
- Pruning time: December to January
- Peach is very susceptible to Fe deficiency
- Peach requires high N and K

Varieties

- **Early:** Alton, Worl's earlist, Red haven, Stark Red Gold, Early Candor, Quetta, Saharanpur Prabhat
- **Mid:** Julie Elberta, Alexander, Co-smith
- **Late:** J.H. Hale, Parrot delux, Peregrine
- **Midhills:** White giant, Cander, Stark earlyglo
- **Subtropical region:** Flordarsum, Dawn rambler, Dawn rose, Sharbati, Nectarine,
- Nectarine: It is a fuzzless peach variety
- **Myran**: Tolerant to drought, poor soil, root knot nematode and verticillium wilt rootstock

- Yellow flush variety is stone free variety
- **Saharanpur Prabhat: Sharbati × Flordasum**
- Nemaguard = P. persia × P. devidiana
- Nematode resistant rootstock: **Nemaguard**, Nemared, Shalin, Yunnan
- For canning purpose varieties: Yellow flush
- For dehydration: White flush

COCONUT

(*Cocus nucifera*, *Arecaceae*; 2n = 32, Origin– South east asia)

- "Cocus" word derived from Spanish word **coco** which means Monkey face
- India's rank 3rd in coconut production after Indonesia and Phillipines
- Monoluron has anti HIV property. It is content of coconut oil
- Dwarf coconut is self pollinated
- Tall coconut is cross pollinated
- Dwarf varieties bearing age is 3–4 years
- Tall varieties bearing age is 6–10 years
- Coconut is heliotropic plant or sun loving plant
- Fully mature nut have 30–40% coir
- Mesocarp–Husk: used for coir making
- Coconut yield: 80–100nuts/palm/year
- Productivity of coconut: 7608 nuts/hac
- India is the first in the world in productivity of coconut
- Maximum productivity of coconut in Maharastra (20,621nuts/ha)
- Secondary growth in coconut stem as well as in root is absent
- Keral's share in coconut production: 45% (Highest) followed by TN and KN
- Fruit is single seeded drupe
- Optimum temperature for growth is 27°C
- Planting: May–June
- It can withastand in waterlogging during rains
- 9–12 month old seedling are generally transplanted
- Spacing: 7.5 × 7.5 m^2 or 9 × 9 m^2

- Below 15°C causes cold injury (abnormal fruit development)
- Below 50% RH affects opening stomata
- Suitable relative humidity for growth is 80–90%
- Immature nuts provide 6–33% and 5–33% less copra and oil respectively
- Tapping is done from unopened inflorescence for toddy making
- Coconut water contains: 94.5% water,
- "Kurumba" an immature coconut containing a refreshing clear liquid
- Endocarp: used for making toys, buttons etc
- First hybrid between Tall and Dwarf coconut was released in year 1932
- Two form of copra:
  1. Edible copra: (a) Ball copra (b) Cup copra
  2. Milling copra
- Improved varieties:
  - Chandra Kalpa
  - Pratap: from Benalin tall
  - Chandratara: from phillipins ordinary
  - Double century: from phillipins ordinary
  - Kera Chandra: from phillipins ordinary
- Laccadive ordinary is suitable for making ball copra and oil extraction
- Laccadive Micro is also suitable for making ball copra
- B deficiency causes: crown chocking , rottning of crown, barrenness of crown
- Zn deficiency causes: Rossete or Little leaf

Varieties

(a) **Tall vars:** West coast tall, East west tall, Laccadive ordinary, Andaman ordinary, Sanroman, Pratap, Laguna

(b) **Dwarf vars:** Chowghat green dwarf, Chowghat orange flower, Gangabondam, Gundanjali, Mangipod, Nuleka

TEA

(*Camelia sinensis*, *Theaceae*/Camelionaceae; 2n=30, Origin – China)

- Tea research institute: Tocklai, UPASI, DTRC and IHBT
- China contributes only 22% of the world production from 44% crop area
- Asia accounts for 89% of the world tea area
- India accounts for 18.5% of the world tea area with 26.2% of total world production
- India rank 1st in production
- Among tea India tea:
  - Darjeeling: famous for unique muscatel flavor
  - Assam: famous for cup character
  - Nilgiris: famous for taste flavor
- Tea processing method:
- Orthodax method: Light strength tea
- CTC (cut, tear and curl) method: Strong strength tea
- Tea stimulant due to: Thein
- Tea aroma due to: Theol
- Tea bitter taste due to: Tannin
- Tea colour due to: Thearubigens and Thearuflavins
- Tea is calcifugre crop
- Skiiffing (Light pruning) is practiced in tea
- Severe pruning is also known as Collar pruning
- The first plucking of recovering bushes is called ' tipping'
- First step in processing of tea is 'withering'
- Main objective of the withering is remove about 15–20% moisture from the leaves
- Most of the tea garden are located at altitude ranging from 1000–1200 m.
- Below 30°C temperature is good for tea cultivation
- Tea contains 2.5–3% moisture
- Single and double hedge system of planting is recommended in tea
- Tea requires 18–20 month to reach from planting to plucking
- CAN is the best source of the nitrogen in winter in south India

Varieties

- Sundaram: High yielder variety
- Singara: canbe grown in high elevation
- Athrey: withstand on slight pH
- Jayram
- Golconda
- Brooklands

COFFEE

(*Coffee Arabica/C. robusta, Rubiaceae*; 2n= 22, Origin– Ethopia)

- Central Coffee Research Institute [CCRI] is situated at Karnataka
- India's rank in coffee production: VIth
- Coffee is the IInd important commodity in world trade after petroleum products
- Two races:
  1. C. arabica: 2n=44, Self pollinated and fertile
  2. C. robusta: 2n=22, Cross pollinated and sterile
- Processing methods:
  1. Wet method: to produce parchment coffee
  2. Dry method: to produce cherry coffee
- In India
  1. C. arabica: Processed as parchment coffee
  2. C. robusta: Processed as cherry coffee
- Arabica coffee for higher elevation while robusta coffee for lower elevation
- Fruit: Single seeded berry or "pea berry"
- Single seeded berry is known as: Pea berry
- Double seeded berry is known as: Common berry
- Three ovules in trilocular ovary is known as: Triangular berry
- Developed bean by pseudo–polyembryone is called: Elephant bean
- Tree coffee (Coffee liberica) is source of resistance to leaf rust
- Coffee contains **Niacin** which is useful to cure skin diseases
- Single stem training system is followed
- Green coffee: it is also called cured coffee which is traded in the market

- Pruning: June–July to August–September
- Scuffling (Soil stirring): practiced in coffee
- Arabica coffee is widely grown
- Major pest: White stem borer
- Major disease: Coffee leaf rust caused by Hamelia vestatrix (Fungus)
- Coffee leaf rust is introduced in India from Srilanka

Varieties

- S.795 (Robusta): most popular variety
- C.congensis × C. conephora: Interspecific hybrid
- Cauvery = Cattura × hybrid de timor, rust resistant variety suitable for HDP
- Chicks
- Kent: Mutant variety
- Blue mountain
- San ramon: Mutant variety
- Cioccie

CASHEWNUT

(*Anacardium occidentale, Anacardiaceae*; 2n=42; Origin– Brazil)

- Cashewnut is a tropical plant
- Ideal temperature for its cultivation is 20–30°C
- Above 39–42°C temperature during fruit development causes fruit drop
- Propagation: Soft wood grafting
- Top working is essential intercultural operation
- Dwarf rootstock of cashew– *Anarcardium pumilum*
- Spacing: 4×4 m^2 or 8×8 m^2
- Inflorescence: Panicle (Poly gamomonocious)
- Commonly used drier for drying of kernels: Broma dryer
- Flower colour: White to Pink colour
- About 3–10% fruit setting
- Collection of fallen nuts is called as gllining
- Planting: July–August (5–12 month old grafts)

- Pruning: August–September
- Most popular method of roasting: steam method
- Best quality kernels are obtained from: Dream roasting
- Maximum recovery of oil: Oil bath roasting
- Cashew is very sensitive to waterlogging
- Moisture content of dried kernel: exceeds 75% kernels
- There are 26 grades of export cashew kernels
- Yield: 2.1 kg nuts/tree/year or 11–12 qnt/ha
- On an average 1 ton on raw nut provides 1 ton of kernels
- Shelling percentage of cashew is 20–25%
- Sound kernels are named as " Whole"
- Popular grade of kernels is 320
- **Terracing** is also culture operation
- Above 36°C adverse affect on fruit setting and retention
- India is largest producer and export of raw Cashewnut
- India is second largest consumer of cashew kernels
- Harvesting: Feb–May
- Yield:
  - 2kg – 3–5 years age old
  - 4 kg– 6–10 year old
  - 5–10 kg– 11–15 year old

Varieties

BPP, Ullal-1, 2,3, UN–50, Chintamani-1, Dhana, Madakhathara, Vengurla-1to 10, VRT-1 to 3, Priyanka-Export variety

Hybrid

- Ven-3: Ven 1× Vector 56
- Ven-4: Midnapur Red × Vector 56
- Ven-6: Vector 56 × Ven-1
- Damodar- Anakkayam–1 × H-313

COCOA

(*Theobroma cocoa, sterculaceae*; 2n=20, Origin–Mexico)

- Cocoa improvement work was started in 1980 in Karnataka
- Bearing habit: Cauliflorus
- Cocoa is a shade loving plant
- Propagation: seed
- Seed viability of cocoa: 7 days
- Suitable temperature for its growth and development is 15–32°C
- Branches:
- Fan or Jorquette: Horizontal branches
- Chupan: Vertical continuous stem
- Young cocoa fruits are called: Cherelle
- Wiches broom is the major disorder of cocoa

Varieties

- Forestero
- Criollo
- Trinitarion = Criollo × Forestero

RUBBER

(*Hevea brasiliensis*, Euphorbiaceae; 2n=36, Origin–South America)

- In world, consumption ratio of natural to system rubber is 39:61
- Tapping is done in rubber for removal of latex
- India ranks 3rd in rubber production
- India ranks 5th in rubber area
- India ranks 1st in rubber productivity
- Latex contain 32% dry matter
- Notional yield: 1.6 t/ha/year
- Processed product – sheet rubber (latex + acetic or formic acid)
- In smoke house 40–60°C temperature is maintained
- Tapping cut (tapping panel) should be at a slope of 30° in budded plants and 25° in seedling trees

- A budded tree is regarded as tappable when it attains a girth of 50 cm at a height of 125 cm from the bud union
- Best yield is obtained by tapping a depth of less than 1 mm close to cambium
- Ridley–Tapping technique
- Matrola – latex meter to measure% of rubber
- 70% of rubber is used in tyres and tubes
- Powdery mildew in rubber – Odium hevea
- Abnormal leaf fall disease due to *Phytophthora palmivora*
- Major physiological disorder: Brown blast or TPD (Tapping Panel Dryness)

Varieties

- RRII–105: occupy 80% area under rubber cultivation

OIL PALM

(*Ealias guinenesis*, *Arecaceae*; 2n = 32, Origin– West Africa)

- Palm wine is prepared by tapping mal inflorescence
- Palm wine is important source of vit–B complex
- Palm oil is used in production of margarine
- Propagation: Seeds
- Suitable temperature for proper growth and development is 22 to 30°C
- At least 1 meter depth of soil is necessary
- Germination: 10–12 days after sowing
- Planting: at 13 leaves stage or 10–14 month old seedling plants
- Spacing: 9 × 9 m^2
- Flowering: 14–18 month after planting
- Yield: 4–6 tonees oil/ha
- Pollinator: Weevil
- Oil palm is the highest edible oil yielding crop among perennial crops
- **Ablation:** Removal of male and female flowers produced in early stage of plantation
- **Palmolin** is prepared from crude oil
- Palm oil is rich in palmitic acid
- Oil is called as crude palm oil rich in vit–A and E
- Stripping: it is done in oil palm

- About 80% area is located in Andhra Pradesh and Karnataka
- Oil palm improvement work was started in 1976 in Andhra Pradesh

Type of races

1. **Dura:** Thick shell (2–8mm) is present
2. **Pisifera:** Shell is absent
3. **Tehera:** Dura × Pisifera (Thin shell)

Hybrids

1. DD × AVROS
2. DD × DUMPY AVROS

PALMYRA PALM

(*Borasus flaballifer, Arecaceae*; 2n = 32, Origin – Malaya peninsular)

- It growa mainly in Tamil Nadu
- It is tropical crop
- It is also known as "Kalpaka Viruchum"
- Jaggery obtained from palm is called Neera
- Dioecious in nature
- 30–40 years old mother palm is ideal for seed collection
- Single seeded nut gives female trees
- Double seeded nut gives male and female trees
- Tri seeded nut gives: 2 male + 1 female tree
- Planting time: August – September
- Tender stage palm is used for making jelly while in mature stage used for making juice
- Tapping is done in January
- Neera on fermentation becomes toddy·
- 3 seeded drupe
- Toddy – 5% alchol
- Tebder fruit is called Nungu
- It is known as source of sweetening agent since time immemorial
- It is tropical crop
- Propagation method: Seed
- **Yield:** Normally 1 liter Neera/day and average yield is 10–12 li/ha/day

Section 'C'
Vegetable and Spice Crops

Important points

- Olericulture is that branch of horticulture science which means vegetable production. Olericulture from latin word meaning " Olerus". Olerus means herb or Ole meaning cabbage.
- **15 agro climatic zone by planning commission** and **21 agro ecological regions** by **soil survey and national land use planning**.
- Vegetable are rich in and cheaper source of vitamins and minerals.
- Vegetables which are rich source of carbohydrate are potato, sweet potato, colocasia, yams, tapioca, elephant foot yam etc.
- Vegetable which are rich source of protein Such as pea, cowpea and all beans like French bean, dolichus bea n, broad bean, cluster bean etc.
- Vegetable are not rich in fat content which is less than 0.1% in most of them.
- According to ICMR, an average man with vegetarian or non vegetarian food habit should consume:

    1. Green leafy vegetable: 125g
    2. Roots and Tuber crops: 100g
    3. Other vegetables: 75g

Vegetable production in India

- India share about 11.5% of the total production in the world while china shares about 48% of the total production.
- Potato ranks first among vegetable crops production in the world followed by cassava, sweet potato, cabbage, onion and melons.
- State which have highest productivity of vegetable: Tamilnadu > kerala > UP > HP > Punjab.
- State which have highest production of vegetable: West Bengal > UP > Bihar > Orissa > Tamilnadu.
- State which have highest area of vegetable:
- Highest productivity of vegetables: Tapioca > Cabbage > Potato > Cauliflower > Brinjal
- Highest production of vegetable: Potato > Brinjal > Tomato
- Highest area of vegetable: Potato> Brinjal > Onion > Tomato > Okra
- Dried and preserved vegetable have the major share of 23.7% followed by fresh onion 14.7% and other fresh vegetable 11%

TOMATO

- Botanical name: *Lycopersicon esculatum*
- Family: Solaceae
- Origin: Peru/Mexico
- CN: 24
- India is the second largest producer of tomato in the world after China followed by Turkey, USA and Italy.
- Highest producing state:Orrisa > Andhra pradesh > KN
- Highest productivity: KN > MH > Assam
- Tomato is universally treated as 'Protective food'.
- The total sugar content is 2.5% in ripe fruit.
- Vitamin-C: 16–65mg/100g of fruit weight.
- The total amino acid is 100–350mg/100g of fruit weight.
- Processed product of tomato like puree and paste have great demand in export.
- Tomato is a herbaceous, annual to perennial plant.
- Tomato is a climatric fruit in which ripening is associated with increase in both respiration and ethylene production
- *Lycopersicon esculentum* has five forms:
  1. Cherry tomato– L. cerasifome (Small fruited spp.)
  2. Pear tomato– L. pyrifomae(Pear type fruits)
  3. Common tomato– L. commune
  4. Potato leaf type tomato– L. grandifolium
  5. Upright tomato– L. validium
- Muller(1940) divided the genus lycopersicon into two sub–genus:
  1. Eulycopersicon
  2. Eriopersicon
- Eulycopersicon is a red fruited type genus.
- Eriopersicon is a green fruited type genus.
- Other useful spp. Of lycopersicon include L. pimpinellifolium, L. cheesmani, L. peruvianum, L. hirsutum and L. chemelewskii, L. parviflorum and L. chionese.
- Determinate type: Plants are dwarf where growth is restricted with appearance of terminal flower. Ex. CO–3, Hissar Anmol, Hissar Arun, La–Bonita, Punjab chhuhara, Punjab Kesari, Pusa early dwarf, Pusa Sheetal.

- Indeterminate type: Growth is continued and there is less initiation of flower and fruit on the stem. Ex. Arka vikash, BT–12, Pusa Uphar, Pusa Rubi,
- Semi determinate type: Arka Saurabh, Hissar Lalit, Pant T–3, Sel 120.
- Optimum temp. is 20–24°C.
- Lycopene, responsible for red colour is highest at 21–24°c while the production of this pigment drops off rapidly above 27°C.
- Breaker stage (10% Lycopene) is suitable for distant market.
- Cluster of flower in tomato is known as **Truss**
- Tomato is a botanically Fruit as well as berry and have kidney shaped seed which surrounded by jelly like parenchyma cells.
- B and Zn are important micronutrient required for long distance transportation
- Tomato grade: Super A, Super, Fancy and commercial
- The "Flavor savar" tomato is first genetically engineering whole food to reach us consumer. It was developed by " Calgene fresh" company.
- Green colour of immature fruit is due to chlorophyll a and b. During ripening the chloroplast are transformed into chromoplast.
- The foliar application of parachlorophenoxy acetic acid (PCPA) 50–100 ppm at the flowering stage increase the fruit setbat low and high temperature.
- Seed treatment of tomato with 2,4–D @ 2–5 ppm increase fruit set earliness and induce parthenocarpy.
- Pruning and training is generally followed in indeterminate varieties.
- Single stem training gives better yield.
- In order to enhance the ripening of tomato fruit, ethrel 100ppm can be sprayed on plants at the time of initiation of ripening.
- Disorder: Puffiness, Catface, Blossom end rot, Sun–scalding, Blotchy ripening and chilling injury.
- Puffiness: it is due to poor pollination, resulting in poor development od seed bearing tissue.
- Blossom end rot: It is due to Ca deficiency and water problem. Symptoms appear at stylax end of the fruit.

Varieties

- Introduction– All varieties are introduced from USA

  Roma (pear Shaped) Sioux Best of all

  Tip Top: Labonita Marvel

  Marglobe Agethe Money Marker

- Selection–

  Improved Meeruti HS 110 (potato leaf type) Pant bahar
  Arke Saurabh Arka Vikash Sonali
- Mutation–

  Selection–12 (S12)– By X–rays (Dwarf type), PKM–1
  Pusa Lal Meeruti– By gamma rays by Maruthan
- Hybrids–

  Pusa Rubi=Sioux ×Improved Meeruti
  Pusa early Dwarf= Improved Meeruti ×Rad cloud
  Pusa Gaurav= Glamour×Watch
  Marglobe= Marvel × Globe
  Other hybrid varieties are: Hisar Anmol, Hisar Arun, Hisar Lalit, Hisar Lalima, Pusa Sheetal, Pusa Uphar
- Bacterial wilt resistant varieties–

  Shakti Arka Alok Arka Abha
  Sonali Arka Shreshta Arka Abhijit
  BT–1 BT–10
- Leaf curl resistant varieties–

  Hisar Gaurav Hisar Anmol
- Root knot nematode resisitant variety– Selection 120
- Fruit borer resistant varities–

  Angurlata, Punjab Chuhara Sabor Prabha
  Atkinson HT 64 Hybrid 37
- Suitable for fresh market

  Pusa early Dwarf Pusa Rubi Arka Vikash
  Arka Saurabh Punjab kesari Pant bahar
- Processing varieties–
- Pusa gaurav Roma Punjab Chuahara, Pusa Uphar Arka Saurabh, Low temperature resistant– Pusa Sheetal
- High temperature resistant– Pusa Hybrid 1
- Both Low and High temperature resistant – Pusa Sadabahar

BRINJAL

- Botanical name: *Solanum melongena*
- Family: Solaceae
- Origin: India
- CN: 24
- India is the second largest producer of brinjal in the world after China followed by Egypt and japan.
- Highest producing state:West Bengal > Orissa > Bihar
- Highest productivity: KN > Bihar > MH
- Largest area:
- It is also known as Aubergine, Egg plant
- There are three botanical var. of solanum namely:

  Solanum serpentinum: which have slender type fruits
  Solanum depressum: which have early and Dwarf type fruits
  Solanum esculentum: which have round and egg shaped fruits
- Brinjal is a self pollinated crop. Although there is some cross pollination (1–2%), by insect.
- Fruit is a multiseeded berry and are born on the fleshy placenta
- Brinjal flowers are pentamerous, hermaphrodite and solitary
- Heterostyle is common feature (except in bunchy type cultivars) which favours cross pollination
- Brinjal flowers are divided into four types:

  1. Long style: 70–80% fruit setting
  2. Medium style: 12–55% fruit setting
  3. Pseudo short style: No fruit set
  4. Short style: No fruit set
- In brinjal, opening of flower (Anthesis) takes place at 6:00– 7:30 am in summer and in winter which is delayed to 11:15 am
- Brinjal is day neutral plant.
- The optimum temp. for normal growth and development of brinjal is 21–30° C
- The optimum temp. for seed germination is 20–25°C with 50% and above relative humidity
- High temp and high humidity in the morning hours hasten the opening of flower and dehiscence of anther
- The brinjal grown in warm season shows luxurious growth and starts bearing from the initial flower while in cool season its growth is poor and slow and fruit size, quality and production are adverse affected

- The glycoalkaloid present in brinjal is solanine.
- The egg plant contains about 7.6 mg alpha solanine in 100g fresh fruit weight.
- Highest amount of solanine (20mg/100g fresh fruit weight) produce a bitter taste and off flavor
- Dry brinjal fruit contain goitrogenic principles
- Purple colour of brinjal due to Anthocynine pigmement
- Dark purple brinjal have more Vit-C content than the white skinned brinjal
- White coloured brinjal is preferred by diabetic patients
- Dried fruit of brinjal good source of Vitamin–B
- In brinjal, the highest yield obtained from plants whose roots were dipped in GA_3+Ascorbic acid at 250 ppm solution
- Application of Cu and Mn increase the No. of flower and fruit while Zn improved the weight of fruit
- Leaves contain more vit-C than that of the fruit
- Bumble bee and honey bee are the insect which do most of the pollination
- *Mimosa pudica* plants should be planted in vicinity of brinjal
- Eleven solanum species were classified into three groups on the basis of their interspecific compatibility:

  1. *Solanum melongena, S. incanum* and *S. macrocarpum*
  2. *S. integrifolium, S. gilo and S. nodiforum*
  3. *S. indicum, S. mammosum, S. torum, S. sisymbrifolium.*
- Crosses were compatible within group A or group B and between group B and group A but were otherwise incompatible
- November sowing– it takes 6–8 weeks for transplanting
- June–july sowing– it takes 4 weeks for transplanting
- Orobanchae is one of the serious weeds affecting solanaceous crops in some areas.
- Orobanchae is a root parasite.
- Brinjal fruits are better stored at 20°C than at 6°C and in perforated polythene bags
- Fruit can also be stored for 7–10 days in fairly good condition at 7–10°C with 85–95% RH
- Fruit rot also occurs during storage which is prevented by 200 ppm NAA in combination with 900ppm Prochloraz that retards fruit senscence and decaying
- Shoot and fruit borer (*Ealis vitella*) these are the major insect of this crop

- Little leaf of brinjal caused by mycoplasma and it transmitted by leaf hopper
- NDB 25 have soft joint cultivar and is easy to harvest

Varieties

- **IARI released–**
- Pusa Purple Long, Pusa Purple Round, Pusa Purple Cluster, Pusa Kranti, Pusa Bhairav, Pusa Anupam, Pusa Uttam, Pusa Uokar, Pusa Bindu, Pusa Ankur, Pusa Shyamala
- **IIHR released–**
- Arka Shirish, Arka Sheel, Arka Kusumakar, Arka Nidhi, Arka Keshav
- **SAUs released–**
- Hisar Shyamla, Hisar Pragati, Hisar Jamuni, Pant samrat, Pant Rituraj, MDU–1, PKM–1
- **IIVR released–**
- Kashi Sandesh, Kashi Taru, Kashi Prakash, Kashi Komal

Hybrids

- Pusa Bindu and Pua Uttam: GRX Pant Rituraj
- Pusa Kranti: PPL × Hyderpur ×***nod local
- Arka Navneet: IIHR 22–1 Supreme, Pusa Anupam:- PPL × Pusa Kranti
- Arka Anand: Punjab Neelam: Jamuni × Globe Pant Rituraj
- Arka Neelkanth: Punjab Barasti: PPC × PH-4, Pant Rituraj : - T-3 × PPC
- Vaisali: Arka Kusumakar × Manjiri Gota, Pragati: Vaishali × Manjiri Gota

CHILLI and CAPSICUM

- Botanical Name: *Capsicum annuum var. hortense* (chilli)
  Capsicum annuum var. grossum (Bell pepper)
- Family: Solanaceae
- Origin: New world (American) – Mexico
- Types of Capsicum
  - Hot pepper: Pungent due to crystalline volatile alkaloid capsaicin, located mainly in the placenta of fruit.
  - Sweet Pepper/Bell Pepper Capsicum (Shimla Mirch): Bears bell shaped, non pungent/mild and thick pericarp/fleshed fruit.
  - Paprika

- The fruits are rich in vitamins A and C.
- Suitable soil pH range of 5.8–6.5 for its better growth and development.
- It is not very sensitive to soil acidity.
- Chilli requires a warm humid climate and it is highly sensitive to frost.
- The most ideal temperature for its better growth and development is 20–25°C.
- Temperature 16–32°C is the most congenial for fruit set but maximum fruit set occurs at 16–21°C.
- It is mostly grown as a rainfed crop.
- Sowing time: In South India: July to October
  In North India: October to December
  In hills area: March–May
- Seedlings are ready for transplanting when they attain a height of 15cm with 4 leaves in 4–6 weeks (30–45 days).
- Seed Rate: For seedling: 1–1.5 Kg/ha
  For direct sowing: 2–3 Kg/ha
  Hybrid: 400–500 g/ha
- Spacing: **Chilli**– 45 × 45 cm or 60 × 45 cm
  Capsicum– 60 × 45 cm
- The most critical stages for irrigation are blooming (flowering), fruit setting and development.
- Foliar application of NAA (50ppm) at full bloom stage can effectively control flower drop with an increase in yield.
- Planofix (10–20ppm) as foliar spray at flowering stage can reduce flower and fruit drop in chilli.
- It needs 5– 6 pickings for harvesting the whole crop.
- The ripe chillies are dried under sun for 8–15 days, while commercially it is dried at about 54.4°C in 2–3 days.
- Yield:

  Irrigated conditions: Green Chilli 200–300 q/ha,
  Dry chili 15–25 q/ha

  Rainfed: Green Chilli 50–60 q/ha,
  Dry chilli 5–10 q/ha
- Capsicum yield:
  - Open pollinated Varieties: 125–150 q/ha
  - Hybrid: 250–300 q/ha

- Important Diseases: Anthraçnose/Ripe fruit rot/die back, Powdery Mildew, Cercospora leaf Spot,Bacterial Wilt, Chilli leaf curl virus.
- Important Insect: Tomato fruit Borer, Aphids and Thrips.

Varieties

- Chilli: G-3, Pusa Jwala, Pusa Sadabahar, Bhagya Lakshmi (G-4), HC-28, HC-44, Andhra Jyoti, Punjab Lal, Punjab Surkha, Punjab Guchhedar, NP-46A, Pant-C-1, Sindhur, Pant-C-2, X-235,
- Chilli hybrids: CH-1, CH-3, Arka Meghana, Arka Harita, Arka Sweta, CCH-2, CCH-3
- **Bell Pepper/Capsicum:** California Wonder, Yolo Wonder, Arka Mohini, Solan Hybrid 2, Arka Basant, Arka Gourav, Bharat (hybrid), Solan Bharpur, Pusa Deepti (hybrid)

POTATO

- Botanical Name: *Solanum tuberosum* L.
- Family: Solanaceae
- Origin: Peru and Bolivia in South America
- CN: 48
- It produces best when soil pH is 6.0–6.5
- It is a cool season crop.
- It requires 20°C soil temperature for better germination.
- Young plant growth is good at 24°C but later growth is favoured by a temperature of 18°C.
- No tuberization takes place when the night temperature exceeds 23°C.
- Maximum tuberization occurs at 20°C.
- Tuber formation stops completely at about 29–30°C.
- Planting time:
  - North India: Feb–March
  - South India: June–July
  - Hilly areas: March–April
- True Potato Seed (TPS): 100–150g/ha
- Potato is propagated by tubers.
- The tubers have a dormancy of nearly 8–10 weeks after harvesting.

- Dormancy breaking chemicals:
  - **Thiourea (Sodium Potassium thiocynate):** 1–2% solution which is used as a treatment to cut tubers for 1–1 1/2 hours and about 1 kg of thiourea is sufficient for 10 quintals of seed tuber.
  - GA_3:Tubers are kept in 5ppm solution of GA_3 for 10 seconds.
  - Treat the tuber with aqueous solution of thiourea for one hour followed by dipping in 2 ppm solution of GA for 10 seconds.
- Propagation:
- 40–50 g tuber with 40–50 mm diameter– 10–15q/ha
- 25–30 g tuber 30–40mm diameter–20–35q/ha
- Suberization/healing: The cut pieces should be allowed to heel at 18–21°C and 85–90% relative humidity for 2–3 days which prevents rotting of cut tubers as seed.
- Irrigation is stopped about 10 days before harvesting of crop to allow firming of tuber skin.
- Yield:
  - Early varieties 200 q/ha
  - Late varieties 300 q/ha
- Grading: 3 grades according to the size and weight of the tubers.

1. Grade A (Large): Tuber weight more than 75g
2. Grade B (Medium): tuber weight between 50–75g
3. Grade C (Small): Tuber weight less than 50g

Physiological Disorder

- Hollow heart: It is caused by rapid growth of tubers or over dose of fertilizers.
  - Control: Adequate fertilizer applied in the field.
- Black heart: It is caused by deficiency of oxygen. It is also due to high temperature and excessive moisture, blackening of tissues in the centre occurs.
  - Control: Proper ventilation should be provide in a storage house
- Greening: It is due to exposure of tubers to sunlight. High glycoalkaloid contents lead to solanin production which is slightly poisonous. Above 5mg solanine is harmful for human consumption.
  - Control: Earthing up should be done after 30 and 45 days of days.
- Knobbiness: It occurs due to uneven growth of tuber cells/tissues. Heavy irrigation after a long dry spell leads to fast growth of some cells and as a result knobs are formed.
  - Control: Ensure frequent and optimum irrigation.

- Cracking: It is due to boron deficiency or uneven water supply.
  - Control: Application of Borax @ 20kg/ha. Ensure frequent and optimum irrigation.
- Sun scalding: It is due to high temperature and sunshine. It appears when temperature is more than 30°C.
  - Control: Water should be passed through the furrows to lower the soil temperature.
- Black spot: It is also known as Internal Browning of potato tubers. It is due to low temperature.
  - Control: Provide proper storage and growing conditions.
- Freezing injury: It occurs due to the exposure of tubers to freezing temperature during or after harvest. It takes place at –1.5°C or below temperature. There is discolouration of the tissues and affect the vascular tissues at the ring and this is called as called ring necrosis and when fine elements or cells of vascular ring are affected, then it is called as net necrosis. Tubers show more damage towards proximal end.
  - Control: Avoid exposure of tubers to freezing temperature during storage or harvest.
- Sprouting: It is a storage disorder.
  - Control: It can be inhibited by spraying borax or iron sulphate @ 1000–1500 ppm about 2–3 weeks before harvesting.
- Important diseases: Early Blight (Alternaria solani), Late Blight (Phytophthora infestans), Brown Rot (Ralstonia solanacearum), Black scurf (Rhizoctonia solani), Wart disease, Black Leg and Soft Rot (Erwinia czotovera) (synchytricum ondosioticum)
- Important insect–pests: Cut worm (Agrotis ipsilon), Potato tuber moth (Phthorimaea operculella),

Varieties

- Early varieties: These varieties are ready for harvest in 70–80 days such as Kufri Ashoka, Kufri Chandermukhi, Kufri Jawahar, and Kufri Lauvkar.
- Mid season varieties: They are ready for harvest in 90–95 days. Among the white coloured varieties, Kufri Jyoti, Kufri Sutlej, Kufri Pukhraj, Kufri Megha, Kufri Badshah, Kufri Anand, Kufri Bahar, Kufri Sadabahar, Kufri Deva, Kufri Sherpa, Kufri Swarna, Kufri Shailza, Kufri Surya, Kufri Himalini, Kufri Girdhari and Kufri Khyati are important.
- Late varieties: Kufri Jeevan, Kufri Neelamani, Kufri Khasigaro, Kufri Naveen
- Varieties for processing: Kufri Chipsona 1, Kufri Chipsona 2, Kufri Chipsona 3, and Kufri Himsona

OKRA

- Botanical name: *Abelmoschus esculentus* (L.) Moench)
- Family: Malvaceae
- Origin: Ethiopia
- CN: 130
- The most ideal pH range for its cultivation is 6.0–6.8.
- It is a warm season crop.
- Optimum temperature for its better growth is 24–27°C and temperature above 42°C causes flower drop.
- A temperature range of 30–35°C is desirable for improved pollination and subsequent seed setting.
- Sowing times:
  - Spring–summer crop: February–March
  - Autumn–winter crop: July– September
  - Hilly region: April–June
- The poor seed germination and erratic crop stand are the major problems in spring–summer crop due to low temperature and in rainy season crop, the major problems are incidence of Yellow Vein Mosaic.
- Seed Rate (kg/ha):
  - 15–20 (Spring–summer crop)
  - 10–12 (Rainy season)
- Seed germination can be enhanced by soaking the seed in water for 12–24 hours or GA_3 at 10 and 50 ppm or immersing the seeds for 5 minutes in pure acetone.
- Spacing: 30–45cm × 15 cm(Spring–summer) and 60cm × 20–30 cm (Rainy season).
- Yield: 80–100q/ha (Spring–summer) and 120–150q/ha (Rainy season).
- **Storage:** Fresh okra fruits can be stored at 7–9°C at 70–75% relative humidity for a couple of days without much loss of colour, texture or weight.
- Fruit can be stored for 2 weeks at 8–10°C at 90% relative humidity.
- Important Disease: Powdery Mildew, Cercospora Leaf Spot, Yellow Vein Mosaic Virus, Root rot, Fruit borer, Flower feeding beetle/Blister beetle, White fly.

Varieties

- Open Pollinated varieties: Parbhani Kranti, Punjab Padmani, Arka Anamika, Arka Abhay, Pusa A–4, Varsha Uphar, Hisar Unnat, Hisar Naveen, HBH–142(Hybrid) Azad Kranti, Azad Bhindi1, Kashi Pragati, Kashi Vibhuti, Kashi Kranti,Phule Utkarsh, Kiran, Salkeerthi, Aruna , Susthira, Pusa Sawani, Parbhani Kranti, Varsha Uphar and Pusa A–4

COLE CROPS

- This group of vegetables includes cauliflower, cabbage, broccoli, knolkhol, kale and Brussels- Sprout.
- The word "cole" seems to have derived from the abbreviation of the word "caulis" meaning stem.
- Wild ancestor *Brassica oleracea* var. *oleracea* (*sylvestris*), commonly known as wild cabbage.
- Order of cole crop: Papaverals
- Excessive use of cole crop result in swelling of thyroid glands and goiter disease.

CAULIFLOWER

- Botanical Name: *Brassica oleracea* var. *botrytis* L.,
- Family: Brassicaceae
- Origin: Mediterranean region
- CN: 18
- It was introduced in India in 1822 by Dr. Jenson from London.
- Cauliflower is only crop in group of cole crop in which the intermediate stage of curding lies between vegetative and reproductive stage.
- Highest producing state: West Bengal
- Highest productivity: West Bengal
- Inflorescence: Racemose
- Interculture operations:
- Blanching: It is a method to protect curd from direct exposure to sun for maintaining their colour. Curd covered by their own leaves.
  - Pusa Himjyoti is a self branched variety.
  - Duration period of blanching:
  - In summer season: 3–5 days
  - In winter season: 10 days.

- **Scooping:** Removal of central portion of curd for easier initiation of flower stalk in cauliflower.

- It prefers soil pH 6 to 6.5.
- It is a thermo–sensitive crop.
- Temperature 10–21°C is good for germination. It is highly sensitive to temperature
- Optimum temperature for growth of young plant is 23°C in initial stages while for growth in later stages, favourable temperature range is 17–20°C.
- Varieties description on the basis of their temperature and maturity time

Group	Nursery sowing	Transplanting time	Maturity	Opt. temp. range for curding
Early I (A)	Mid May	July beginning	mid Sept–mid Nov.	20–25°C
Early I (B)	May end to Mid June	Mid July	Mid Oct–mid Nov	20–25°C
Mid Early	July end	Sept beginning	Mid Nov–mid Dec	16–20°C
Mid late	Aug end	Sept end	mid Dec–mid Jan	12–16°C
Late	Sept end to mid Oct	Oct end– mid Nov	Jan–March)	10–16°C

Seed Rate:

Early varieties: 600–750g
Mid–Early–season varieties: 400–500g
Mid–late varieties: 300–400 g
Late varieties: 250–300g

- Early crop should be transplanted on ridges or raised beds while the mid and late cultivars can be planted on flat beds.
- Transplanting should be done during late afternoon to avoid losses due to sun heat.

Spacing:

Early varieties: 45 cm × 30 cm
Mid and Late season Varieties 60 cm × 45 cm

- Cauliflower is a shallow rooted crop.
- Transplanting: 3–4 weeks after sowing.
- Delayed harvesting leads to the elongation of flowering stalk, loose, ricey, fuzzy and over matured curds which deteriorates the quality of the curd.
- When late sowing: produce button head
- When early sowing: delay head forming

- Breaking seed dormancy: CO_2 @ 3–5% for 8–24 hrs at 100% RH
- Yield (t/ha):
  - Early varieties: 12–15 t/ha
  - Mid and late season varieties: 20–30 t/ha.
  - Snowball group may produce yield upto 500 q/ha.

Physiological disorders

- Buttoning: It means development of small curds or buttons. It is due to early variety grown in late or late varieties are sown in early. It is also doe to high temperature.
- Riceyness: Due to temperature higher or lower than the optimum required for curding or high application of nitrogen result in riceyness.
- Control:Manage proper soil moisture and fertility during curd development stage
- Fuzzyness: It is the elongation of pedicels of the individual flower. It is due to high or low temperature.
- Blindness: They do not form curd. It is due to poor fertility of the soil or damage to the terminal portion during handling at the time of planting or by insects, diseases *etc.*
- Control: Healthy and vigorous seedlings with terminal portion intact should be planted.
- Bracting: Temperature higher than the optimum during curding leads to this disorder.
- Purple colouring: Various pigmentations develop on the curd which deteriorates the quality of the final produce. Fluctuations in the temperature are the main reason for this disorder.
- Whip tail: It is caused by the deficiency of Molybdenum (Mo). In olde plants, the lamina of the newly formed leaves is irregular in shape and leaves have only a large bare midrib.
- Control:Apply molybdenum @ 1kg/ha to manage the deficiency.
- Browning (Red or Brown rot): It is caused by boron deficiency. Control: Application of borax @20kg/ha.

Varieties

- Early varieties (Yellow coloured): Early Kunwari, Pusa early synthetic, Pusa Deepali, Pusa Ketki
- Mid Early(Off white coloured): Improved Japanese, Pusa sharad, Pusa Aghani

- Mid Late (Off white coloured): Pusa Synthetic, Pant Shubhra, Pusa Shubhra, Pusa Himjyoti
- Late varieties (Milky white coloured): Pusa Snowball, Pusa Snowball K–1
- Introduced variety: Improved Japanese
- Selection: Pusa Himjyoti, Pusa Snowball K–1, Pusa Ketki, Pusa Deepali, Pant Shubhra, Pusa Aghani
- Synthetic varieties: Pusa early synthetic, Pusa synthetic, Pant Gobi–3
- Hybrid: Pusa shubhra, Pusa Aghani
- Private sector hybrid: White flesh, Himani, Early himlata, Himani, Nath Ujwala, Nath shweta
- Sclerotia rot resistant variety: Pusa Snowball K–2
- Blackrot, curd and inflorescence blight resistant varieties: Pusa Shubhra, Pusa Snowball K–1
- Pusa Himjyoti: It is grown in April to July in the hills
- Pusa Hybrid–2: First hybrid in public sector

CABBAGE

- Botanical name: *Brassica oleracea* var. *capitata*
- Family: Brassicaceae
- Origin: Mediterranean region
- CN: 18
- Cabbage can tolerant to salt.
- It can withstand extreme cold and frost better than cauliflower.
- It thrives best in a relatively cool and moist climate.
- The optimum temp. for seed germination is 12.6–15.6°C.
- The optimum temperature for growth and head formation is 15– 20°C whereas, the growth is checked above 25°C.
- Flower: Protogynous
- Inflorescence: Racemose
- Fruit type: Siliqua (In a bicarpellary pod)
- Planting time:
  - In northern place: October to January
  - Hilly areas: April to May
- Seed Rate: 400–500g/ha

- Transplanting: 30–45 days after sowing.
- Spacing:
  - Early varieties: 45 cm × 30 cm or 30 cm × 30 cm (round & smaller heads)
  - Late varieties: 60 cm × 45 cm or 60 cm × 60 cm (Ovule shape)
- Earthing up is important in rainy season as roots get exposed after every shower.
- Cabbage is very sensitive to soil moisture.
- Yield (t/ha):
  - Early varieties: 25–30 t/ha,
  - Late season varieties: 40–50 t/ha

Physiological disorder

- Cracking: It is due to Excess nitrogen fertilizer. Hot, dry weather. Control: Apply fertilize properly.
- Tip–burn speck and Black petiole: It is a non–pathogenic internal disoreder
- Black Petiole: It is complex disorder.
- Cytoplasmic and genetic male sterility found in cabbage is also helpful for the production of F–1 hybrid
- It has anti–cancer property due to presence of Indol–3–carbinol.
- Saurkraut: It is a value added product prepared from white cabbage. It is used to cure scurvy disease.
- Species of cabbage:
- Wild cabbage: B. Oleracea var sylvestris (colewart)
- White cabbage: B. Oleracea var alba
- Red cabbage: B. Oleracea var rubra
- Savoy cabbage: B. Oleracea var sabuda
- Cabbage grown in saline soil is more prone to black leg disease.
- Cabbage produces seeds in the temperate aeas only

Varieties

- Early Group: (It takes 55–70 days for maturity): Golden Acre, Pride of India, Copenhagen Market, Pusa Ageti,
- Pusa Mukta, Pusa Cabbage Hybrid–1 (KGMR–1).
- Mid season Group: September, Pusa Drum Head.
- Late Group: (It takes about 85–130 days for maturity): Large Drum Head

- Introduction varieties: Golden Acre, Red acre Copenhagen Market, September, August, glory of Enkhuizen, August
- Selection: Pride of India, Pusa Ageti (Both varieties are selected from Copenhagen), Pusa drum Head (from Japanese Material EC6774)
- Hybrid: Pusa Drum Head, Pusa Mukta, Pusa synthetic, Pusa Sambandh
- Private sector varieties: Oquesto, Sree Ganesh Gol (Developed by Mahyco comp.), Uttam, bajrang, Green Boy, Green Express
- September variety: Introduced from Germany
- Golden Acre: Introduced from Denmark
- Pusa Drum Head: Black leg or Dry rot resistant variety
- Pusa Sambandh: suitable for HDP, Early maturity
- Pusa Ageti: 1st tropical variety developed for cultivation under high temperature condition.

BROCCOLI

- Botanical name: *Brassica oleracea* var. italica
- Family: Brassicaceae
- Origin: Mediterranean region
- CN: 18
- It is mainly grown as a winter crop in most parts of the country, however in high hills it may be grown as a spring summer crop.
- It is sensitive to temperature as bud clusters grow loose quickly and give rise to bracts under warm weather conditions.
- Rich source of sulphoraphane– compound associated with reducing risk of cancer.
- Inflorescence: Cymose
- It has 130 times more vitamin–A than cauliflower and 22 times more than cabbage.
- The optimum temperature of 12–18°C is suitable for proper head development.
- Planting time:
  - In north India: August to mid September
  - In south India: October to December
- Seed rate: 400–500g/ha
- Transplanting: 30–45 days after sowing.
- Spacing: 30– 40 cm×20–25 cm.

- Yield: 15–20t/ha.
- Varieties: Palam Samridhi, Palam Haritika, Palam Kanchan, Palam Vichitra, Pusa Broccoli Kt Selection–I, Punjab Broccoli–I, Decicco, Pusa KTS–1, Sparten early, Coastal Atlantic, Greenbud, Green Mountain, Italian Green, Green Head

KNOL KHOL

- Botanical name: *Brassica oleraceae* var. gongylodes
- Family: Brassicaceae
- Origin: Mediterranean region
- CN: 18
- Tuber or knob develops entirely above the ground. It is stem cole crops.
- Seeds germinate well at temperature of 15–30°C.
- Optimum temperature requirement for its growth is between 15–25°C depending upon cultivars.
- Planting time:
  - North eastern plains: September–October.
- Best time for planting: October
- Seed rate: 0.8 to 1 Kg/ha.
- Spacing: 30– 40 cm × 20–25 cm.
- Generally bright coloured tubers of 5–8 cm diameter along with the foliage are favoured in the market.
- Yield: 200–250gm tuber obtained 12– 25 t/ha.
- Knol–khol is a:
- For flowering and fruiting: Annual
- For seed production: Bienial
- Varieties: Whilte Vienna, Purple Vienna, King of North, Purple Speck, Golith White, Suuton's Early Purple
- Purple Vienna: Late maturity
- Purple speck: Early variety

BRUSSELS SPROUT (Mine cabbage)

- Botanical name: *Barssica oleracia* var. gemmifera
- Family: Brassicacae
- Origin: Mediterranean region
- CN: 18
- It is a frost resistant crop.
- Inflorescence: Racemose
- Excessive application of potash imaperts bitterness, affect quality
- Varieties: Hilds Ideal, Danish Prize, rubine, Jade cross, Amager Market, Catskill, Early Mom, Long Island, Dwarf Improved, Frontier Zuerg, Kvik

KALE

- Botanical name: *Barssica oleracia* var. acephala
- Family: Brassicacae
- Origin: Mediterranean region
- It is the hardiest crop
- Varieties: Dwarf Green, Dwarf Moss, Hamburger Market, Scotish, Siberian
- Karamsag: Mostly grown in J & K

ONION

- Botanical Name: *Allium cepa* L.
- Family: Alliaceae/Amaryllidaceae
- Origin: Central and South Western Asia
- CN: 16
- It relieves heat sensation.
- Bulb juice is used as smelling on hysterical fits in faintness. It is used to relive insect bites and sour throat.
- Red colour is due to anthocyanin pigment.
- Yellow is due to quercetin pigment.
- The soil pH should be in the range of 5.8–6.5. It is sensitive to high acidity and alkalinity.
- 20–25°C temperature is required for seed germination.
- It requires 13–21°C temperature for vegetative growth before bulb initiation and 16–25°C for bulb development and 25–30°C for bulb maturation.

- Low temperature and short photoperiods (LTST) are required for vegetative growth, while relatively high temperature and long photoperiods (HTLT) are needed for bulb development.
- Seed Rate: 8–10 kg/ha.
- About 10qnt. Sets are enough to plant one–hectare area.
- Spacing: 5–10 × 5–10 cm^2.
- Seedlings become ready for transplanting in 8–10 weeks.
- Seedlings must be about 15–20cm in length at the time of transplanting.
- Sowing time: In rainy season– June – July
- In winter season– Oct – Nov
- Transplanting: In rainy season: July – Aug
- In winter season: Dec – Jan
- Onion is a shallow rooted crop.
- Insufficient moisture tends to slow down bulb growth while over supply causes rotting.
- Generally, 10–12 irrigations are given in Rabi season. Stop irrigation when the tops mature and start falling down.
- Harvesting time: In rainy season: Nov – Dec
- In winter season: May – June
- A maturity index for harvesting is 50% neck fall.
- The green onions can be harvested when they reach pencil size until bulbing begins.
- It is desirable to leave 1.5–2.0 cm of the tops attached to the bulb as it helps to close neck and reduce storage losses.
- **Curing:** To remove the excess moisture from the outer skin and neck of onion bulb. Curing helps to reduce the chances of disease infection, minimizes shrinkage due to loss of moisture from the interiors and helps to develop good skin colour.
- Bulbs are cured in field for 3–5 days in wind row method. Then bulbs are placed in shade and cured for 7–10 days to remove field heat. This shade curing improves bulb colour and reduces losses during storage.
- Yield: Rabi crop: 250–300q/ha,
- Kharif crop: 200–250q/ha
- Storage: Temperature: 0°C and 60–65%RH for 2 months.

Physiological disorders

- Bolting: It means emergence of seed stalk prior to time of bulb formation. It is due to early sowing of seeds in the nursery beds, which result in the formation of small sets or Low temperature (10–12°C) for prolonged period, or low temperature.
  - Control: Time of planting..
- Sprouting: An important disorder in storage. It is due to excessive moisture at maturity and supply of nitrogen.
  - Control: Stop irrigation as soon as bulbs reach maturity.

    Spray iron sulphate or borax @ 500–1000 ppm 2–3 weeks prior to harvesting.
- Important disease: Purple blotch **(Alternaria porri),** Downy Mildew (*Peronospora destructor*), Onion Smut (*Urocytis cepulae*), Stemphylium blight.
- Important insect– pests: Onion thrips, Onion maggot, Mites.

Varieties

- There are 4 classes on the basis of colour of bulb: – White, Yellow, Red and Brown.
- Red Coloured: Agrifound Dark Red, Agrifound Light Red, Arka Niketan, Arka Kalyan , Pusa Madhavi, Pusa Ratnar, Pusa Red, Pusa Riddhi ,Udaipur 101, Udaipur 103, Bhima Raj, Bhima Red
- Kharif Onion: Arka Kalyan, Arka Pragati, N–53, Arka Niketan
- Rabi season varieties: Palam Lohit, Patna Red, Agrifound Dark Red, Palam Lohit
- White skinned varieties: Pusa White Flat, Pusa White Round, Punjab–48, Udaipur–102
- Yellow skinned varieties: Brown Spanish (Long day variety, suitable for growing in hills), Early Grano (Good for salad, suitable for green onions).
- Multiplier Onion: Agrifound Red, CO–1, C–2 (resistant to purple blotch), CO–3 (resistant to thrips), CO–4 (moderately resistant to thrips), MDU–1.
- Small Onion: Agrifound Rose (pickling type, suitable for export), Arka Bindu

GARLIC

- Botanical name: *Allium sativum* L.
- Family: Alliaceae
- Origin: Central Asia

- CN: 16
- Largest area of garlic in the world: China>India
- Highest production of garlic in the world: China> India> Bangladesh
- Highest Productivity: Egypt
- Highest producing State in India: Madhya Pradesh (In area also)
- Garlic is sexuallt sterile diploid.
- Pungency in garlic is due to the compound: Diallyl–disulphide.
- Allicin is the antibacterial substance of garlic.
- Allin water soluble amino acid present in garlic.
- Loam soils are best suited for cultivation of garlic.
- The soil pH 6–7 favours for its cultivation.
- It is sensitive to high acidity and alkalinity.
- It is a winter season crop requiring cool and moist atmosphere (12–18°C) during growth and relatively dry weather (20–25°C) during bulbing.
- Temperature 25–30°C at bulb maturity is required.
- It is a frost hardy plant.
- Low temperature and short days are favourable for proper bulb formation and hence the pre–requisites for higher yield.
- Sowing time: September to November
- Propagation: Vegetatively propagated by cloves.
- Seed rate: 5–7 qt/ha of cloves are required.
- Propagating clove size: 8–10mm
- For large clove varieties like GHC–1, the seed rate is 15–20q/ha.
- Bulbs are separated into single segment i.e. cloves.
- Spacing: 15–20 cm × 10 cm.
- Sowing depth: 2–4 cm.

Planting methods

- Dibbling: Cloves are dibbled 5–7.5 cm deep keeping their growing ends upwards.
- Furrow planting: Cloves are dropped in the furrows by hand and covered lightly by loose soil.
- Critical stages of irrigation are bulb formation and bulb enlargement.
- Harvesting: When the tops turn yellow or brownish and show signs of drying up.

- Harvesting time: March– April
- Curing: Bulbs are cured in field for one week. Then, these bulbs are cured in shade for 7–8 days either with tops or after cutting tops, leaving 2.5cm of the stalk. Roots are also trimmed leaving 1cm of root.
- Export quality: 40–60mm diameter bulb with 10–15 cloves in each bulb.
- Yield: 100–200q/ha.
- Storage: Cold storage at 0–2.2°C and 60–70% RH is congenial.
- The storage life is prolonged and loss in weight is reduced by spraying MH @ 2000–3000 ppm, 2–3 weeks before harvesting.
- Diseases: Purple blotch, Downy mildew
- Insect–pests: Mites, Aphids, Thrips

Varieties

- GHC-1, Agrifound Parvati, Large Segmented, Solan Selection, Selection 1, Godavari, Sweta, Yamuna Safed, Agrifound Parvati, G-282
- Big size clove varieties: G-282, Agrifound Parvati
- G-282: Early maturity and Export variety.
- About 25–50% crop losses due to without stored maintenance.
- Borax @ 10 kg/ha or application @ 0.5–1ppm increases bulb size and yield.

CARROT

- Botanical Name: *Daucus carota* L.
- Family: Apiaceae
- Chromosome No: 2n=18
- Origin: South western Asia (Afghanistan)
- Black carrots are used for the preparation of Kanji.
- Kanji is to be a good appetizer.
- Carrots prefer sandy loam to loam soil with a slightly acidic reaction.
- It is a cool season crop.
- A temperature range of 7.2 to 23.9°C is suitable for seed germination and 18.3 to 23.9°C for better root growth.
- The optimum temperature for better colour development of roots is 15.6–21.1°C.
- Sowing time: In north Indian plains: August to December.

  In south India: July to Sepember

- Seed Rate: 5–6 kg/ha
- Seeds are to be mixed with fine sand before sowing to facilitate even distribution.
- Spacing: 30cm × 8–10cm
- Sowing depth: 1–1.5 cm deep on the ridges.
- Transplanting: 30–40 days after sowing.
- Earthing up is also essential for better growth and development of roots.
- Cracking of roots occur due to exposure to dry weather followed by wet weather.
- Harvesting: The common Asiatic varieties attain the marketable stage at 2.5–4.0 cm diameter at the upper end.
- A light irrigation before 2–3 days of harvesting is to be given to facilitate the pulling of the roots from the soil without any damage.
- Roots harvested with top are called bunch carrot
- Roots harvested without tops are called bulk carrots.
- Most carrots for fresh market are now topped which greatly reduces water loss from the roots and increases storage life.
- Yield: Asiatic types: 250–300 q/ha.
- European Types: 100–150 q/ha
- Storage: At temperature 0–4.4°C with 93–98% RH roots can be stored for 3–4 months.
- Protoandry found in carrot.
- Physiological disorders:
- Root splitting: It is due to wider spacing as larger roots tend to split more or dry weather followed by wet weather is conducive to cracking of roots or high nitrogen application or early cultivars tend to split more readily than late ones.
- Cavity spot: It is due to calcium deficiency.
- Forking: It occurs on heavy soils due to soil compactness.
- Important diseases: Leaf blight, Leaf spot or Cercospora blight, Powdery mildew, Watery soft rot, Black rot, and bacterial soft rot.
- Insect–pests: The serious pests are rust fly and turnip moth.
- Temperate or European type form root both under temperate and tropical climate but seed setting only in temperate climate.
- Asiatic type carrot: roots are long, high yielding, poor in quality and carotene, rich in anthocyanin

- European type carrot: requires chilling (4.8–10 °C) for flowering, roots are medium in size, Orange coloured, rich in carotene, stump and blunting core
- Temperate type carrot: Low

Varieties

- **Asiatic or tropical type:** Pusa Kesar, Pusa Meghali
- **European or temperate type varieties:** Nantes, Nantes half long, Early nantes, Chantney, Pusa Yamdagini, Zeno, Danvers, Solan Rachna
- **Selection variety:** Hisar garlic

Hybrid

- Imperator: Nantes × Chantenay
- Pusa Kesar: Local Red × Nantes half long
- Pusa Meghali: Pusa Kesar × Nantes
- Pusa Yamdagni: EC–9981 × Nantes
- Other varieties: Pusa Vristi, Pusa Rudhira, Pusa Ashita (black coloured), Black Beauty, oty, Pusa Nayan jyoti
  - Cylindrical shape root variety: Nantes
  - Heart shaped variety: Oxheart
  - Oval shaped variety: Early Scarlet Horn
  - Round shaped variety: French Forcing

RADISH

- Botanical Name: *Raphanus sativus* L.
- Family: Brassicaceae
- Origin: Western Asia
- CN: 18
- The roots are good appetizer, effective in curing liver, gall bladder and urinary disorders, piles and gastrodynia.
- The characteristic pungent flavour is due to the presence of volatile iso–thiocynates.
- The optimum soil pH 5.5–7.0 is suitable.
- It is a cool season crop.
- The optimum temperature for best flavour, texture, root growth and development is 10– 15°C.

- The Asiatic types are tolerant to high temperature than European types.
- During the hot weather, the roots become tough, pithy and pungent before reaching the edible type.
- Long days coupled with high temperature leads to premature bolting without adequate root formation.
- Sowing time: In Northern plains

  European type: September–March

  Asiatic type: August–January
- Seed Rate: 9–12 kg/ha
- 1 g seed contains 80–125 seeds
- Spacing: European type – 30cm × 5–10cm

  Asiatic types – 45 cm × 6–8 cm
- Sowing depth: 1.5– 3 cm deep on the ridges for semi–long type \
- Harvesting: European types are ready to harvest– 50–90 days.

  Asiatic types are reasy to harvest– 25–35 days.

  Mid maturity group– 40–60 days.

Yield

European type 50–80 qt/ha
Asiatic type 200 –500 qt/ha

- **Storage:** At 32°F temperature and 95–100% relative humidity radish can be stored for 3–4 weeks. Roots can be stored for 2 months at 0 oC and 90–95% relative humidity.

Physiological disorders

- Pithiness: Delay in harvesting is the main reason for this disorder. Therefore, harvesting should be done at an appropriate time.
- Elongated root or Forking: It is due to excessive moisture during root development in heavy soils which leads to soil compactness. Use well decomposed organic manure to overcome this problem and ensure irrigation at proper time.
- Important diseases: Damping off, Alternaria blight, White Rust
- Important Insect: Aphids

Varieties

- **Asiatic or tropical type:** Pusa Desi, Pusa Reshmi, Pusa Chetki, Japanese White, Pusa Mridula, Punjab Safed, Punjab Pasand, Arka Nishant, Chinese

Pink, Hisar Mooli No. 1, Kalyanpur No. 1, Kalyani White, CO-I, Jaunpuri Mooli, Kashi Sweta, Kashi Hans

- **European or temperate type varieties:** Pusa Himani, White Icicle, Rapid Red White Tipped, Scarlet Globe, Scarlet Long, Silver Queen, Kvarta, French breakfast, and Palam Hriday

TURNIP

- Botanical name: *Brassica rapa* L.
- Family: Brassicasea
- Origin : Mediterranean (European type varieties)
- CN: 20
- In India, Purple Top White Globe (PTVWG) is the most common variety.
- Sowing time: September– October
- Inflorescence: Terminal raceme.
- It has strong sporophytic self incompatibility.
- Nacl and CO_2 is used to overcome self incompatibility.
- Seed rate: 4–4.5 kg/ha.
- Spacing: In plains: 45 × 45 cm^2.
  In hills: 60 × 60 cm^2
- Thinning is important culture practices in turnip.
- Thinning is done 10–15 days after germination.
- Germination: 4–6 days after sowing.
- Large roots have poor texture and bitter taste.
- A light irrigation may be given before harvesting to facilitate lifting.
- Yield: Fruit: 20–40 t/ha.
- Seed: 5–6 qt/ha
- Seed viability: 4–5 years.

Varieties

There are two types of turnip varieties

- Asiatic/Tropical/Subtropical: Pusa Kanchan, Pusa Swati, Punjab Safed 4
- European/Temperate type: Purple Top White Globe, Pusa Chandrima, Golden Ball, Early Milan red Top, Pusa Swarnima

BEET ROOT

- Botanical Name: *Beta vulgaris* sp *vulgaris*.
- Family: Chenopodiaceae
- Origin: Europe
- CN: 18
- Inflorescence: Spike
- Beet root is rich in protein, carbohydrates, Ca, P, Fe and vitamin C.
- Red colour of table beets is due to betacynin (β-cyanine)
- Yellow pigmentation is due to betaxanthin (β-xanthin).
- It is a cool season crop that can tolerate mild frosts and light freezes.
- Optimum seed germination occurs between 65 and 75°F.
- Beets are very sensitive to low temperature and if exposed to 4.5°C – 10°C for 15 days, bolting occurs.
- It grows well in warm weather but the best colour, texture and quality are achieved in a cool weather condition.
- Excessive hot weather causes: Zoning
- Sowing: September: November in north India
  July to November in South India.
- The seed rate: 7–9 kg/ha.
- Spacing: 45–60 cm × 8–10 cm.
- Beet root has multigerm seeds in a fruit containing usually 2–6 seeds.
- A gram of seed ball counts about 50 seeds.
- Thinning is an essential operation in beet cultivation.
- Generally, the plants emerge in groups unless segmented seed or monogerm seed is used.
- The soil should be kept sufficiently moist until emergence of seedlings.
- The marketable maturity is just depending on the size ranging from 3–5 cm diameter.
- Yield: 250–300 q/ha.
- Physiological Disorder:
- **Internal black spot:** It is due to boron deficiency.

Variety

Detroit Dark Red, Crimson Globe, Early Wonder, Crosby Egyptian

PALAK/BEET LEAF/SPINACH BEET

- Botanical name: *Beta vulgaris* var. *bengalensis* L.)
- Family: Chenopodiaceae
- Origin: Indo–China
- CN: 18
- It grown well in sandy loam soil.
- It is highly tolerant to saline conditions and can be successfully grown in saline sodic soils.
- It is a cool season crop.
- It tolerates frost and high temperature.
- Palak leaves contain low oxalic acid.
- Sowing time: Early spring, July–Aug, and Sept.–Nov.
- Seed rate: 15–20 kg/ha.
- Spacing: 30 cm × 5–10 cm
- Thinning is essential operation.
- Harvesting: 3–4 weeks after sowing.
- Winter crop gives more cuttings than spring–summer crop.
- Yield: 8–12 tonnes/ha leaves.
- Storage: 0°C with 90–95% RH for 10–14 days.

Varieties

- Selection: Pusa Bharti, All Green, Pusa Jyoti, Punjab green.

Hybrid

- Pusa Palak: Swiss chord × Local Palak
- Pusa Harit: Sugar beet × Local Palak
- Banerjee's Giant: Local Palak × Beet root
- Mutant variety: Jobner Green

SPINACH/VILAYATI PALAK

- Botanical Name: *Spinacea oleracea* L.
- Family: Umbelliferae
- Chromosome no: 2n=12
- Origin: Central Asia

- Among vegetable crops, it ranks second only to broccoli in total nutrient concentration.
- It is not commercially grown in India except hilly areas.
- Spinach is an annual. Plants are usually dioecious. Some monoecious plants may develop rarely in certain cultivars.
- Dioecious types produces two different kinds of male plants:
    - Extreme males: small with very little vegetative development and tend to bolt quickly.
    - Vegetative males and females: slower to flower and produces considerably more foliage, making them the preferred plants type for commercial cultivation.
- Eliminate the extreme males from commercial strains by selection.
- It is susceptible to injury by high acidic soil.
- It is a hardy, cool season crop that does best at temperature of 60–65°F.
- The plant is very intolerant of warm temperature above 77°F.
- Seed germination at 10–15.5°C (50–60°F) and decreases at higher temperature
- Sowing time: North Indian Plains: September–October
- Seed Rate: 37–45 kg/ha
- Spacing: 30 cm × 5–10 cm.
- Harvesting: Ready for harvest about 4 weeks after sowing.
- Yield: 8–10 tonnes/ha.
- It gives about 3– 4 cuttings in the season.
- **Diseases:** Damping off, Leaf spot, White rust, Downy mildew
- **Insects:** Aphids and Catterpiller

Varieties

These are classified in two groups;

On the basis of seed:
Further in two groups:

(a) Pricklyseeded (b) Round seeded

On the basis of leaf:

(a) Smooth leaved e.g., Early Smooth Leaf
(b) Savoy leaved: Virginia Savoy

- Prickly seeded varieties best suited for autumn winter crop in the hills

- Smooth seeded varieties best suited for spring summer crop in the hills.
- Other varieties: Khara Palak, Khara Lucknow
- Sex form: It is a tetramorphic. Such as

1. Extremely male 2. Vegetative male 3. Female 4. Monoecious

FENUGREEK

- Botanical name: There are two types of fenugreek which are of economic importance:

1. *Common methi: Trigonella foenum–graecum*
2. *Kasuri methi: Trigonella corniculata.*

- Family: Fabaceae
- Origin: Europe
- CN: 16

Kasuri Methi

- Yellow coloured flowers and sickle shaped pods
- The seeds are very small in size.
- Mostly preferred in North India.

Common methi

- White or light violet coloured flowers.
- It is quick growing upright crop.
- The pods are straight and seeds are bold.
- Soil: Clay loam soil is the ideal.
- It is a cool season crop.
- Sowing time for common methi: Mid September –Mid March.
  Low hills: Oct–Nov.,
  Mid hills: Aug.–Oct
  High hills: April–July.
- Seed rate: Common methi– 25 kg/ha
  Kasuri type– 20 kg/ha
- Spacing: 20–30 cm × 5–7 cm.
- Manures and fertilizers: FYM @ 10–25 t/ha, 30:40:45 kg $N:P_2O_5:K_2O$/ha, respectively.
- Irrigation during early vegetative and grain formation stages is more critical than later stages.

- Excess irrigation is likely to make the crop susceptible to root rot disease.
- The young shoots are nipped off in about 3 weeks of sowing.
- More number of cuttings may be taken from the Kasuri types.
- The first cutting is ready in about 25–30 days after sowing and the subsequent cuttings may be taken after an interval of 12–15 days.
- Yield: Common methi: 80–100 q/ha
  Kasuri methi: 90–100 q/ha
- Important diseases: Powdery mildew, downy mildew, root rot, damping off, leaf spot, rust, mosaic and Important pes: Aphid.
- The climate, soil and cultural practices for the cultivation of fenugreek are as under:
- The common cultivars are Lam Selection 1, Pusa Early Bunching, Kasuri Selection, CO-I Fenugreek, Rajendra Kranti, RMT-1, Methi No. 47, Methi No. 14, and Palam Soumya
- Varieties for For Himachal Pradesh: IC–74, Palam Soumya, Kasuri Methi, Pusa Kasuri

CUCUMBER

- Botanical name: *Cucumis sativus*
- Family: Cucurbitaceae
- Origin: India
- CN no.: 14
- Sowing: In south India: Oct – Nov
  In North India: Nov– Jan
- Optimum temperature required for growth and yield – 26.4°C (18–24°C)
- Seed rate– 2.5–3.5 kg/ha
- Vit–C presence in cucumber:2mg/100g
- 2nd most widely cultivated crop after water melon crop
- It is thermophilic and frost susceptible crop
- White spine colour is indication for edible maturity in slicing cucumber while blacknin pickling cucumber
- Open pollinated cultiver of cucumber are monoecious
- Ethral increases number of female flower and fruit yield (150–200 ppm)
- GA_3 and Silver Nitrate ($AgNO_3$) induce male flower on gynoecious cucumber
- Yield: 80–120 qnt/ha

Varieties

(i) Introduction: Japanese long green Straight eight Poinsett China long

(ii) Selection: Sheetal

(iii) Public sector hybrid: Pusa Sanyog– It has gynoecious female parent

(iv) Private sector hybrid: Priya

(v) Hybrid: Himangi – Poinsett × Kalyanpur Ageti, resistant to Bronzing Phule Subhangi – Poinsett × Kalyanpur Ageti

- Poinsett resistant to PM, DM, Anthracnose, Angular leaf Spot
- Poinsett is a multiple disease resistant crop
- Japanese long green, Straight Eight and Pusa Sanyog: restricted to temperature region only
- Cucumber mosaic resistant Varieties

1. Tokoyo Long Green
2. Chinese long
3. Winscrimson
4. Table Green

WATERMELON

- Btanical name: *Citrulus lunatus*
- Family: Cucurbitacea
- Origin: Tropical Africa
- CN: 22
- It requires hot and dry climate
- Required temperature:
  - Seed germination: 25–30°C
  - Plant growth: 28–30°C
  - Fruiting: 24–27°C
- Seed rate: 4–5 kg
- It contains 95% water
- White heart at central position shows poor quality fruits
- Harvesting at full mature stage
- Cucurbitacin is main bitter substance (Tetracyclic teiterpense)

- Training system:
  - Archway system: 9500plants/ha
  - Vertical cordon: 12000plants/ha
- Harvesting: 90–120 days after sowing
- Yield: 20–250 qnt/ha
- Storage: 2.2–4.4°C temperature with 80% RH for 1–3 weeks
- TSS range: 8–13%
- Yield losses upto 30% have been observed due to weeks
- Metalic sound at the time of harvesting shows: Immaturity
- Heavy dull sound at the time of harvesting shows: Maturity
- Yellow tinge/brown spot where iot rests on ground, indicate maturity
- Presence of pigment: Anthocyanin and Lycopene
- Pusa Bedana is triploid variety
- Pusa Rasal is seedless variety

Varieties

- **Introduction**

  Asahi Yamato, Sugar Baby– 11–13% TSS
  Improved shipper, Dixie Cream, Furken, New Hemisphire midget

- **Selection**

  Durgapura Meetha
  Durgapura Kesar: Yellow fleshed
  Pusa Rasal: Seedless variety

Hybrid

Arka Manik: IIHR × Crimson sweet, 11–12% TSS
Arka Jyoti: IIHR–20 × Crimson sweet, 11–12% TSS
Pusa Bedana: Tetra-2 × Pusa Rasal

- Private sector hybrid: Madhur, Milan,

MUSKMELON

- Botanical name: *Cucumis melo*
- Family: Cucurbitaceae
- Origin: South America
- CN: 22

- Whole some fruit
- Pickling melon: C. melo var cocmom
- Mango or Lemon melon: C. melo var chita
- Sowing time: November–January
- Edible part: Seed Kernels
- Seed rate:
  - Dibbling method: 1 kg/ha
  - Kera or Pora method: 2.5–3.5 kg/ha
- Temperature required for seed germination: 27–30°C
- High temperature at the of fruit maturity and ripening increases the sweetness
- Musk melon is harvested at full slip stage (except Hara Madhu) – Netting
- Maximum number of fruits with highest TSS is produced between 9th and 12th bud or nodes on the main stem
- TSS range 11–17% present in most of varieties
- Downey mildew resistant variety: Punjab Rasila
- Powdery mildew resistant variety: Arka Rajhans (excellent keeping quality)
- Arka jeet: excellent flavor and high vit–C, relative dwarf habit

Varieties

- **Selection:** Durgapura Madhu, Hara Madhu, Pusa Madhura, Arka Rajhans, Arka Jeet,

Hybrid

- Pusa Sharbati: Kutana × Cantaloupes, Early variety, 11–12% TSS
- Punjab Sunhari: Hara Madhu × Edisto, 11–12% TSS
- Hissar Madhur: Pusa Sharbati × 75
- MHY–5: Durgapura × Hara Madhu
- Punjab Rasal: Resistant to Powdery mildew and Downey mildew
- **Public sector hybrid:** Pusa Rasraj
- **Private sector hybrid:** Shweta, Swarna

BOTTLE GOURD

- Botanical name: *Lagenaria siceraria*
- Family: Cucurbitaceae
- Origin: South Africa

- CN: 22
- Kofta and Petha are most popular preparation from Bottle gourd
- It is highly photosensitive
- Dry shell is used for preparation of musical instrument
- Processed product: tooty–fruity
- Fruit pulp is very good source of fibre free carbohydrates
- Germination: 25–30°C, Brownish or whitish brown seeds germinate well
- High temperature and high N_2 induce maleness in bottle gourd
- Heterosis is present through its life cycle in all stage

Varieties

- **Selection:** Pusa summer prolific, Arka Bahar, Pusa Navven, Pusa summer prolific, Punjab round, Punjab long, Samrat

Hybrid

- Punjab Komal, Pusa Manjari, Varad, Pusa Sandesh, Gutka, Harit, NDBG-1, PBOG-1

BITTER GOURD

- Botanical name: *Momordica charantia*
- Family: Cucurbitaceae
- Origin: India
- CN: 22
- Bitter principle– Momordicin
- Bitter gourd fruit are rich in iron
- If temperature goes above 40°C, induce maleness
- Sowing time: Jan–Feb
- Fruits are ready for 60–70 days after sowing

Varieties

- Selction: Pusa-Do-Mausami, Pusa Vishesh, Preethi, Coimbatore long Priyanka, Konkan Tara

Hybrid

- Phule green gold: Green long × Delhi local, Pusa hybrid-1

PUMPKIN

- Botanical name: *Cucurbita moschata*
- Family: Cucurbitaceae
- Origin: Mexico
- CN: 40
- Amphidiploid (2n=40) in nature
- Orissa – 85% area and 90% production
- Yerusseri: Prepared from immature fruits
- Cucurbita ficifolia: Fig leaf gourd or Malabar Gourd
- "Channel and hill" system of cultivation is most useful for higher yield
- Chief pollinator: Honey Bees
- Suitable temperature for growth: 13–18°C
- Seed rate: 5–6 kg/ha
- Storage temperature: 15–20°C temperature with 75% RH for 2–3 weeks
- Male and Female parent can be grown in a 1:3 ratio
- Flowers of pumpkin are more nutritive than fruits
- Arka Chandan: Pleasant aroma
- Arka Surya Mukhi: Resistant to Fruit fly

Varieties

Arka Chandan, Arka Surya Mukhi, Pusa Viswas, Pusa Vikash, Ambili

POINTED GOURD

- Botanical name: *Trichosanthus dioca*
- Family: Cucurbitaceae
- Origin: India
- CN: 22
- Propagation: Vine cutting @ 2000–2500 cuttings/ha
- 10% male plant is necessary to get high yield
- 15 female plant/male plant to get high fruit yield

Varieties

Bihar Sherif, Dandi, Kalyani, Damodar, Shankolia, Swarna Alaukik, Swarna Rekha, Chhota Hilli

ASH GOURD

- Botanical name: *Benincasa hispida*
- Family: Cucurbitaceae
- Origin: Japan
- CN: 24
- Fruits at maturity have white waxy surface
- Annual hispid (Rough with bristle like hairs)
- It is also known as "Chinese preserving melon"
- Longest storage life among all the cucurbits crop
- **Varieties:** Mudlier, Pusa Ujjwal

CHOW–CHOW

- Botanical name: *Sechium edule*
- Family: Cucurbitaceae
- Origin: Mexico
- CN: 28
- It is also known as Chayote, Choco or Askas
- Fruit: single seeded fruit
- It is Herbaceous, Perennial, Monoecious and Climbing vine
- High calcium content crop
- Highest nutritional crop among all the cucurbits crop
- Propagation: By fruit
- It is a Vivipary type of fruit

RIDGE GOURD

- Botanical name: *Lufa acutangola*
- Family: Cucurbitaceae
- Origin: Asia
- CN: 26
- Warm hot climatic crop
- Optimum temperature for its proper growth is 25–30°C

- Above 38°C causes maleness
- Spray of ethrel 250 ppm increases female flower
- Seed rate– 1–1.5 kg/ha
- Commercial trained on kniffin system
- Surekha and Arka Sujat are hybrid varieties
- Satputia is hermaphrodite variety
- Anthesis time: Evening
- Yield: 150–200 g/ha

Varieties

Pusa Nasdar, Punjab Sadabahr, Konkan Harit, Satputia, Surekha, Arka Sujat

SPONGE GOURD

- Botanical name: *Lufa cylendrica*
- Family: Cucurbitaceae
- Origin: India
- CN: 26
- It contains high protein than ridge gourd
- It contains gelatinous compound called – Luffien
- Anthesis time: 4–8 am (morning)
- Yield: 150–200 q/ha
- Harita is a F1 hybrid variety

Varieties

- Pusa Chikni, Pusa Supriya, Phule Prajakta, Harita

SUMMER SQUASH

- Botanical name: *Cucurbita pepo*
- Family: Cucurbitaceae
- Origin: Mexico
- CN: 40
- It is also known as: Bushy cucurbit, Ornamental cucurbit
- Harvesting stage: 1/3rd maturity

Varieties

Introduced: Patty Pan, Australian Green

Selection: Early Yellow Prolific

F1 hybrid: Pusa Alankar = Chappen × Early Yellow Prolific

WINTER SQUASH

- Botanical name: *Cucurbita maxima*
- Family: Cucurbitaceae
- Origin: Mexico
- CN: 40
- It is also known as Vilayati Kaddu
- It can tolerate to frost
- Optimum temperature for its cultivation: 25–30°C

Varieties

- Arka Suryamukhi, Pink Banana

SNAKE GOURD

- Botanical name: *Trichosanthus anguina*
- Family: Cucurbitaceae
- Origin: India
- CN: 22
- Seed rate: 2–3 kg/ha
- Yield: 180–200 qt/ha
- Bower syatem of training is best for its cultivation
- MDU–1: F1 hybrid variety

Varieties

- Konkan Shweta, PKM-1, CO-1, CO-2

SPINE GOURD

- Botanical name: *Momordica dioca*
- Family: Cucurbitaceae
- Origin: India
- CN: 22
- It is also known bristly balsam pear or Kakrol
- Dioecious crop
- Propagation: Tuberous root

PEA

- Botanical name: *Pisum sativum*
- Family: Leguminoceae
- Origin: Central Asia
- CN: 14
- **Field pea:** Pisum sativum var. arvense
- **Garden pea:** Pisum sativum var. hortense
- Garden pea is widely grown in India
- Favorable temperature for pea is 15–25°C
- Pea sensitive to saline and alkaline soil
- Maturity of pea is mmeasured by Tensiometer
- F1 hybrid seed production is almost restricted due to less number of seeds per in pod
- Seed rate: 80–100kg/ha
- Pea is a rich source of protein
- Arkel: Introduced from England
- Bonneville: Suitable for dehydration
- Whole pod is edible: JP-19, Sylvia, UN-53
- JP-6 variety is also known as JM-9
- Bonneville is introduced from USA
- Arkel is introduced from England
- Sylvia is introduced from Sewden
- Sylvia is pod edible vriety

- Arka Ajit and Palam Priya are powdery mildew resistant varieties

Varieties

Introduction: Bonneville, Arkel, Early Badger, Early Superb, Lincoln, Little Marvel, Sylvia, Meteoror

Selection: Arka Ajit, Harbhajan, Pant Upkar, Palam Priya

FRENCH BEAN

- Botanical name: *Phaseolus vulgaris*
- Family: Leguminoceae
- Origin: Mexico
- CN: 22
- Edible portion: 94% of the pod
- Staking is important operation in pole type varieties
- Most of varieties are day neutral except semipole type– they are short day types
- It is sensitive to both water excess and water stress condition
- Blossom drop and ovule abortion are common problems at high temp.(35°C)
- Semi moisture below 12% enhance craking of cotyledon
- Pusa Parvati: developed by mutation
- Contender: tolerant to powdery mildew and mosaic

Varieties

1. Pole type: Kentuky wonder, Tweed wonder, Pusa Himlata
2. Bush type: Contender, Pusa Parvati, Arka Komal, Arka Suvidha, Pant Anupamma, Top Cross, Giant Stringless, Bountiful, Jampa
3. Semi pole type

COWPEA

- Botanical name: *Vigna unguiculata*
- Family: Leguminoceae
- Origin: Africa
- CN: 22

- It is also known as Southern pea or Black eyed pea
- Most probable progenitor of cowpea spp.- Mensensii
- There are three groups of cowpea

1. Common cowpea: *Vigna unguiculata*
2. Catjang bean or Kidney bean: *Vigna cylindrica*
3. Asparagus bean or Yard long bean: *Vigna sesquipedalis*

- Sensitive to water logging
- Seed rate:
  - In rainy season: 12–15 kg/ha
  - In summer season: 20–25 kg/ha
- Germination temperature: 12–15°C
- It is grown as cash crop
- It is drought tolerant crop
- Pods are rich in Vit–B and Vit–A (941IU/100g)
- Pusa Phalguni: Dwarf variety
- Yield:
  - Green pod: 50–80 qnt/ha
  - Dry seed: 12–15 qnt/ha

Varieties

- **Introduction:** Phillipins Early, Yard long bean
- **Selection:** Pusa Barsati, Arka Suman, Arka Garima, Arka Samrudhi, Pusa Phalguni

Hybrid

- Pusa Dofasali: Pusa Phalguni × Phillipins bush
- Pusa Komal: Pusa Rituraj × P-246
- Pusa Rituraj: Bush type and Dua purpose

CLUSTER BEAN

- Botanical name: *Cyamopsis tetragonolobus*
- Family: Leguminoceae
- Origin: India
- CN: 14

- It is drought and hardy tolerant crop
- Some varieties are suitable for extraction of gum
- Pusa Sadabahar: Non branching variety and suitable for summer and rainy season
- Pusa Navbahar is a hybrid variety

Varieties

- Pusa Sadabahar, Pusa Mausmmi, Sharad Bahar, Pusa Navbahar

DOLICHUS BEAN

- Botanical name: *Dolichus lablab*
- Family: Leguminoceae
- Origin: India
- CN: 22
- It is grown for its whole pod
- Seed rate:
  - Pole type: 10–12 kg/ha
  - Bushy type: 20–30 kg/ha
- Pusa Early prolific– Pole type, suitable for autumn and spring season
- Mutant variety: CO–10
- Pusa Sem 3: Tolerant to mosaic
- Arka Ajay: Photoinsensitive and bush type variety
- Varieties: Pusa Early Prolific, Pusa Early Rajni, Arka Ajay, Konkan Bhushan, Rajni, Deepali

LIMA BEAN

- Botanical name: *Phaseolus lunatus*
- Family: Leguminoceae
- Origin: Guate mala
- CN: 22
- It is used to prepare Wine

Varieties

1. Pole type: King of Garden, Karolina butter, Challenger, Florida butter
2. Bush type: Baby Potato, Baby Fordhook, Handerson Bush
3. Semi–pole type: Wilbur, Hopi

BROAD BEAN

- Botanical name: *Vicia faba*
- Family: Leguminoceae
- Origin: India
- CN: 12
- It is pollinated by insect
- It is he only bean which is grown in autumn and winter crop

Varieties

Red Epicure, Windsore, Pusa Sumeet

SWEET POTATO

- Botanical name: *Ipomea batata*
- Family: Convolvulaceae
- Origin: South America
- CN: 90
- Most probable ancestor of sweet potato: Ipomea trifida
- It is a perennial vine
- China: 1st rank in area and production in sweet potato
- Propagation: Vine cutting 82000 cuttings/ha
- Cercospora leaf spot of sweet potato was first reported in Africa
- Fusiform variety: Varsha
- Sree Bhadra: Excellent trap crop for root knot nematode

Varieties

Kalmegh, Samrat, Kiran, Gouri, Shankar Varsha, Bhuban, Pusa Suffaida, Pusa Lal, Pusa Sunderi

- **Sree series:** Sree Vardhani, Sree Nandini, Sree Arun, Sree Varun, Sree Bhadra

CASSAVA/TAPIOCA

- Botanical name: *Manihot esculenta*
- Family: Euphorbiaceae
- Origin: Brazil
- CN: 36
- The plant is perennial shrub
- Yellow colour of flesh is due to presence of carotene
- It is drought tolerant crop
- "Vascular blue lining" or "Vascular streaking" is present in cassava
- Cassava is photo insensitive crop
- Important processed food product from cassava: Sago or Sabudana
- Sree Harsha: Triploid clone from Sree sahya
- Sree Vishakam: Conical tuber
- Sree Sahya: Cylindrical tuber

Varieties

Sree Harsh, Sree Prakash, Sree Jaya, Sree Vijaya, Sree Vishakam, Sree Sahya, Nidhi

ELEPHANT FOOT YAM

- Botanical name: *Amarpholhalus companulatus*
- Family: Araceae
- Origin: South Asia
- CN: 26
- It is also known as Suran or Whitespot gaint arum
- It works as a Blood Purifier
- Propagation: Tubers
- Planting time: Feb–March
- Harvest: 7–8 month after planting

Varieties

- Gajendra, Santragachi, Kovvur, Sree Padma, Bidham Kusum

YAMS

- White yam: *Dioscorea rotundata*
- Greater yam: Dioscorea alata
- Lesser yam: Dioscorea rotundata
- Family: Dioscoraceae
- Chromosome number: 2n=40
- Origin: Indo-Burma
- Greater yam is also known as Ratalu or Water Yam
- Lesser yam is also known as Chinese yam or Asiatic yam
- Lesser yam matures early as compared to other spp.
- Yam flour is also used for human consumption as Kokonte
- Fuyu is a product made from yam
- Africa alone produce 90% tubes and covers 95%

Varieties

- **Greater yam:** Sree Kirthi, Sree Roop, Sree shilpa
- **Lesser yam:** Sree Latha, Sree Kala, Konkana Kanchan
- **White yam:** Sree Subhra, Sree Priya, Sree Dhanya
- Lesser yam is sweeter than other yams

BLACK PEPPER

- Botanical name: *Pepper nigrum*
- Family: Piperaceae
- Origin: Indo– Burma
- CN: 128
- Chemical compound found in black pepper is piperine
- King of spices
- Largest producers – Vietnam
- India accounts for 54% of total area and 26.6% of total production in the world
- It can tolerant 10–40°C temperature
- Suitable pH is 4.5–6.0
- Fruiting branches: Plagiotropes

- Hanging branches: Geotropes
- Top shoots: Orthotropes
- Propagation: Runner shoot cutting
- Spacing: 2.7 × 2.7 m^2
- Maturity: 180 – 200 days after sowing
- Yield: 273 kg/ha
- Harvesting: Nov–Feb
- Triploid stand for harvesting
- North America – Major importer of India pepper
- The mean anuual rainful, maximum and minimum temperature for black pepper is 2000–3000 mm, 10°C and 40°C

Varieties

- Karimunda, Panniyur, Sree Kara, Subhakara Poornima, Panchami,

Hybrid

- Panniyur-1, Panniyur-3

SMALL CARDAMOM

- Botanical name: *Elettaria cardamomum*
- Family: Zingiberaceae
- Origin: India
- CN: 48
- Queen of spices
- 2nd important national spices
- Planting: used 10–18 month old seedling
- Inflorescence: Panicle
- Propagation: Rhizomes
- Spacing: 2 × 2 m^2
- Harvesting: Oct–Nov
- Yield: 500 kg/ha
- Summer showers are essential for flowering
- The mean anuual rainfall, maximum and minimum temperature for cardamom is 1500 mm– 5750 mm, 10°C and 35°C

Varieties

- Mysore type, Malabar type, PV–2, Mudigree-1, Vazukha type

LARGE CARDAMOM

- Botanical name: *Amomum subulatum*
- Family: Zingiberaceae
- Origin: India
- CN: 48
- Sikkim is the largest producer
- It is shade loving plants (Seophyte)
- Propagation: Suckers

Varieties

Bebo, Golsey, Ramla, Ramsey

GINGER

- Botanical name: *Zingiber officinalis*
- Family: Zingiberaceae
- Origin: South East Asia
- CN: 22
- India accounts 70% of total world production and 50% in world export
- Kerala leading producer of ginger (60% area and 25% production)
- Propagation: Rhizome bits of 15–20 g @ 1200–1800 kg /ha
- Spacing; 30 × 30 cm^2
- Yield: 15–30 qnt/ha
- The yield of dry ginger is 16–25% of the green ginger
- Cochin ginger/India ginger best in the world
- Riode Janario introduced from Brazil
- Surbhi is a mutant variety
- Himgiri is tolerant to rhizome rot

Varieties

Riode Janerio, Surbhi, Suphrabha, Suruchi, Wynad manantody, Himgiri, Bombey Desi

TURMERIC

- Botanical name: *Curcuma longa*
- Family: Zingiberaceae
- Origin: South East Asia
- CN: 63
- India accounts 76% of total world production
- Andhra Pradesh is the highest producer state
- Crop period:
    - Short duration crop: 7 month crop
    - Medium duration crop: 8 month
    - Long duration crop: 9 month
- Propagation: Rhizome @ 2500 kg/ha
- Spacing: 30 × 15 cm^2
- Yield: 25–30 t/ha
- Trade type: Allepe finger turmeric
- Allepe turmeric is famous for its colour in trade
- Trade name: Allepe, Erode, Duggirala, Nizamabad, Rajapuri etc.
- Turmeric is antioxidant due to phenolic character of curcumin
- The mean annual rainfall, maximum and minimum temperature for turmeric is 640 mm to 4290 mm and 18.2°C to 27.4°C

Varieties

Rajedra Sonia, Prabha, Pratibha, Kranti, Krishna Rashmi, Roma, Saguna, Suroma, Suvarna, Sudarshana, Sugandham

Section 'D'
Medicinal and Aromatic Crops

Medicinal plants: A medicinal plants are those plants rich in secondary metabolites and are potential sources of drugs. These secondary metabolites include alkaloids, glycosides, coumarins, flavonoids, steroids etc.

- Pharmaceutical drugs: A pharmaceutical drugs is a drug that is produced in a laboratory to cure or help an illness. Typically, pharmaceutical drugs are modeled after compound found in medicinal plants.
- WHO has listed over 21000 plant species used around the world for medicinal purpose and in India 8000 spp. listed is available. ISM (Indian Systems of Medicine) uses nearly 2500 plant spp. belonging to more than 1000 genera. Of the nearly 800 spp. used in the industries, 25% are cultivated.

Example: Isabgol, Sarpagandha, Opium, Goggle, Ashwagandha, Medicinal yam, Fox–glove, Pyrethrum, Senna, periwinkle, Belladonna, Rye Ergot, Coleus, Neem, Datura, Stevia, etc.

Aromatic plants: Those plants which possess essential oil in them. These essential oils are the odoriferous steam volatile constituents of the aromatic plants.

- Essential oil: They are mainly a complex misxture of acyclic and cyclic monoterpenoids. These terpenoids are basically secondary matabolites and they have no apparent function in the plant's primary metabolism.
- **Example:** Indian Basil, Keweda, Abrette/Muskdana, Celery, Rosemary, Jamalgota, Davana, Lemon grass, Vetiver grass, Java citronella, Palmrosa grass, Patcholi, Japanese mint, Eucalyptus, Sandal wood, Patchouli, Lavender etc.

Medicinal Crops

OPIUM

- Botanical name: *Papavera somnifera*
- Family: Papaveraceae
- Origin: Europe
- Useful part: Fruit/Capsule
- Chemical content: Morphine, Narcotine, Codine
- Flowering time: 95–115 days after sowing
- Capsule maturity: 15–20 days after flowering
- Uses: It is also called "God of sleep". It is used in Painkillar, hypotonic effect and cure to leukaemia

- It is a licence crop and grow in Aari
- One aari equals to 100 m^2
- Seed rate: For broadcasting: 7–8 Kg/ha
  For line sowing: 4–5 Kg/ha
- Thinning is important cultural practices.

Lancing

- It is the process of latex collection from capsule.
- It is done with a knife having 3–4 equispaced pointed ends which dose not penetrate more than 1–2 mm in the capsule.
- The length of incision should be 1/3 or less than the full length of capsule.
- Lencing is done in the early morning at 2 days interval in each capsule.
- **Yield:** raw opium: 50–60 kg/ha

Varieties

- Jawahar Aphim 16, JO 539, JO540, Kirtiman, Chetak, Trishna, Talia, Ranghatak, Shama

ISABGOL

- Batonical name: *Plantago ovate*
- Family: Plantaginaceae
- Origin: West india
- Useful part: Husk and Seed
- Chemical content: Mucilage
- Uses: It is soothing and cooling agent. It also used against irritation in gastrointestinal tract. It has laxative property.
- It is a **stemless** annual herb.
- Fruit: Capsule
- Each seed is ancased in a thin, white, translucent memebrane, which is odourless and tastless is called: **Husk**
- Seed rate: 4–6 Kg/ha
- Husk : Seed = 25 : 75 by weight
- Yield: 1 tonn per hectare

Varities

Niharika, Gujarat Isabgol 1, GI 2, Haryana Isabgol 4

SARPAGANDHA

- Botanical name: *Rauvolfia serpentine*
- Family: Apocynaceae
- Origin: India
- Useful part: Root
- Chemical content: Serpentine, Reserpine, Saponine
- Uses: It is used as treatment for hypertension as a sedative
- Seed rate: 5–6 kg/ha
- Yield: 2000 kg root/ha

Varities

RS–1, CIM–sheel

ASHWAGANDHA

- Botanical name: *Withania somnifera*
- Family: Solanacea
- Origin: Africa
- Useful part: Root
- Chemical content: Withanine, Somniferine
- Seed rate: 3–4 kg/ha
- Uses: It is used for making general tonic

Varities

Jawahar Asgandh

PERIWINKLE

- Botanical name: *Catheranthus rosae*
- Family: Apocyanaceae
- Origin: West Indies

- Useful part: Roots and Leaves
- Chemical content: Vincrestine, Vinblastine, Ajmacline
- Uses: It is used for cancer therapy, Blood pressor control

  Seed rate: For direct sowing: 2–3 kg/ha
  For nursery: 500g/ha
- Yield: Under rainfed condition: Root– 0.75 tonne/ha
  Stem– 1 tonne/ha
  Leaves– 2 tonnes/ha
  Under irrigated condition: Root– 1.5 tonne/ha
  Stem– 1.5 toone/ha
  Leaves– 3 tonnes/ha

Varieties

Nirmal, Dhawal, Prabhat

Aromatic plants

LEMON GRASS

- Botanical name: *Cymbopogon flexuosus*
- Family: Graminae
- Origin: India
- Useful part: Leaves
- Oil content: Citral, Farnesol
- **Uses:** Used for Vit–A manufacturing
- Lemon grass oil is known as: Cochin oil
- Seed rate: 15–20 kg/ha
- Yield: Oil–25 kg/ha from first year
- 80–100 kg from 2nd to 6th year

Varieties

Pragathi, Nima, Krishna, Sugandhi, Chirharit, Kalam

VETIVER GRASS

- Botanical name: *Vetevaria zizanoides*
- Family: Vitaveraceae

- Origin: India
- Useful part: Root
- Oil content: Viteverol
- **Uses:** It has carminative poperties. It is used as a stimulant, refrigerant and stomachic.
- Propagation: Slip (50,000 to 2,25000 slips/ha)
- Yield: 5–7 tonnes roots/ha and 15–16 kg of oil/ha

Varities

Dharini, Gulabi, Sugandha, Keshari

JAVA CITRONELLA GRASS

- Botanical name: *Cymbopogon winterianus*
- Family: Graminae
- Origin: Cylon
- Useful part: Leaves
- Oil content: Citronellal
- **Uses:** Making Deodrants, Mosquito repellents and scented soaps
- **Propagation:** Slips
- **Yiled:** Oil– 140–150kg/ha from first year
- 200–300 kg/ha from 2nd to 4th year

Varieties

Manjusha, Mandakini, Jamrosa, Medini, Manjari, Bio–13

INDIA BASIL/TULSI

- Botanical name: *Occimum* spp.
- Family: Labiatae
- Origin: Africa
- Useful part: Leaves and Inflorescence
- Oil content: Methyl chevicol, Linalool
- Uses: Flouring food
- Seed rate: 200–250g/ha

- Yield: 25–30 tonnes of herbage/ha from first year

Varieties

Soumya, Vikarsudha, Kusmohak, Angana, Kanchan

Some important points

Distillation of essential oil

1. Water distillation: best for finely powder form material like rose petal
2. Water and steam distillation: Seed and roots
3. Direct steam distillation: Herb and leaf materials

- National Aromatic and Medicinal Plant Board (NAMPB): New Delhi
- National Research Centre for Medicinal and Aromatic Plants (NRCMA): Lucknow, UP
- Central Institute for Medicinal and Aromatic Plants (CIMAP): Anand, GJ
- Largest family of medicinal crops: Astaraceae
- Maximum demand of the medicinal plants in the world market:

  Senna > Isabgol > Cassia tora
- India's first rank in case production: Kewada, Senna, Davana oil, Isabgol
- USA is largest producer and consumer of essential oil
- **Winter chum** or **Indian Ginseng** is known as; Ashwagandha
- Psyllium is also known as: **Isabgol**
- **Cinchona** is used for the treatment of malaria
- **Liquorice or Mulathi** is 150 times sweeter than sugar
- Safes Musli is also known as: Second Shilajeet
- Arka Upkar is a variety of Medicinal yam
- Sher-A-Kashmir is a variety of Oil bearing rose
- Johori is the variety of Pachouli
- Rosemary has anticancer and antioxidant property

Section 'E'
Floriculture and Landscape Gardening

ANNUALS

Those plants which are completed their life cycle in a season or a year, is called annuals. Thre are many types of annuals.

1. On the basis of seasons:
   (a) Rainy annuals: Balsam, Cock's comb, Amaranths, Gaillardia, Torenia, Gompherena etc.
   (b) Summer annuals: Zinnia, Kochia, Tithonia, Sunflower, Cosmos, Coreopsis.
   (c) Winter annuals: Remaining annuals.
2. On the basis of colour
   (a) Blue colour: Corn flower, Blue larkspur, Ageratum, Linaria, Browallia
   (b) White colour: Allysum, China Aster, Phlox, Zinnia, Stock
   (c) Yellow colour: Pot marigold, Tropaeolum, Zinnia, Wall flower, Coreopsis, Helichrysum
   (d) Pink colour: Candy tuft, Acroclinum
3. On the basis of pollination:
   (a) Self pollinated: Lupin, Sweet pea, Salvia
   (b) Often cross pollinated: Antirrhinum, Larkspur, Linaria, Phlox, Pancy
4. On the basis of photo period
   (a) Short day annuals: Amaranthus, Cosmos, Chrysanthemum, Salvia, China aster
   (b) Long day annuals: Carnation, Petunia, Sweet william, Antirrhinum, Rudbeckia
   (c) Day neutral annuals: Gomphrena, Balsam
5. Other important annuals:
   (a) For fragrant annuals: Carnation, Sweet pea, Sweet sultan, Sweet william, Sweet alyssum, Stock.
   (b) For hanging annuals: Daisy, Verbena, Phlox, Sweet alyssum, Portulaca, Torenia, Lobelia, Nasturtium
   (c) For shady situation: Salvia, Cineraria
   (d) For rock garden: Ice plant, Verbena, Phlox, Gamolepsis, Nasturtium
   (e) For screening purpose: Hollyhock, Sweet pea
   (f) For peculiar shape: Clianthus
   (g) For dry flower: Statice, Helichrysum, Nigella, Lady's lace

SHRUBS

A woody plant which is smaller than a tree and has several main stems arising at or near the ground is known as Shrubs.

- Classification of shrubs:
  - Foliar shrubs: Acalypha tricolour, Nandina domestic, codium variegatum, Manihot variegata
  - Flower and foliage shrubs: Bouganvillea, Hamelia, Buddleia asiatica
  - Fragrant flower: Queen of night, King of day, Jasminum sambac, Kamini
  - Specimen shrub: Hibiscus, Hamelia, Bouganvillea, Thevtia peruviana
- Propagation:
  - Seed: Thevetia peruviana, Calliendra
  - Cutting: Hibiscus, J. sambac, Hamelia patens, Bouganvillea, Queen of night, King of day
  - Layering: Bouganvillea, J. sambac, J. multiflora

TREES

Trees are perennial, tall with marked trunk and grow several years, bear flower and fruit.

- Classification of trees
  - For screening purpose: Grevillea robusta, Eucalyptus spp., Poplar spp, Polyanthia longifolia
  - For checking pollination: Morus spp, Poplar hybrida, Plumeria acutifolia, Ficus infectoria
  - For Alkline and Saline soil: Cassia fistula, Parkinsonia aculeata, Casuarina

CLIMBERS

Climbers are the group of plants which have week stems and ability to climb up the support with the help of modified organs for sunlight and air.

- Modified organs
  - Tendrils: Coral vine, Golden shower, Clematis
  - Thorn: Bouganvillea, climbing rose
  - Roots and rootlets: Campsis grandiflora, Ficus repens

- Sticky substance: Ficus repens

- Classification of climber
  - For sunny situation: Bouganvillea, Rangoon creeper, Campsis grandiflora, Antigonon leptopus, Pyrostegia venusta
  - For partial: Clerodendron splendons, Petra volubilis, Lonicera japonica
  - For pots: Bouganvillea, Clitoria
  - Making hedge: Clerodendron inerme, Bouganvillea
  - For screening: Vernonia, Pyrostegia venusta
  - Annual climber: Sweet pea, Ipomea lobata, Clitoria ternatea

BULBOUS PLANT

- It is herbaceous perennials grown for ornamental purpose, which have underground or near ground storage organs.
- Botanists distinguish between true bulb, corms, rhizome, tubers and tuberous roots any of which may be termed "bulb" in horticulture.
- Warm season bulb: Canna, Dalia, Tuberose, Crinum, Zephyranthes
- Cool season bulb: Gladiolus, Narcissus, Daffodils, Fressia
- Propagation:
  - Bulb: Amaryllis, Tuberose, Zephyranthes, Crinum(Lily)
  - Tuber: Dahlia
  - Corms: Gladiolus, Fresia
  - Rhizomes: Canna, Iris

CACTUS AND SUCCULENTS

Cactus:

- Cacti are succulent perennial plants.
- Cacti genrally have thick herbaceous or woody chlorophyll containing stems.
- Cacti can be distinguished from other succulent plants bt the presence of areoles (Hairs/Spine/bristles).
- It belongs to family of Cactacaea.
- The cactacaea is one of the most distinctive families of dicotyledons flowering plants, with around 90 genera and 2500 species.

■ Examples: Opuntia, Sea onion, Chin cactus, Rat's tail

Succulents:

■ Succulents from more than 60 families and 300 genera have evolved special water storage tissues in thickened or swollen leaves, stems or roots as an adaptation to arid environment.

■ Examples: Agave, Aloe, Euphorbia, Lithops, Yucca, Portulaca

PALMS

■ Palms: Palm trees are a botanical family of perennial lianas, shrubs and trees.

■ It belongs to family of Arecaceae. Family of flowering plants belonging to monocot order.

■ There are roughly 202 currently known genera with aroung 2600 species.

Example: Royal palm, Chinese palm, Bottle palm, Sago palm, Date palm, Butterfly palm, fish tail palm.

ROSE

(*Rosa* spp., Rosaceae; 2n=14, Origin– India)

■ The fleshly berry like fruit is known as **Hip**.

■ Fruit seed is called **Achenes**

■ It is also known as Queen of flower

■ Rose is a National flower of England, Iran and UK

■ Rose is a symbol of love

■ B.K. Roy Choudhary : 1st India rose breeder who raised variety Dr. S.D. Mukherjee in 1935

■ B.S. Bhattachatarjee (Father of rose breeding) was IInd rose breeder, evoluted variety Ramkrishnadev

■ Dr. B.P. Pal evolved Ist rose variety: Rose Sherbat

■ Bud union is most susceptible to low temperature than any other part of rose

■ Winter chilling is necessary in flower bud formation in Rosa damascene

■ Preservative solution: 1–3% + 100–200 ppm HQC

■ Flowers yield was highest in plants kept at night temperature between 15–18°C and day temperature of 20 to 25°C.

■ Suitable pH of 6.0 and 7.5

- Sowing time: In plains – September to October
  In the hills – October to November or February–March.
- Planting Distance
  (a) Cut flower production – 60 × 30 cm
  (b) Oil extraction – 2.5 × 0.5 m
  (c) Vigorously growing cultivars. 60 × 75 cm /75 × 75 cm
  (d) Polyanthas – 45 cm
  (e) Miniatures – 30 cm
  (f) Climbing types – 3 m
- Propagation : Commercial method– budding (T-budding)
  Traditional method– Cutting.
  1. Hard wood Cuttings: Polyanthus, Climbers, Ramblers types rose
  2. Soft or semi hardwood cuttings: Miniatures
- **Rootstock**
  R. multiflora (Edward rose) : Commonly used in Western India
  R. indica var *odorata*: Commonly used in North India
  R. canina: Dog rose
  R. gallica: French rose
  R. moschata: Musk rose
  R. centifolia: Cabbage rose
  R. pendulina, R. Bourboriana: Thornless rose
- Time of pruning: Exactly 45 days prior to the date of requirement of flowers during October–December.
- Pruning is necessary when the yield and quality declines.
- Rejuvenation: After 5–6 years the plants are to be rejuvenated.
- Economic yield 2nd to 10th year.
- Yield:
  Loose flowers : 7.5 t/ha
  Cut flowers : 1st year : 100–120 flowers/m^2
  2nd year: 200–240 flowers/m^2
  3rd year: 300–360 flowers/m^2
- **Important pest:** Aphids (*Macrosiphum rosae),* Red scale (*Lindigapsis rosae),* Chaffer beetles (*Onycetonia varsicolor)*
- **Important diseases:** Dieback (*Diplodia rosarum)* , Black spot (*Diplocarpon rosae)* , Powdery mildew (*Sphaerotheca pannosa var. rosae)*

Varieties

- I[st] var in Hybrid Tea is " La France" produced by Guillot (1867)
- I[st] var in Floribundas are " Rodhatte" produced by Poulsen (1912)
- I[st] var in Grandiflora is " Buccaneer"
- I[st] var in Polyantha is "La Paquerette"

(A) Hybrid Tea

- Red: First Red, Avon, Happiness, Mr. Lincoln, Raktagandha, Black Lady, Montezuma, etc.
- Yellow: Aalsmeer Gold, Gold Medal, Golden Star, Golden Time, Yellow Success, Pusa Sonia
- Orange: Super Star, Summer Hoilday, President and Grand Gala
- Bi–colour: Anvil Spark, Mudhosh, Double Delight, Supriya, Abhisarika, Kiss of Fire, Tata Centenary.
- Scented: Avon, Granda, Papa Meilland, Blue Perfume, Eiffel Tower, Oklahoma

(B) Floribunda

- White: Iceberg, Summer Snow, Margette Maril, Chitchor, Chandrama
- Pink: Prema, Sadabahar, King Arthur, Bridal Pink
- Yellow: Arthur Bell, Dr. Foun, Allgold, Sea Pearl, Golden Times
- Mauve: Neelambari, Angel Face, Africa Star
- Orange: Doris Norman, Suryakiran, Jorina, Jambra
- Bi–colour: Charisma, Mask Red, Paint Box, Nav Sadabahar, Red Gold, Rare Addition
- Scented: Angel Face, Delhi Princess

(C) Polyantha: Anjani, Rashmi, Nartaki, Priti, Swati, etc.

(D) Miniature

- Red: Beauty Secret, Dark Beauty, Fast Fire
- White: Green Ice, Z-Trail, Aany
- Pink: Windy City, Sweet Fairy, Dizzler
- Yellow: Baby Gold Star, Kale Gold, Delhi Star Late
- Mauve: Silver Tip, Blue Bird
- Orange: Angel Ripyance, Petayit Foly
- Bi-colour: Star and Strip, Jainy Williums, Over the Rainbow

(E) Climber

- Red: Climbing Crimson Glory, Blaze, Cocktail, Black Boy
- White: Delhi White Pearl, Shelderer White, Rambler, American Pear, Lamark
- Pink: Climbing Show Girl, Lady Water Loo, Climbing of Silk, Soft Silk, Climbing Piece, Pink Meradan
- Lemon: Miracle Neel, All Gold, Golden Shower, High Moon

CHRYSANTHEMUM

(*Chrysanthemum indica/Dendranthema grandiflora*; Asteraceae, 2n=24, Origin– China)

- It is also known as Guldavadi, Queen of eastern, Glory of East and Autunm Queen
- Suitable pH is pH of 6.5
- It is a shallow fibrous rooted plant
- It is very sensible to water logged conditions
- Planting time: June – July
- Spacing: 30×30 cm^2
- Propagation: Stem cutting
- Blooming period: September – October
- Transplanting: 1 month after sowing
- Harvest: 3–4 month after transplanting
- Yield: 9–10 tonnes/ha
- It is symbol of Royalty in Japan
- Chrysanthemum is National Flower of Japan
- Chrysanthemum is aperennial plant
- It is a short day plant
- Urea is not applied as it causes phytotoxicity
- Chrysanthemum has two types of florets

  Disc florets: Central part of the flower
  Ray florets: Outer part of the flower
- Intercultural operation: Pinching, Disbudding, Desuckering etc
- Pinching: To encourage side branches for cut flowers
- Pinching is also known as stopping

- Disbudding: To encourage single crown branch for standard flower
- Auxillary shoots produce buds called crown buds
- Petal burn is due to deficiency of boron
- Sen, Rin tsukisi: Japanese style of chrysanthemum culture (growing 1000 blooms)
- Optimum temperature for long holding of chrysanthemum is 2.5°C
- By use of plant biotechnology the colour of money maker cultivar has changed from pink to white
- Blooming time:

  Himanshu: April–July
  Maghi: February–March
  Meghdoot: July–August

Varieties

- Large flowered varieties: Sonar Bangla, Redwest field, Cresta, City beauty, Day dream, Peach blossom, Sweet heart, Regalia, Green Sensation, Rupasi Bangala, Mahatma Gandhi, Hommand Philip, J.H. Salisburry, Indra, Kirti, Chandrakanta, Kasturba Gandhi
- Small flowered varieties: Gul–e–Sahir, Birbal Sahni, King Fisher, Golden Dust, Manbhavan, Anokha, Red star, Stella, Sharad Kumar
- Off Season varieties: Haldi Ghati, Himanshu, Jwala, Maghi, Meghdoot
- Export varieties

  1. Standard: Dignity, Wild Fire, Detroit News
  2. Spray: Parliament, Dazzler Florida Marble
  2. Pot mums: Fantasy, Albert, Mandarin, Alpine

International varieties

1. Kokovarouri: Standard type and yellow coloured
2. Nanako: Spray type and yellow coloured

GLADIOLUS

(*Gladiolus grandiflora/G. tritis; Iridaceae,* 2n=30 and 60, Origin– Europe and Africa)

- Origin:

  Diploid spp. – Europe
  Tetraploid spp. – Africa
- Chromosome number

  Diploid: 30
  Tetraploid: 60
- Gladiolus is also called as sword lily
- Optimum temperature for growth 16–30°C
- It requires open sunny situation
- Longer day length improve spike quality
- Suitable pH range is 5.5–6.5
- Propagation: Corms and Cormels (Size 5 cm in diameter)
- Corms require 15–20 days to germinate
- Dormant cormels contains 5–10 times ABA than non dormant
- Breaking dormancy:
- GA_3
- Stored in 4–5°C for 3–4 month
- Ethylene chlorohydrine
- Planting: July–December
- Spacing: 20 × 20 cm^2
- Corm should be treated with 0.2% Bavistin
- Ethylene chlorohydrins is used to break dormancy of corm
- Gladiolus is 7 month crop
- Hilling is important operation of gladiolus
- Preservative solution: 20% sucrose + 200 ppm HQC
- For cut spikes storage temperature: 1–2°C for 2 weeks
- Geotropism disorder is due to transporting
- Short days at 1–2 leaf stage in gladiolus leads to blind shoot
- Floride toxicity seen on tip of leaves, absorbed from air
- Floride toxicity is due to heavy application of SSP, Rock phosphate which contains hydrogen floride

- Dhiraj variety is resistant to fusarium wilt
- Sagar is fragrant variety of gladiolus
- Friendship is a Tetraploid variety
- Pusa Suvasini: Mutant variety of wild rose
- Chrysanthemum Kirti is a new released variety

Varieties

Jawala, Gazal, Priyadarshani, Melody, Suchitra, Friendship, Happy end, Prabha, Oscar, Windsong, Hunting song, Her Majesty, Blue sky, Mayur, Agnirekha, Peter Pears, Chrysanthemum Kirti

CARNATION

(*Dianthus caryophyllus, Carypphyllaceae*; 2n=30, Origin– France)

- National flower of Spain
- Quantitatively long day plant
- It is a cool season crop
- Ideal temperature range is 10–20°C
- Pinching and Disbudding is regular practice in carnation
- Staking is also done in carnation
- Storage temperature: 2–4°C
- Pre–conditioning of cut flower in solution of $AgNO_3$ is important to avoid ethylene injury and prolong shelf life
- Propagation: Terminal stem cuttings (8–10 cm long with 4–6 leaf pairs)
- Planting time: September – October
- Spacing:

  Standards: 20 × 20 cm

  Spray: 30 × 30 cm
- Intercultural operation: De–shooting, Pinching, Disbudding, Staking etc.
- Tinting: Colouring of white carnation
- Pinching: normally done in 6–7 pairs leaf stage
- Calyx splitting of carnation is due to genetic nutritional and environmental factors
- Harvesting stage: 2–3 petals unfurl

Varieties

- **Standard cultivars**

  Red: Scania, Tanga, Red William, Granda, Espana, Master, Killer.
  Pink: Pamir, Nora, Lena, Sharina, Pink Sim, candy, Manon, Oriana.
  Yellow: Pallas, Raggio di Sole, Candy, Yellow Dusty, Murcia,Tahiti.
  White: White Sim, Roma, Candy, Calypso, Sonsara.
  Orange: Tangerine Sim, Orange Triumph.
  Others: Charmeur, Aurthor Sim, Toledo, Solar, Laurella,Vanessa.
  Indian cultivars: Arka Flame and Arka Tejas
- Spray cultivars:

  Red: Rony, Karma, Enzo, Etna, Peach Delight, Vermillion Protruding.
  Pink: Annelies, Barbara, Silvery pink, Madea, Karina, Medley.
  Yellow: Yellow Odeon, Alicetta, Lior, Goldilocks.
  White: White Royallete, Tibet, Iceland, Excel, Equisite, White Lilia.
  Others: Twinkle, Exquisite, Kissi, Luna, Mirage, Macarena.
- Perpetual types varieties: D. cryophillus × D. Chinensis, Winter cheer, Britania, Jokar, Mr. Thomas Lawson, Day Break, William Sim, Lipstick, Pink dona
- Marguerite types varieties: D. Chinensis × D. cryophillus
- Malmaison types varieties: Princess of wales, Mr. Martin smith
- Royal types varieties: Malmaison × Perpetual, Royal fancy, White perfection, Wivel's field
- Modern types varieties: Pico

MARIGOLD

(*Tagetes erecta/T. patula*, *Compositae*; 2n=24 and 48, Origin– South America)

- African marigold: Tagetes erecta, 2n = 48
- French marigold: Tagetes patula, 2n = 24
- It is also known as Gainda, Hazari and Rose of Indies
- Marigold can be sown throughout year
- Marigold is a herbaceous plant
- Male sterility in African marigold is due to female character
- Genetic male sterility is very common in marigold
- Optimum temperature: 18–30°C
- Seed rate: 1–2 kg /ha

- Spacing: Tagetes erecta: – 40 × 30 cm
  T. patula : –20 × 20 cm or 20 × 10 cm
- Pinching of rainy crop is beneficial to avoid water logging
- Transplanting: 1 month after planting
- S.P.S Raghava is associated with marigold
- Nugget: Triploid variety of marigold
- Important Pest: Red spider mite (*Tetranychus sp.),* Hairy caterpillar (*Diacrisia oblique*)
- Imporatant disease: Damping off (*Rhizoctonia solani),* Collar rot (*Phytophtora sp., Rhizoctonia solani, Pythium sp.),* Flower bud rot (*Alternaria dianthi.),* Powdery mildew (*Oidium sp.*)

Varieties

- African marigold: Cracker Jack, Climax, Golden Age, Crown Gold, Star Gold, Chrysanthemum Charm, Pusa Narangi, Pusa Basanti
- French marigold: Rusty Red, Butter scotch, Valencia

TUBEROSE

(*Polianthes tuberosa, Asparagaceae;* 2n=24, Origin– Mexico)

- It is also grown for perfumery as its flowers contain about 0.1 per cent oil
- The suitable temperature for its cultivation 20–35°C as low
- High temperatures (above 35°C adversely affect the growth and floral quality.
- Propagation: Tuberose is propagated by bulbs (2–3 cm diameter).
- About 15–20q bulbs are required for tuberose cultivation in one hectare area
- Planting spacing: 20 × 20 cm or 30 × 20cm
- Planting depth of 8–10 cm is ideal for production of quality cut flowers and bulbs
- Intercultural operations: Staking, Earthing up
- Earthing up: It is done at 10–15 cm height
- Tuberose flowers are ready for harvesting after 100–120 days of planting
- Yield:

First: For cut flower 3.5–5.0 (Lakhs/ha)
For Loose flower 6.0–10.0 (Ton/ha)

Second: For cut flower: 5.0–6.0
For loose flower: 10.0–12.0

- Bulb production: 18.0–20.0 (Lakhs/ha)
- Important diseases: Stem rot (Sclerotium rolfsii), Alternaria leaf spot (Alternaria polyanthi), Blue mould (Botrytis elliptica), Flower bud rot (Erwinia species)
- Important pest: Grasshopper, Aphids, Thrips, Caterpillars, Red, Spider Mites, and Nematodes

Varieties

- Single flower type: Rajat Rekha, Shringar, Prajwal, Mexican, Calcuttia and local types
- Double flower type: Swarna Rekha, Suvasini, Vaibhav, Arka, Nirantara, Mexican, Calcuttia and local

GARDEN STYLE

There are two types of garden style

1. Formal style

- A formal garden is a garden with a clear structure, geometric shapes.
- This design is symmetrical layout.
- The hedge, edge and topiary are maintained in a proper shape by regular training and pruning.
- *Examples:* Mughal Garden, Persian Garden, Italian Garden and French style garden.

2. Informal style

- In this design, the plants and features of the garden are arranged naturally without following any hard and fast rules.
- This design is asymmetrical pattern.
- This style reflects **naturalistic effect** of total view and represents natural beauty
- *Examples:* English and Japanese gardens

3. Free style:

- Combination of both formal and informal style
- *Examples:* Rose garden of Ludhiana, English Garden, Lal Bagh

Some important garden styles

Mughal gardens

- Father of Mughal garden: **Babar**
- Key Features: Site and Design, Terraces, Running water, Bardari, Entrance gate, High protecting wall, Tomb or Mosque, Trees and flower

Symbolism in Mughal gardens

- Water: Source of life
- Flowering trees: renewal of life
- Cypress: Immortality
- White flowering Bauhinia alba: Youth and life.
- Running water: Life

Italian gardens/Roman gardens

- Key features: Terraces adorned with marble pillars, rose gardens, fountains, pools, sculptures among plants

- **British garden/English Garden**
  - Key Features: Lawn, Rockery, Herbaceous border
  - Examples based on English Garden: Cottage Garden, Royal Botanical Garden at Kew, Royal Horticulture Society, Chelsa Physic Garden, Indian Horticulture Society

French Garden

- The moral of French garden style is "how to think big"

Japanese garden

- Key features: Trees, Ornamental water, Garden lanterns, Garden Pagoda, Garden Bridge, Dry Landscape, Gate, Fances, Wells
- Japanese gardens style is **'nature in miniature'** which enables them to meditate, be in harmony with nature.
- Both the Persian and Japanese garden designs were based on their respective ideas of heaven.
- A most important teaching of the Japanese garden is possibly that "unless a garden has an air of peace it's not worth a place visiting.
- Example based on Japanese style: Hill garden, Tea Garden, Flat Garden, Sand Garden, Roshnara Park, Budha Jayanti Park
- Flower arrangement in Japanese garden style
  - Ikebana: Japanese flower arrangement
  - Moribana: When Piled flower and Dwarf vase are used in this flower arrangement

- Jiyubana: Free flower arrangement
- Morimona: When fruits, vegetables flowers are arranged. This is type of "English flower arrangement"
- Nagiere: When tall vase are used in this flower araangement
- Zeneika: When Straight material with uneven height are used
- Zeneibana: Wood, Stone, Rocks etc are used in this flower arrangement

■ Basic line in Japanese flower arrangement
- Heaven: Shin
- Man: Soe
- Earth: Hikaie
- Jushi: Fillers

FAMOUS GARDEN OF INDIA

Lal Bagh

■ The Lal Bagh situated at Bengaluru, Karnataka

■ The garden was started in 1760 by Hyder Ali

■ The most attractive feature of the garden is a large glasshouse where the annual flower show is held.

Bridavan garden

■ It is located at Mysore, Karnataka in India.

■ The garden lies adjoining the Krishnarajasagara dam which is built across the river Cauvery

■ The work on laying out this garden was started in the year 1927 and completed in 1932

■ The main attraction of the park is the musical fountain in which movement of water is synchronized to the music of songs.

Byrant Park

■ It is situated at Kodaikanal, Tamilnadu

■ The park was actually laid out in 1909, but it completed in 1961

Rashtrapati Bhavan Garden

■ It is located at New Delhi

■ It was renamed as 'Rashtrapati Bhavan' in 1950.

■ It was designed by the British architect **Sir Edwin Lutyens.**

Shalimar Garden

- It is located at Sri Nagar, Jammu & Kashmir
- This garden was initiated by Jehangir for his wife Nur Jehan in 1619
- It was extended in 1630 by Zafar Khan
- This garden is also known as the 'garden of love'

The Mughal Garden

- It is situated at **Pinjore (Haryana)**

Rose Garden

- Rose Garden is situated at Chandigarh
- It is an Asia's largest rose garden.
- This garden was created in 1967, under the Dr M.S. Randhawa

The Sim's Park

- It is located at Coonoor in Tamil Nadu

The Indian Botanical Garden

- It is located at Kolkata (West Bengal)
- The Acharya Jagadish Chandra Bose Botanical Garden (previously known as Indian Botanical Gardens, Howrah)
- It is situated in the twin city of Howrah, on the opposite side of the river Hoogly.

Llyod Botanic Garden

- It is situated at Darjeeling in West Bengal
- Established in 1878

National Botanical Research Institute

- It is situated at Lucknow in Uttar Pradesh
- The National Botanical Research Institute popularly known as Sikander Bagh

Rock Garden

- It is situated at Chandigarh in Punjab
- It is also known as Nek Chand's Rock Garden
- It is sculptured by **Nek Chand Sainy**

The Ramoji Film City Gardens

- It is situated at Hyderabad in Telangan
- Ramoji Film City is the world's largest integrated film studio

Tulip Garden

- It is situated at Sri Nagar, J& K

Botanic Garden

- It is located at Coimbatore in Tamil Nadu

Sayaji Park

- It is located at Vadodra in Gujarat

Mandoor Garden

- It is located at Jodhpur in Rajesthan

Botanical Garden or Forest Research Institute

- It is located at Dehradun in Uttrakhand

Rose Garden

- It is located at Chandigarh in Punjab

PRINCIPLE OF LANDSCAPE GARDENING

Colour:

- Primary colour: Red, Blue, Yellow
- Secondary colour: Orange, Green, Violet
- Unity: Unity means that all parts of the landscape go together. It achieved by using mass planting and epetation.
- Balance: The balance in landscape design is visual equilibrium of different garden elements. Balance can be created in a garden either formal or informal by grouping the components, structures and plants equally on both sides of the imaginary central axis.
- Proportion: Proportion refers to the share of the different parts or components to the whole. It is the relation of the component with other in magnitude

Vista

- It is the three dimensional confined view of a terminal object along eye line at focal point.

  Example: Taj tomb, Hanging garden of Babylon.
- Prospect: It is the three dimensional confined view of a terminal object along eye line at focal point. E.g. Taj tomb as viewed from its opposite.
- Restraint: Overuse of any component including grouping of plants in a particular location masks the scenic beauty.

- Rhythm: Rhythm is measured as cyclic repetition of an object, effect and event. In a garden, rhythm can be infused through cleverly repeated colours and shape, topiaries and hedges etc.
- Harmony: Harmony is the pleasing effect obtained due to appropriate arrangement and collation of the various garden features. It is the overall effect of various features styles, colours and structures in the total landscape.
- Movement or Mobility: The concept of mobility is vital to garden as breath to human. Mobility can be introduced in the garden by the magnificent sway of tall trees, birds in the sky, butterflies circling over flowers, dispersal of clouds in the sky, surging water in fountains, the gentle curvature of roads, trunks, branches of trees, etc.
- Scale: Scale is a relative dimension. The height and spread of trees and shrubs and the spread of the water garden are determined by adopting a scale.
- Space: The aim of every garden design should be such that the garden should appear large than its actual size.

Axis

- Axis is an unifying element.
- In formal garden: Axis is central
- In informal garden: Axis is oblique
- Contrast: It is most useful in emphasizing the best features of an object.
- Accent or emphasis: It is created in the garden to avoid the monotonous view. Mostly unusual object like tall fountain, tree, statue etc. are used to create the effect on accent or emphasis.
- Transition: Transition can be obtained by the arrangement of object with varying texture forms or size in a logical sequential order. It is gradual change.
- Focalization: It involves the leading of visual observation toward a feature by a placement of this feature at the vanishing point between radical or approaching lines.
- Repetition: It refers to repeated use of features like plants with identical shape, line, form texture and colour.

LAWN

- It is also known as " Heart of Garden"
- 60–65% area of garden should be devoted to lawn
- Axis of lawn never divergent
- Most widely used fungicide: Glyphosate
- Important weed: Cyperus rotundus, Euphorbia spp.

Selection of grasses

- Bermuda grass/Doob or Haryali: Cynadon dactylon
- Korean grass: Zoysia japonica
- Manilla grass: Zoysia matrella
- Korean valvet grass: Zoysia tenuifolia
- Carpet grass: Axonopus affinis

Planting of grasses

- Dibbling of roots: Most common and cheapest method
- Seedling: 12 kg/Acre or 25–30 kg/ha or 2.5 g/m^2
- Bricking: To replace the few unhealthy patches in well maintained this method is used
- Turfing : Quickest method
- Planting on polythene
- Turb plastering

Disease of lawn

- Fairy ring: Caused by fungus (Marasmius ordeades)
- Pale or yellow lawn: Due to N_2 deficiency

MISCELLANEOUS

- Carnation: Susceptible to ethylene injury or sleepiness
- Anthurium: Resistant to ethylene injury or sleepiness
- Modified part of Anthurium: Spathe
- Protandry: Rose, Chrysanthemum
- Jasmine is substitute for saffron
- Marigold are used to produce natural colour
- For defoliation in jasmine, Penta chlor isophenol is used
- China Aster is true short day plant
- Dahlia is known as King of flower
- Leading flower product exporting country: Netherlands (57%) > Columbia (14%)
- Leading flower product importing country: German > Netherland
- Leading country with highest per capita consumption of cut flower: Swizerland > Norway

- Leading country with highest per capita consumption of live plants: Norway > German
- Country having largest market of cut flower: German > USA
- Leading dry flower product exporting country: Australia
- Leading dry flower product importing country: U.K.
- Leading bulbous plant producing country: Netherland
- Leading bulbous plant importing country: USA
- Largest producer of perfumery products: Bulgaria
- International flower market is situated at Alsmeer in the Netherland
- International Registration authority for rose: USA
- International Registration authority for Bouganvillia: New Delhi, India
- International cut flower growers association: USA
- International society for horticulture science: Belgium
- No-1 foliage plant at global level: Diffenbachia
- No-1 cut flower at global level: Rose
- No-1 pot plant in global flower market: Hadera (Ghost tree)
- 1st rank in dried ornamentals in global flower market: Helichrysum
- 1st rank in cut green in global flower market: Asparagus
- India's share in global floriculture trade: 0.6%
- State having highest maximum area under floriculture in India: Karnataka
- State having maximum production under floriculture in India: Tamilnadu
- State having maximum cut flower production in India: West Bengal
- Share of dry flower product in India's total export: 60%
- Division of ornamental crops started at IIHR in: 1969
- Division of floriculture and landscaping started at IARI in: 1983
- 1st AICRP on floriculture started in: 1971
- Flower crop covering maximum area in India: Jasmine
- India is largest producer of loose flower in the wolrd
- Flower capital of world: California, USA
- Foliage capital of world: Florida, USA
- Hogarth course is also known as line of beauty
- Biggest formal garden: Brindavan garden, Mysore
- Heaven of man: Italian Garden

- Stevia: Wonder plant and Seetners of future
- Kadam tree is associated with Lord Krishna
- Semal tree is associated with Shiva
- Bauhinia tree is associated with Saraswati
- Amaranthus tree is associated with Kali
- Yellow Amaltas tree is associated with prosperity in trade
- Ashoka, Sal and Palash tree is associated with Budha
- Bulgaria is largest producer of rose perfume
- Egypt is largest producer of jasmine perfume
- France is largest producer of tuberose
- France is largest producer of carnation perfume
- Concrete: Non purified form of essential oil obtained by solvent extraction method
- It contains 45–55% absolute
- Bonsai: Japanesd art of growing miniature trees and shrubs by extreme dwarfing

Book

- Beautiful Garden: Written by M.S. Randhawa
- Garden Flower: Written by V. Swarup
- Garden Through Ages: Written by M.S. Randhawa

Section 'F'

Post-Harvest Management and Value Addition in Fruits and Vegetables

HISTORY

- Fruit and vegetable processing was 1st started in organized manner in 1857
- Canning of fruit and vegetable started in 1927
- Needham (1729) 1st time explained: cause of spoilage of stored food
- Nicholus Appert (1804) 1st preserved the food in glass containers
- Cooking of food by means of preserve started by Papin in 1861
- In India, 1st fruit and vegetable processing industry was established in 1935 at Mumbai
- In 1950, CFTRI was established at Mysore
- FPO: Food Product Order was passed by Govt of India in 1955
- 1st fruit preservation and Canning Institute was established in 1949 at Lucknow

PRE–HARVEST FACTORS AFFECTING POST–HARVEST QUALITY

Related to plants

- **Crops:** Quality of the fruit and vegetables are varies from crop to crop.
- **Cultivars:** The quality of seed or plant material is an important factor that controls the quality of the fruit and vegetable produced. Several parameters of quality are controlled genetically.
- **Cultural practices:** All cultural practices have direct effect on the final quality of the produce.
- **Planting period:** Many plants are very sensitive to environmental conditions, and thus quality will not be optimized when crop is produced under adverse conditions. Producing summer plants during the winter or vice–versa will not be appropriate, unless protection practices are implemented.
- **Planting density:** It affects both the quantity and quality of the produce.
  - High density planting increases competition between plants, reduces light availability, and thus may decrease quantity.
  - Low density planting lead to large size, better colored fruit or vegetable which may have shorter shelf life.
  - Larger fruits are commonly more sensitive to physiological disorders.
- **Irrigation**: Irregular watering usually reduces fruit size, increases splitting, physiological disorders, reduces water content in the plant or plant part, etc.

- **Fertilization**: Poor management of fertilizers will increase physiological disorders due to deficiencies of some minerals or increase of other leading to toxicity. In both cases, quality will be negatively affected.
- **Pruning**: It reduces the load and increases the growth of fruit and chemical use after harvest.
- **Thinning**: This operation reduces the competition between fruits or plants and thus promotes a good balance between the vegetative and fruit parts and improves quality.
- **Protection**: Pathogens and insects have a very negative effect on quality. Poor management of plant protection programmes can lead to very poor quality and reduced yield.

Related to environments

- **Temperature:** It is the most important environmental factor that affects quality.
- Very low or very high temperature may injure sensitive crops.
- Adequate high intensity and quality is important for the formation of some colour.
- Fruits and vegetables should always be harvested when temperature is mild. Because, higher temperature leads to faster respiration.
- Wind and rain may cause negative effects on some crops.

Related to chemicals

- Many hormones and growth regulators are used in agriculture and they can affect quality in different ways.

During harvest factor

- **Season**: Quality of produce are greatly influenced by season e.g.
- Winter season harvest having more shelf life as compared to other season.
- Off season fruits and vegetables give more remunerative price.
- Harvesting during or immediately after rains should not be carried out since it creates most favourable conditions for multiplication of micro–organisms.

Time

- Morning harvest of horticultural crop prefer for local market because they are fully fresh and turgid and having dew drop in this time.
- Evening harvesting is preferred for distant market due to higher accumulation of reserved carbohydrates and less amount of moisture which give the better quality of the produce to consumer.

- Leafy vegetables harvested in the latter part of the morning or late in the afternoon.
- Cucumber is harvested in the late morning when it to be transported under less than ideal condition because it is less prone to injury when it contains less water.
- **Method of harvesting:** Selection of suitable method for harvesting of the produce is necessary otherwise bruises or injuries during harvesting. Injury to peel may become an entry point for microorganisms, causing rotting.
- **Stage of harvesting:** Fruits and vegetables must be harvested at right stage of maturity.
  - Vegetables harvested immature or over mature usually do not keep long.
  - Fruit vegetables harvested too early lose water fast and are more susceptible to mechanical damage and microbial attack.
  - An over mature vegetable is more susceptible to decay, has passed its best eating quality, and deteriorates fast.
- **Consumer demand:** Harvesting time and harvest maturity can be altered by the requirement of the consumer's demand which may affect the quality of the produce at some extent.

POST–HARVEST FACTORS AFFECTING POST–HARVEST QUALITY

Curing

- Curing is done immediately after harvesting.
- It strengthens the skin.
- In the field, curing is done at 37.8°C for 3–5 days
- Potato tubers are held at 18°C for 2 days and then at 7°—10°C for 10—12 days at 90% relative humidity.
- Sweet potato are held at 33°C with 95% RH
- Artificial curing of onion is done at 40°C temperature for 16 hrs.
- The process is induced at relatively higher temperature and humidity, involving suberization of outer tissues followed by the development of wound periderm which acts as an effective barrier against infection and water loss.
- It is favoured by high temperature and high humidity.
- Potato, sweet potato, colocasia, onion and garlic are cured prior to storage or marketing.

- Curing also reduces the moisture content especially in onion and garlic.
- Drying of superficial leaves of onion bulbs protects them from microbial infection in storage.

Degreening

- It is the process of decomposing green pigment (Chlorophyll) in fruits usually applying ethylene or similar metabolic inducers to fruit.
- It is applicable to banana, citrus and tomato.
- Low concentration of ethylene (20 ppm) is applied for degreening.
- Degreening temperature: 27°C
- Relative humidity at the time of degreening: 85–90%
- Below 1% CO_2 levels: does not allow higher colouring
- Kerosene fumes better coloured fruit than ethylene
- Ethylene accelerate decomposition of chlorophyll without significantly affecting the synthesis of carotenoids pigment
- **Pre–cooling**: Pre–cooling is a means of removing the field heat.
- It slows down the rate of respiration, minimizes susceptibility to attack of micro– organisms, and reduces water loss.
- Peas and okra which deteriorate fast need prompt precooling.
- **Washing and drying:** Most of the fruits and vegetables are washed after harvesting to improve their appearance, to prevent wilting and to remove primary inoculum load of microorganism.
- **Sorting and grading:** Fruits and vegetables require sorting and grading for uniform packing at field level.
- Sorting is done on the basis of size and colour
- Grading practice is performed as per the defect or on the basis of marketable and unmarketable produce.

Disinfection

- Papaya, mango, melon and other fruits are susceptible to fruit fly attack.
- Disinfection is done either by vapour heat treatment (VHT) at 43°C with saturated air with water vapour for 6–8 hr by Ethylene dibromide fumigation.

Waxing

- Fruits and vegetables have a natural layer on their outer surface which is partly removed by washing.

- An extra discontinuous layer of wax applied artificially with sufficient thickness and consistency to prevent anaerobic condition within the fruits provides necessary protection against decay organism.
- There are 2 types of wax emulsions and both contain 12% TSS
  1. Wax 'O': For impart gloss to fruits and vegetables
  2. Wax 'W': It does not impart gloss to fruits and vegetables
- Waxing also improves the appearance and glossiness, making them more acceptable
- **Packing**: Packing not only protects the horticultural produce but also makes a favourable impression on the buyers and May able to fetch higher income.
- **Delivery**: Moving the harvest produce from the farm to the customer in good condition is important.

POST HARVEST LOSSES

Postharvest loss: It can be defined as the degradation in both quantity and quality of a food production from harvest to consumption.

Food losses: It refer to the decrease in edible food mass (dry matter) or nutritional value (quality) of food that was originally intended for human consumption (FAO, 2013). Food losses take place at production, postharvest and processing stages in the food supply chain. Food losses are mainly due to poor infrastructure and logistics, lack of technology, insufficient skills, knowledge and management capacity of supply chain actors, and lack to markets.

Food waste: It refers to food appropriate for human consumption being discarded, whether or not after it is kept beyond its expiry date or left to spoil. Food waste occurs at the food chain (retail and final consumption) and relates to retailers and consumers behaviour.

Note– **Food wastage refers to any food lost by deterioration or waste. The term "wastage" includes both food loss and food waste**

FACTORS OF POST HARVEST LOSSES

There are internal and external factors contributing to postharvest loss.

- **Internal Factors:** The following sections describe PHL occurring at all stages in the food supply chain from the moment of harvesting, to handling, storage, processing and marketing.

1. **Harvesting:** The time of harvesting is determined by degree of crop maturity and weather conditions.
2. **Pre-cooling:** Loss at this stage is primarily due to the high cost and lack of availability of pre–cooling facilities, inadequate training on pre–cooling technology at the commercial scale, and lack of information on cost benefits of pre–cooling technology.
3. **Transportation:** Primary challenges in the transportation stage of the supply chain include poor infrastructure (roads, bridges, etc.), lack of appropriate transport systems, and a lack of refrigerated transport.
4. **Storage:** Facilities, hygiene, and monitoring must all be adequate for effective, long-term storage. In closed structures (granaries, warehouses, hermetic bins, silos), control of cleanliness, temperature, and humidity is particularly important.
5. **Grading**: Proper packing and packaging technologies are critical in order to minimize mechanical injury during the transit of produce from rural to urban areas.
6. **Packaging and labelling**: After harvest, fresh fruits and vegetables are generally transported from the farm to either a packing house or distribution centre. Farmers sell their produce in fresh markets or in wholesale markets.
7. **Secondary processing:** Causes of post–harvest loss in this stage include limited availability of suitable varieties for processing, lack of appropriate processing technologies, inadequate commercialization of new technologies and lack of basic infrastructure, inadequate facilities and infrastructure, and insufficient promotion of processed products.
8. **Biological:** Biological causes of deterioration include respiration rate, ethylene production and action, rates of compositional changes (associated with color, texture, flavour, and nutritive value), mechanical injuries, water stress, sprouting and rooting, physiological disorders, and pathological breakdown. The rate of biological deterioration depends on several environmental factors, including temperature, relative humidity, air velocity, and atmospheric composition (concentration of oxygen, carbon dioxide, and ethylene), and sanitation procedures.
9. **Microbiological:** Micro–organisms cause damage to stored foods (e.g., fungi and bacteria). Usually, microorganisms affect directly small amount of the food but they damage the food to the point that it becomes unacceptable. Toxic substances elaborated by molds (known as mycotoxins) cause loss in food quality and nutritional value

10. **Chemical**: Many of the chemical constituents naturally present in stored foods spontaneously react causing loses of colour, flavour, texture and nutritional value. One such reaction is the "maillard relation' that causes browning and decolouration in dried fruits and other product. There can also be harmful chemicals such as pesticides or obnoxious chemical such as lubricating oil.

External Factors: Factors outside of the food supply chain can cause significant postharvest loss. These factors can be grouped into two primary categories: environmental factors ic and socio–economic patterns and trends.

1. **Environmental factors:** Climatic conditions, including wind, humidity, rainfall, and temperature influence both the quantity and quality of a harvest
2. **Temperature:** In general, the higher the temperature the shorter the storage life of horticultural products and the greater the amount of loss within a given time, as most factors that destroy the produce or lower its quality occur at a faster rate as the temperature increases.
3. **Humidity:** Fresh horticultural products have high moisture content and need to be stored under conditions of high relative moisture loss and wilting (except for onions and garlic). Dried or dehydrated products need to be stored under conditions of low relative humidity in order to avoid adsorbing moisture to the point where mold growth occurs.
4. **Altitude:** Within a given latitude the prevailing temperature is dependent upon the elevation when other factors are equal. There is on the average a drop in temperature of 6.5°C for each kilometre increase in elevation above sea level. Storing food at high altitudes will therefore tend to increase the storage life and decrease the losses in food provided it is kept out of direct rays of the sun.
5. **Time:** The longer the time the food is stored the greater is the deterioration in quality and the greater is the chance of damage and loss. Hence, storage time is a critical factor in loss of foods especially for those that have a short natural shelf life.
6. **Socio-economic factors:** Social trend such as urbanization has driven more and more people from rural area to large cities, resulting in a high demand for food products at urban centres, increasing the need for more efficient and extended food supply chains.

TECHNOLOGIES AND PRACTICES TO REDUCE POST HARVEST LOSSES

Some strategies for reducing postharvest losses are listed below:

1. A systematic analysis of each commodity production and handling system is the logical first step in identifying an appropriate strategy for reducing postharvest losses
2. **Harvest**: Harvesting should be carried out as carefully as possible to minimize mechanical injury such as scratches, punctures and bruises to the crop. Provision of the proper tools and equipment for harvesting and training workers in their correct use should be a priority prevention of food loss activity.
3. **Handling**: Mechanical injury provides sites for pest attack and increases physiological losses. Therefore, avoid mechanical injury to the crop while handling.
4. **Packing**: Packing should minimize deterioration of the roots within the container and cushion against impact and compression. During packing in the field care must be taken to minimize physical damage that results from impact bruises due to stacking and overfilling of bags, abrasion or vibration bruises due to root movement against each other. Therefore packages should be neither loose (to avoid vibration bruising during transport) nor overfilled, and should provide good aeration.
5. **Transportation:** Temperature management is critical during long distance transport, so loads must be stacked to enable proper air circulation to carry away heat from the produce itself as well as incoming heat from the atmosphere and off the road. In many developing countries traditional baskets and various types of trays or buckets are used for transporting produce to the house or to village markets. The selection of suitable containers for commercial scale marketing requires very careful consideration. Among the various types of packaging material that are available: natural and synthetic fibre sacks and bags as well as moulded plastic boxes seem to be more suitable
6. **Storage**: The following three things must be done to ensure successful storage of fresh roots and tubers:
   i. Carefully select only top quality roots and tubers without any signs of handling or pest or disease damage for storage.
   ii. Keep them in specially designed stores.
   iii. Check the stores at regular intervals.

7. **Processing:** Overcoming the perishability of the crops, improving marketing, enhancing nutritional value and adding economic value through processing are the main strategic areas in for reducing postharvest losses. The various processing techniques are listed below: peeling and washing, grating, pressing/fermentation, sieving, frying/drying.

RESPIRATION

Respiration: Through photosynthesis, plants transform sunlight into potential energy in the form of the chemical bonds of carbohydrate molecules. However, to use that stored energy to power their essential life processes – from growth and reproduction to healing damaged structures – plants must convert it into a usable form.

$$C_6H_{12}O_6 \text{ (glucose)} + 6O_2 \text{ (oxygen)} = 6CO_2 \text{ (carbon dioxide)} + 6H_2O \text{ (water)} + 32 \text{ ATP (energy)}$$

- Many external and internal factors affecting the rate of respiration are as follows:

External factors

Temperature

- With every 10°C rise of temperature from 0°C–30°C the rate of respiration increases 2–2.5 times (*i.e.,*temperature coefficient (Q10°) is = 2–2.5.
- Below 0°C the rate of respiration is greatly reduced although in some plants respiration takes place even at −20°C. Dormant seeds kept at 50°C survive.

Supply of oxidisable food: Increase in soluble food content readily available for utilization as respiratory substrate, generally leads to an increase in the rate of respiration upto a certain point when some other factor becomes limiting.

Oxygen concentration of the atmosphere: The amount of oxygen in the environment of plants is increased or reduced upto quite low values the rate of respiration is not affected. On decreasing the amount of oxygen to 1.9% in the environment aerobic respiration become negligible (extinction point of aerobic respiration) but anaerobic respiration takes place

Oxygen poisoning: The significant fall in respiration rate was observed in many tissues in pure O_2. The oxygen poisoning effect was reversible, if the exposure to high oxygen pressure was not too prolonged.

Water: With increase in the amount of water the rate of respiration increases. In dry seeds, which have 8–12 of water the rate of respiration is very low but as the seeds imbibe water the respiration increases.

Light: Respiration takes place in night also which shows that light is not essential for respiration. But light affects the rate of respiration indirectly by increasing the rate of photosynthesis due to which concentration of respiratory substrates is increased.

Carbon dioxide (CO_2)**:** If the amount of CO_2 in the air is more than the usual rate of respiration is decreased. Germination of seeds is reduced and rate of growth falls down.

Inorganic salts: The chlorides of alkali cations of *Na* and *K*, as also the divalent cations of Li, and Ca and Mg, generally increase the rate of respiration as measured by the amount of CO_2 evolved.

Injury and effects of mechanical stimulation: Wounding or injury almost invariably results in an increase in the rate of respiration.

Effect of various chemical substances: Certain enzymatic inhibitors like cyanides, azides, carbon monoxide, iodoacetate, malonate etc. reduce the rate of respiration even if they are present in very low concentration. However, various chemical substances such as chloroform, ether, acetone, morphine, etc., bring about an increase in respiratory activity.

Pollutants: High concentration of gaseous air pollutants like SO_2, NOX and O_3 inhibit respiration by damaging cell membrane. These gaseous pollutant causes increase in pH which in turn affects the electron transport system thus inhibiting respiration. Heavy metal pollutant like lead (Pb) and cadmium (Cd) inhibit respiration by inactivating respiratory enzymes.

Internal Factors

Protoplasm: The meristematic cells (dividing cells of root and shoot apex) have more protoplasm than mature cells. Hence, the meristematic cells have higher rate of respiration than the mature cells. Respiration rate high at growing regions like floral and vegetative buds, germinating seedlings, young leaves, stem and root apices.

Respiratory substrate: With the increase of in the amount of respiratory substrate, the rate of respiration increases.

PRESERVATION

Preservation: Preservation means just protect the foods against the spoilage. It deals with the process for prevention of decay or spoilage of the food is called preservation.

In other words, just controlling the physical, chemical or microbial changes in the foods is called preservation.

1. Physical Changes: Colour, flavour, texture and taste etc.
2. Chemical Changes: Carbohydrate, fats, proteins, vitamins and minerals.
3. Microbial Changes: Mould, yeasts and bacteria

Principles of Preservation

There are three main principles:

1. Prevention/delay the microbial decomposition of the food.
2. Prevention/delay the shelf decomposition of the food.
3. Prevention of damage by insects, animals, mechanical causes etc.

1. Prevention /delay the microbial decomposition of the food

i. By Keeping out the micro organisms-Asepsis
ii. By Removal of micro organisms-Filtration
iii. By Hindering the growth and activity of micro organisms-Anaerobic condition
iv. By Killing the micro organisms-Exposing at high temperature

Asepsis: It means preventing the entry of micro organisms by maintaining of general cleanliness, while picking, grading, packing and transporting of fruits and vegetables, increase their keeping quality and the product prepared from them will be superior quality.

Filtration: Fruits juice, bear, soft drinks, wines etc. enter through a bacteria proof filter which is made of Asbestos pad or unglazed porcelain type of materials. These filters contain the micro organisms and allow the water or juice to percolate though with or without pressure.

Anaerobic conditions: It can be maintained by: (i) Replacing the O_2 by CO_2 carbonation (ii) Evacuating the sealed container (fruit juice) (iii) Use of oils from top of the food (pickles)

Exposing at high temperature: Fruits can be exposed by high temperature such as:

i. **Canning:** Food is exposed to a high temperature (> 1000 C) which prevents spoilage and inactivate the enzyme present in the food.
ii. **Irradiation:** In case of irradiation, the food is exposed to the radiations to kill the survive m.o. by ionizing and non–ionizing radiation like α, β and γ rays. Her, food is exposed to electromagnetic or ionizing

radiation or various frequencies ranging from low frequency electromagnate to high frequency i.e., gamma rays which destroy the micro–organism present in the food.

B. **Prevention/delay the shelf decomposition:**

1. By destruction or inactivate the enzyme: Blanching.
2. Prevention /delay the non–enzymatic chemical reactions: Antioxident

1. Blanching:

- It is a primary treatment which has to soften the tissues to facilitate packaging.
- To preserve the original colour and flavour
- To destroy the certain enzyme which are undersirable
- Elimination of the air
- Mostly for vegetables
- Remove micro–organisms
- Remove astringent taste and toxins

2. Anti-oxidant: Anti-oxidant are substances which are used to protect the food gamma deterioration caused by exposure to the air.

- BHA-Butylactic Hydroxy Anisole Vegetable oils BHT-Butylactic Hydroxy Toluene
- **Gellales:** Animal fat, Vegetalbe oil
- **Tocopherols:** Animal fat
- **Ascorbic acid:** Fruit juices, Citrus oil, Wine, Bears etc.
- **Lactic acid :** Processed fruits and vegetables, Canned fruits,
- **Phosphoric acid:** Vegetable oils, Animal fat and cola drinks

Methods of preservation of fruit and vegetable

There are two main basic methods:

1. Bacteriostatic methods
2. Bactericidal methods

1. Bacteriostatic Methods: a. Drying of foods
b. Use of chemical preservatives
c. Use of food additive
d. Use of low temperature

2. Bactericidal Methods: 1. Pasteurization
b. Cooking
c. Canning
d. Irradiation

A. **Bacteriostatic methods:** In this method, the environmental conditions are change to prevent the growth of micro organisms, such conditions are called bacteriostic. These are –

1. **Drying of foods:** Drying is just removal of moisture from the food to a certain level at which micro organisms can not grow is called drying, it can be done by two methods:

   (i) Application of heat:

   (a) Sun drying: In which food is directly exposed to sunlight.

   (b) Mechanical drying: application of heat is applied by a mechanical dryer under the controlled conditions of temperature, humidity and air flow.

   (c) Vacuum drying

   (d) Freeze drying

   (ii) Binding the moisture in the food:

   (a) Use of Sugar: The use of high concentration (15–70%) of sugar bindup the moisture and make the food have a certain level of moisture at which micro organisms are not able to grow.

   (b) Use of Salt: The concentration of salt (7–20%) causes the high osmotic pressure and tie up the moisture which inhibit the growth of micro organisms. Salt reduces the solubility of O_2 in the food by reducing the moisture.

2. **Use of chemical preservative:** Only two chemical preservatives are used in fruits and vegetables Preservation such as:

(i) Potassium metabisulphate (KMS) [$K_2S_2O_5$]

(ii) Sodium benzoate [$C_7H_5NaO_2$]

(i) Potassium metabisulphate (KMS)

1. It releases the SO_2 gas and it is unstable.
2. It is used for the fruit which have non water solvent pigment (colourless).
3. Best to control **moulds** than **bacteria**.
4. 350–700 ppm KMS is mostly used in fruit juice products.
5. It can not be used in naturally coloured juices such as phalsa, jamun because they have the Anthocynin pigment.

6. It can not be used in the product which are packed in container because it acts on the tin containers and oil, Hydrogen Sulphide (H_2S) which has an unpleasant smell and also form a black compound with the base plate of containers.

(ii) Sodium Benzoate:

1. It is salt of benzoic acid and soluble in water.
2. It delays the fermentation in the juices.
3. It is commonly used in the product which are having natural colour such as anthocynin pigment.
4. It is more effective against the **yeast**.
5. 750 ppm Sodium benzoate is mostly used in fruit juices, squashes and cordials while RTS and Nectar is 100 ppm.

3. **Use of food additives:** Food additives are substances or mixture of substances other than basic foodstuffs, which are present in the foods as reagent of any aspects of production, processing, storage, packaging *etc.*

   Food additives are: (i) Sugar (ii) Salt (iii) Acids (iv) Spices.

   (i) Sugar

   - The concentration of 68–70% is used for preparation of jam, jelly, marmalades etc.
   - Sugar act as a preservative by osmosis.
   - It absorbs most of the available water, so little water available for the growth of micro organisms.

   (ii) Salt

   - The concentration of salt 15–20% is used for the preparation such as pickles.
   - Salt inhibits enzymatic browning and discolouration and also acts as an anti-oxidant.
   - It causes high osmotic pressure resulting in the plasmolysis of microbial cells.

   (iii) Acids

   Many processed foods and beverages need the addition of acids to impart their characteristic flavour and taste in the final product because acid provides desired flavour and taste. Main acids are the following

   1. Acetic acid (Vinegar)
   2. Citric acid (Lime juice)
   3. Lactic acid (Lactose)

1. **Acetic acid:** It is commonly used for pickles, chutney, sauce and ketchup, just to inhibit the growth of micro organisms.
2. **Citric acid:** It is used for preparation of jam, jelly, squash, nectar etc. just to increase the acidity.
3. **Lactic acid:** It is used for the formation of curd from milk, raw flavour, and specific to pickles

   Food additives are work as:

   1. **Antioxidants:** BHA (Butylated hydroxyl anisol), BHT, $SnCl_2$
   2. **Preservatives:** SO_2, Benzoic acid, Sorbic acid
   3. **Surface active agent:** Monosodium phosphate
   4. **Stablizers:** Pectin, CMC (Carboxy methyl cellulose)
   5. **Sweetners:** Aspartane, Glycyrrhizic acid
   6. **Flovouring agent:** Monosodium glutamate
   7. **Bleaching agent:** H_2O_2 (Hydrozen peroxidize), Benzoyl peroxide
4. **Spice:** Spices are plant products which are used in flavouring the foods and beverages to enhance the food flavour, colour and palatability.

4. Use of low temprature: Low temperature retards the microbial growth and enzyme reaction because it retards the chemical reactions. This is not a permanent method because some micro–organisms can also grow at low temperature. Some storages which maintained low temperature:

1. Cellar storage : (Above 15°C)
2. Refrigerated storage : (0 to 7°C)
3. Freezing storage : (–18 to –40°C)

Freezing point:

- Freezing with Cryogenic liquids:
- **Liquid N_2 :** –196°C
- **Liquid CO_2 :** –43°C
- **Frozen temperature:** –12 to –17°C
- **Quick freezing: –18 to –25°C**

B. Bactericidal methods: In this method, food material is exposed to higher temperature. Due to high temperature, kill the micro organisms due to coagulation of protein. It helps in inactivation of enzyme. High temperature can be employed by following methods:

(i) Pasteurization : Below 100°C (85–90°C for 30 minutes)

(ii) Boiling/Cooking : at 100°C

(iii) Canning : Above 100°C

(i) Pasteurization: (Pasteurization done at the temperature of 85–90°C for 30 minutes). There are three methods of pasteurization

(a) **Bottle or holding pasteurization.** The extracted juice is strained and filled in bottles, leaving sufficient head space for the expansion of the juice during heating.

(b) **Overflow method:** Juice is heated to temperature of about 2.5°C higher than the pasteurization temperature.

(c) **Flash pasteurization:** The juice is heated rapidly to a temperature of about 5.5°C higher than the pasteurization temperature.

Juices can be pasteurized in two ways

(1) By heating the juice at a low temperature for a High time **(LTHT)**

(2) By heating the juice at high temperature for a short time only **(HTST)**

(ii) Boiling/Cooking: The primary objective of cooking is to produce a palatable food. Other objectives are:

- Putting the temperature about 100°C. by this method, food can be preserved for 10–24 hours at low temperature.
- Destruction or reduction of micro organisms and inactivation of undesirable enzymes.
- Destruction of potential hazard in the foods which are present naturally through micro–organism.
- Improvement of colour, flavour and texture of the food.
- It improves the digestibility of food component.

(iii) Canning: Canning is done at or above 100°C.

- In case of fruits which are acidic, they are canned at 100°C.
- In case of vegetable those are non–acidic, they are canned at above 100°C (at least 115–121°C).

Canning operation:

1. Grading
2. Washing
3. Peeling
4. Blanching
5. Can filling
6. Syruping
7. Brining

8. Exhaustion
9. Sealing
10. Processing

Peeling types:

- Lye peeling: Potato, Peach and Citrus
- Flame peeling: Onion

RIPENING

- **Definition:** Ripening is associated with physical and biochemical irreversible process which leads to senescence and finally leads to death.

Factors affecting ripening of fruits and vegetables

1. Respiration
2. Transpiration /water loss
3. Ripening Ethylene production
4. Pathological stresses
5. Mechanical stress
6. Temperature stresses.

MATURITY

Definition: It can be defined as the stage at which a commodity has reached a sufficient stage of development.

Maturity Indices

1. **Shape:** (a) Banana· Disappearance
   (b) Pineapple: Flattening of eyes
   (c) Litchi: Flattening of tubercles
2. **Juciness:** Sweet corn
3. **Tapping:** Water melon, Jackfruit
4. **Solidity:** Cabbage
5. **Netting:** Musk melon
6. **Aroma:** Jackfruit
7. **Juice content:** Citrus
8. **Starch index:** Apple, Pear and Banana
9. **Days from fruit set to harvest:** Banana, Sapota, Mandarin etc.

10. **Acidity:**
    (a) Mandarin: 0.4%
    (b) Sweet orange: 0.3%
    (c) Mango: 0.5–0.6%
    (d) Pineapple: 0.5–0.6%
11. **TSS (Total soluble solid): (in°Brix)**
    (a) Grape: 18–22
    (b) Mandarin: 12–14
    (c) Sweet orange: 12
    (d) Papaya: 11.5
    (e) Pineapple: 12–14
12. **Specific gravity:**
    (a) Mango (Alphonso): 1–1.02
    (b) Mango (Dashehari): 1
    (c) Guava: 1
    (d) Pineapple: 0.98–1.02

INJURY

Chilling injury

Definition: It is damage to plant parts caused by temperatures above the freezing point (32°F, 0°C).

Freezing/Frost injury

Definition: It is damage to plant parts caused by temperatures below the freezing point (32°F, 0°C).

COLD STORAGE/CONTROLLED ATMOSPHERE (CA)

Definition: It is a special kind of room, the temperature of, which is kept very low with the help of machines and precision instruments.

ZERO ENERGY COOLING CHAMBER (ZECC)

- It is based on principle of **evaporative cooling system**
- Cool chambers can reduce temperature by 10–15°C and maintain high humidity of about 95% that can increase shelf life and retain quality of horticultural produce
- It does not require any electricity or power to operate
- Materials required like bricks, sand, bamboo etc. available easily and cheaply.

PERISHABLE NATURE OF FRUITS AND VEGETABLES

1. Very perishable (0–4 weeks):

- **Fruits:** Apricot, Ripe banana, Fig, Mango and Water melon
- **Vegetables:** Spinach, Broccoli, Ripe tomato, Lettuce and Cauliflower

2. Perishable (4–8 weeks):

- **Fruits:** Avocado, Grape, Mandarin, Peach and Pineapple
- **Vegetables:** Cabbage and Tomato

3. Semi perishable (6–12 weeeks):

- **Fruits:** Coconut and Sweet orange
- **Vegetables:** Celery and Leek

4. Non perishable (Above 12 weeks):

- **Fruits:** Apple, Grape fruit and Pear
- **Vegetables:** Carrot, Onion, Potato and Turnip

Value Added Products

S. No.	Products	Fruit juice (%)	TSS(°Brix)
1.	Jelly	45	65
2.	Jam	45	68
3.	Sauce	–	30
4.	Ketchup	–	28
5.	Chutney	40	50
6.	Squash	25	40–50
7.	Cordial	25	30

S. No.	Products	Fruit juice (%)	TSS(°Brix)
8.	Syrup	25	65
9.	Nectar	20	15
10.	Crush	25	55
11.	RTS	10	10
12.	Preserve	55	68–70
13.	Natural juice	100	–
14.	Sharbat	–	65

Value added tomato products

S. No.	Products	TSS
1.	Juice	5
2.	Soup	7
3.	Puree	9
4.	Paste	25
5.	Ketchup	28
6.	Sauce	30

Permissible Limts of Preservaties

S. No.	Preservatives	Products	Limits (ppm)
1.	KMS (SO_2)	Fruit juice	700
		Raisins	750
		Squash/Crush/Cordial	350
		Jelly/Jam/Marmalade	40
		Candi	150
		Dry fruits and vegetables	2000
		Cidar	200
2.	Benzoic acid	Fruit syrup	600
		Preserve	200
		Sauce	750
		Tomato puree and paste	250

Some important points

- Syruping temperature: 79–82°C
- Sealing temperature: 74°C
- Exhausting temperature: 82–100°C
- Cooling temperature: 39°C
- Principle of freezing: Crystalization
- Alcohol in wine: 13–20%
- All vegetables are alkaline nature
- 1st rank in pickle making in the world: Cucumber
- 1st rank in pickle making in India: Mango

- Fermentation is the only process in which both donor and accepter are organic
- R–enamal cans used for : Acid fruit, because it are acid resistant cans
- C–enamal cans used for: – Sulphoric nature vegetable, because it are sulphur resistant cans
- Honey is the only product which can not be spoiled
- Selenium is a antioxidant mineral
- Due to excess sugar or less cooking of jelly resulting: Crystal form
- Ultrafilteration is a cold process

Section 'G'

ICAR Institute and Research Centres

ICAR Institutions and Research Centres

Deemed Universities of ICAR

1. **IARI**–Indian Agricultural Research Institute, New Delhi.
2. **NDRI**–National Dairy Research Institute, Karnal.
3. **IVRI**–Indian Veterinary Research Institute, Izatnagar.
4. **CIFE**–Central Institute on Fisheries Education, Mumbai.

Institutes and Research Centres of ICAR

1. **CRRI:** Central/National Rice Research Institute, Cuttack
2. **CRIJAF:** Central Research Institute for Jute and Allied Fibres, Barrackpore
3. **CTRI:** Central Tobacco research Institute, Rajmundary
4. **CICR:** Central Institute of Cotton Research, Nagpur
5. **IGFRI:** Indian Grassland and Fodder Research Institute, Jhansi
6. **IISR:** Indian Institute of Sugarcane research, Lucknow
7. **IISR:** Indian Institute of Spices Research, Marikunnu, Kerala
8. **IIPR:** Indian Institute of Pulses Research, Kanpur
8. **IINRG:** Indian Institute of Natural Resins and Gums, Ranch
10. **SBI:** Sugarcane Breeding Institute
11. **IIW&BR:** Indian Institute of Wheat and Barley Research
12. **IIMR:** Indian Institute of Maize Research, New Delhi
13. **IIMR:** Indian Institute of Millet Research, Hyderabad
14. **IIOR:** Indian Institute of Oilseed Research, Hyderabad
15. **IIOPR:** Indian Institute of Oil palm Research, Pedavegi, West Bengal
16. **VPKAS:** Vivekananda Parvatiya Krishi Anusandhan Shala, Almore
17. **IIHR:** Indian Institute of Horticultural research, Bangalore
18. **CISH:** Central Institute of Subtropical Horticulture, Lucknow
19. **CIAH:** Central Institute for Arid Horticulture. Bikaner, Rajasthan
20. **CITH:** Central Institute of Temperate Horticulture, Srinagar
21. **CTCRI:** Central Tuber Crops Research Institute, Trivandrum
22. **CPCRI:** Central Plantation Crops Research Institute, Kasargod
23. **CPRI:** Central Potato Research Institute, Kufri, Shimla
24. **IISR:** Indian Institute of Spices Research, Calicut
25. **IIVR:** Indian Institute of Vegetable Research, Varanasi

26. **CRIDA:** Central Research Institute for Dryland Agriculture, Hyderabad
27. **CCRI:** Central Citrus Research Institute, Nagpur
28. **CSWCR & TI:** Central Soil and Water Conservation Research and Training Institute, Dehradun
29. **CSSRI:** Central Soil Salinity Research Institute, Karnal
30. **CAZRI:** Central Arid Zone Research Institute, Jodhpur
31. **CRIDA:** Central Research Institute for Dryland Agriculture, Hyderabad
32. **ICAR–NEH:** ICAR Research Complex for North–Eastern Hill Region, Barapani
33. **ICAR–GOA:** ICAR Research Complex for Coastal Agricultural Research Institute, Goa
34. **ICAR–ER:** ICAR Research Complex for eastern region, Patna.
35. **CARI:** Central Agricultural Research Institute for Andaman and Nicobar Islands.
36. **IISS:** Indian Institute of Soil Science, Bhopal
37. **NAARM:** National Academy of Agricultural Research Management, Hyderabad.
38. **NIAM:** National Institute of Abiotic Stress Management, Malegaon, Pune
39. **NIBSM:** National Institute of Biotic Stresses Management, Raipur
40. **IIWM:** Indian Institute of Water Management, Bhubaneswar
41. **CIAE:** Central Institute of Agricultural Engineering, Bhopal.
42. **CIRCT:** Central Institute for Research on Cotton, Bombay
43. **NIRJAFT:** National Institute of Research on Jute and Allied fibre Technology, Calcutta.
44. **CIPET:** Central Institute of Post–harvest engineering and Technology, Ludhiana.
45. **IIAB:** Indian Institute of Agricultural Biotechnology, Ranchi
46. **IISR:** Indian Institute for Seed Research, Mau
47. **NIAE & PR:** National Institute of Agricultural Economics and Policy Research, New Delhi
48. **IASRI:** Indian Agricultural Statistics Research Institute, New Delhi
49. **CSWRI:** Central Sheep and Wool Research Institute, Avikanagar
50. **CIRG:** Central Institute for Research on Goats, Mathura
51 **CARI:** Central Avian Research Institute, Izatnagar
52. **CIRC:** Central Institute for Research on Cattle, Meerut, UP.
53. **CIRB:** Central Institute for Research on Buffaloes, Hisar

54. **NIANP:** National Institute of Animal Nutrition and Physiology, Bangalore
55. **NDRI:** National Dairy Research Institute, Karnal, Haryana.
56. **IVRI:** Indian Veterinary Research Institute, Bareilly, UP
57. **NIVEDI:** National Institute of Veterinary Epidemiology and Disease Informatics, Hebbal, Bangalore
58. **NIHSAD:** National Institute of High Security Animal Diseases, Bhopal
59. **CIFRI:** Central Inland Fisheries Research Institute, Barrackpore
60. **CMFRI:** Central Marine Fisheries Research Institute, Cochin
61. **CIFT:** Central Institute of Fisheries Technology, Cochin
62. **CIBA:** Central Institute of Brackish water Aquaculture, Chennai.
63. **CIFE:** Central Institute of Fisheries Education, Mumbai.
64. **IASRI:** Indian Agricultural Statistical Research Institute, New Delhi.
65. **NCAP:** National Centre for Agricultural Economics and Policy Research, New Delhi.
66. **CIWA:** Central Institute for Women in Agriculture, Bhubaneswar

Directorate of ICAR

1. Directorate of Cashew Research, Puttur
2. Directorate of Cold Water Fisheries Research, Bhimtal, Nainital
3. Directorate of Floricultural Research, Pune, Maharashtra
4. Directorate of Groundnut Research, Junagarh
5. Directorate of Knowledge Management in Agriculture (DKMA), New Delhi
6. Directorate of Medicinal and Aromatic Plants Research, Anand
7. Directorate of Mushroom Research, Solan
8. Directorate of Poultry Research, Hyderabad
9. Directorate of Rapeseed & Mustard Research, Bharatpur
10. Directorate of Soybean Research, Indore
11. Directorate of Weed Research, Jabalpur
12. Directorate on Onion and Garlic Research, Pune
13. Project Directorate on Foot & Mouth Disease, Mukteshwar

National Bureau of ICAR

1. National Bureau of Agricultural Insect Resources, Bengaluru
2. National Bureau of Agriculturally Important Micro Organisms, Mau Nath Bhanjan, Uttar Pradesh
3. National Bureau of Animal Genetic Resources, Karnal, Haryana
4. National Bureau of Fish Genetic Resources, Lucknow, Uttar Pradesh
5. National Bureau of Plant Genetic Resources, New Delhi
6. National Bureau of Soil Survey & Land Use Planning, Nagpur, Maharashtra

National Research centre of ICAR

1. National Centre for Integrated Pest Management, New Delhi
2. National Research Centre for Banana, Trichi
3. National Research Centre for Citrus, Nagpur
4. National Research Centre for Grapes, Pune
5. National Research Centre on Litchi, Muzaffarpur
6. National Research Centre on Pomegranate, Solapur
7. National Research Centre on Camel, Bikaner
8. National Research Centre on Equines, Hisar
9. National Research Centre on Integrated Farming, Motihari
10. National Research Centre on Meat, Hyderabad
11. National Research Centre on Mithun, Medziphema, Nagaland
12. National Research Centre on Orchids, Pakyong, Sikkim
13. National Research Centre on Pig, Guwahati
14. National Research Centre on Plant Biotechnology, New Delhi
15. National Research Centre on Seed Spices, Ajmer
16. National Research Centre on Yak, West Kemang